How to Write a

Books and films by Christopher Keane

BOOKS

How to Write a Selling Screenplay
The Maximus Zone
The Heir
The Crossing
Christmas Babies
The Paradise Pill
The Hunter
Lynda
The Huntress
The Tour
Handbook for the Martial Arts and Self Defense

FILMS/TV

The Hunter
Dangerous Company
Mr. & Mrs. Bliss

How to Write a Selling Screenplay

A Step-by-Step Approach to Developing Your Story and Writing Your Screenplay by One of Today's Most Successful Screenwriters and Teachers

CHRISTOPHER KEANE

Broadway Books

NEW YORK

BROADWAY

Broadway Books titles may be purchased for business or promotional use or for
special sales. For information, please write to: Special Markets Department, Bantam
Doubleday Dell Publishing Group, Inc., 1540 Broadway, New York, NY 10036.

BROADWAY BOOKS and its logo, a letter B bisected on the diagonal, are
trademarks of Broadway Books, a division of Bantam Doubleday Dell Publishing
Group, Inc.

Library of Congress Cataloging-in-Publication Data
Keane, Christopher.
    How to write a selling screenplay : a step-by-step approach to developing your
story and writing your screenplay by one of today's most successful screenwriters
and teachers / Christopher Keane. — 1st ed.
        p.   cm.
    Includes bibliographical references.
    ISBN 0-7679-0071-5 (pbk.)
    1. Motion picture authorship.   2. Television authorship.   I. Title.
PN1996.K34   1998
808.2′3—dc21   97-36109
                                                                        CIP

Designed by Susan Hood

            05   20   19   18   17   16   15   14   13   12

TO MY BROTHER JAY,
AND IN MEMORY OF HIS SON, CHRIS

Contents

Foreword

Based on the assumption that a goodly percentage of young aspiring screenwriters will go on to become professional screenwriters, I think that a few words on the status of screenwriters will be of some value.

A little more than sixty years ago, Irving Thalberg, head of production at MGM, stated—understandably not for publication—that "writers are the most important part of the making of a motion picture, and we must do everything in our power to prevent them from finding out."

Well, we did find out. What good has it done us? Surveys show that most moviegoers believe that the actors make up the words they utter on the screen. In some isolated cases that is true. Weak directors allow stars to indulge in the undisputed evil of *improvisation.* The results are almost always disastrous.

The most recent display of the downplaying of writers occurred during the 1993 Academy Awards ceremonies. There was a filmed segment paying tribute to important figures in the Industry who had died in the past year. Close-ups of actors, actresses, directors, musicians filled the screen. Nary that of a screenwriter. This led some misguided people to believe happily that not one of the nine thousand members of the Writers Guild of America had died during 1993. Unfortunately, not exactly accurate. Among the scores of departed screenwriters, three Academy Award winners come quickly to mind: Michael Kanin, Philip Dunne, and Daniel Fuchs. Their demises were not deemed sufficiently important to be included in the tribute. A posthumous victory, perhaps, for Irving Thalberg.

But now let us agree that you have written a full-length screenplay. A legitimate agent loves it and sends it to the studios, where it must run the gauntlet of a horde of vice presidents with impressive titles. They can and most frequently do say "No!" They have not the power to say yes. That function rests with a tier of top executives whose main concerns are, "Is it high concept?" and "Is it commercial?" Still, miraculously, some scripts do get sold and that is when the vice presidents come to the fore again. To justify their salaries they believe that they have to improve your script, so they chip away and chip away. This is known as the dreaded word, *development,* a procedure that has driven more than a few screenwriters to the Betty Ford Rehabilitation Center in Palm Springs.

But please don't be discouraged. Screenwriting has its rewards. Two, in fact. One is financial. Many scripts sell for six and even seven figures. Two, you will have the admiration and respect of your peers. And even a little jealousy. So, good luck and welcome to the terrible, wonderful world of screenwriting.

Julius J. Epstein
Screenwriter, *Casablanca*
Los Angeles

Acknowledgments

I wish to thank the following for their invaluable contributions:

My students at Emerson College, the Rhode Island School of Design, and the International Film & Television Workshops.

A deep appreciation to Lauren Marino, editor extraordinaire at Broadway Books, for her wisdom, guidance, and wit.

A special thanks to Alix Taylor for all her help in the initial stages.

To Pamela Tien and Mandy Syers.

To Michael Blowen, Scott Neister, William Martin.

To Martha Frisoli, Tracy Winn, Connie Biewald, and Kati Steele.

To Susan Crawford of The Crawford Literary Agency, with love.

And to David H. Lyman, keeper of the faith.

Introduction

My introduction to screenwriting came on the day I met Steve Mc-
Queen, a few months before he died. I rode the elevator to the eleventh
floor of the Beverly Wilshire Hotel in Beverly Hills, where some of the
top movie stars kept their private suites when they were in town.

It was a heady time for me. I was in my late twenties and McQueen
had just announced that he wanted to turn my book, *The Hunter,* into
his next movie. I wasn't that nervous. Not much!

We sat for five hours going over, detail by detail, how McQueen saw
the book becoming the movie. I couldn't help but notice a chair in the
next room. It was a beautiful chair, high-backed and Victorian, except
for a huge hole blown out of the back of it with the stuffing spread all
over the floor. After a while, I got up enough courage to ask him about
it. He said a director whom he had hired for the picture turned out to be
such an insufferable bore that he wanted to teach him a lesson.

"I told him to sit in the chair," McQueen explained, "and I pro-
ceeded to tell him what a huge mistake I had made in hiring him, that
he was an imbecile, and thought far too much of himself to direct this or
any other picture. I told him that he made me so mad I wanted to shoot
him, but I couldn't do that for a number of reasons. So, I told him to get
up out of the chair and stand over by the bar."

"When he did, I pulled this out." McQueen reached down beneath
the table where we sat and came out with an ancient .45 caliber hog-leg
revolver with a long barrel. "I aimed at the chair and pulled the trigger.
I told him that I would have shot him if I could have gotten away with it,

1

but in this case I had just killed the terrible aura he carried around with him, and to get the hell out of my sight."

A long silence filled the room. Was I supposed to laugh?

He laughed and said that the most important thing in this business was focus, and the reason he fired the director was that all his focus was on himself and not where it should have been, on the making of the movie.

If there was one thing I learned that afternoon, it was what focus was all about. Everything we discussed, whether it seemed important or not, McQueen grabbed onto and fed into a greater power—the motion picture he was about to star in. Nothing else mattered.

In the ensuing weeks, as I struggled to learn this strange form of writing, someone said to me, "So you're doing the screenplay? And you like it? Watch out. If I were you I'd go off into a dark corner and wait for the feeling to pass." It didn't. This new challenge excited me. It was another way to get things down on paper. I had no alternative.

What is this strange and compelling need to write things down? To get things out of us? They say there's a deep wound in us that needs to heal and the only medicine, for most of us, is to write the wound away. Or to cut into the wound and find the source of the pain and then, by writing it down, extract the poison.

We write in a solitary place, all alone, by ourselves. For a writer, solitude becomes a companion for life. One reason I write is to control what little of the universe I can. The universe I can control—if control is the word—lives inside my head. I can bring characters to life, kill them off at will, go to Argentina, fall in love. I can do these things while sitting in a dark room, looking at a computer screen, and watching my characters do what they will. What *they* will; for eventually, after I have given them what I can, the story belongs to them. Contrary to some popular belief (usually by stubborn writers who never get produced), the writer is not master of, but servant to, the story.

The art and craft of writing is just this: a collaboration between the writer and the characters.

My best work comes after I've let the characters go, when I've allowed them to make sojourns of their own. In the beginning, I work with an outline and character sketches. Good solid foundation work happens at this stage, called *building the story.*

Here you create a world in which the characters begin to breathe. You can bring them to life, kill them off, and play God in the process. Imagine killing off your adversaries in real life. With the same swift strokes that you dispatch them in your stories, you'd be whisked off to the gallows.

There is also the matter of knowing a good story when we see one. Some of the great stories in history may have never been recorded because a writer was not there to record them, or the writer wasn't able to recognize the jewel for what it was.

I knew long ago that I do not take orders well, nor do I like to give them. I am happiest creating dreams, playing with characters in my head and on the page. This is the world in which I'm most comfortable, that seems to heal the wounds of my childhood and past. To infuse them with some kind of meaning, to shake my troubles out of trees, to give them shape. To write them into being and in so doing begin to heal myself.

Some of my most vivid memories of childhood are of the movies. Sitting alone in a dark theater, I watched characters up there on the huge screen accomplish remarkable things, solve seemingly impossible problems. In real life, people were too frightening, and so these imaginary characters became my friends and enemies, my heroes and villains. The movies replaced a world in which I didn't want to live, with one in which I did. And later on, writing became the life-long means of transportation from one world to the other. This book is about one way to make that journey. Through screenwriting.

Screenwriting is a bastard art. Think about it. You write the story down on paper, fifty messy pairs of hands—from the agent, producer, and director to the actor, the actor's agent, and even the grip—screw around with it without your permission, and then—then!—it comes out not on the page where you'd think it would, but on celluloid.

After completing several drafts of *The Hunter*—working with Mc-Queen, the producer, and the studio—I was horrified by what was happening to my book. "Stop," I shouted, "you are defiling my work." They told me to calm down. I cried louder. They ignored me. Then McQueen, who saw my problem, came over to me and said, "Hey, kid, take it easy. You'll give yourself a heart attack. This is a movie now; it's no longer your book. Your book will always live, as a book. This is a different form. If you want to be in this business, learn the ropes." So off I went to learn the ropes of the movie business. In the years that followed, I wrote a number of screenplays. Some made it to the screen, the vast majority did not.

I learned the art and craft of screenwriting from reading scripts, seeing thousands of movies, and teaching at places like Emerson College, The International Film & Television Workshops, the Rhode Island School of Design, and in foreign countries—where everyone is even more movie-crazy than in this country—where I've been invited to talk on "the American screenplay form."

In writing this book, I've tried to follow George Bernard Shaw's advice—"My method is to take the utmost trouble to find the right thing to say, and then to say it with the utmost levity"—and to say it, I might add, in one of the sacred dictums of screenwriting, with the utmost brevity.

Christopher Keane
Cambridge, Massachusetts

I

Getting Started

The first draft of anything is shit.

Ernest Hemingway, novelist
and author of *The Sun Also Rises*
and *A Farewell to Arms*

The process of writing a screenplay knows no rules. You get up in the morning and drag yourself to your yellow pad or computer and go to work. Or you come home from your day job and spend every night banging out pages until you reach the end. Many writers begin slowly. They ponder, they think, they outline, they do a little here, a little there, basically gathering steam, researching as they go—until by the end, having gained momentum, they work at a furious clip.

Some people get up at four in the morning, as I do, and write for two or three hours before going back to bed, their reward. I love the early morning: no phones, day breaking over the land, headphones pressed against my ears, lost in another world. I also like rewards when I work.

John Milius *(Geronimo, The Wind and the Lion)* works between five and six in the afternoon, seven days a week. Paul Schrader *(Taxi Driver)* works in his head for months, tells his story to everybody, watches for reactions, then sits down and writes the screenplay in two weeks.

These people have a schedule, and they stick to it. They write every day, and so should you.

If you write three pages a day for forty days, you'll have 120 pages, a first draft. Forty days is less than a month and a half in return for possible fame and fortune, and a profound sense of accomplishment.

Every year we waste that much time grousing about how unfair the movie business is. After listening to me complain one too many times, my agent advised me, "Take all that negative energy and turn it to write a good script." He was right.

The important thing is getting it out of your head and onto the page.

Who cares if it's not perfect? Just get it down. You'll worry about editing later. If you don't get it down on paper you'll never reach the editing stage anyway. Write the first draft in a hurry.

First you write the story in four pages and then expand it into a step outline or scene breakdown. Along the way you write character sketches. You've transferred the scenes onto index cards, which you've thumbtacked to a cork board on the wall. This way you get to see the entire movie in front of you. You're ready to write. You've taken all the right steps. So what's the problem?

Fear. Ah, fear. Of course. Fear of failure. Fear of success. Fear of taking risks. And so you make excuses: Not enough time. I can't do it that well. I don't have the story down. I have kids. My computer doesn't work. I don't have a computer. I'll do it next spring, next summer, next year. Next millennium. Or: I'll never get it finished. I've never finished anything. What if it doesn't work? I have a much better idea. Let me work on that one, and I'll get back to this one when I can. It's a waste of valuable time. What the hell am I thinking about here? They'll never take it. It's a pipe dream. I have more important things to do. Don't I?

Fear. What an obstacle. *F.E.A.R.—False Events Appearing Real.*

Okay, so then forget about it. Do something else. Admit it: you never wanted to write a screenplay in the first place. You just wanted to be a little decadent, in this pipe dream; now you realize it. You really only wanted to *think* about writing a screenplay, not actually *do* it.

So, close this book, throw it away, rip it up. It'll just be a reminder of what you never wanted to do anyway.

Sound familiar? It does to me. I've used these excuses, and still do, but not to the extent that I used to. Just sit down and do it, one day at a time. Don't worry about the future. The future will take care of itself. All you've got is today. You might as well make use of it. Do four pages or one paragraph. What's the rush? Who's counting? As long as you show up everyday and log some time, twenty minutes will do for starters. Don't set ridiculous goals for yourself. You do that, and after five days, when you haven't gotten twenty pages done, you say to yourself: "See, you're way behind. You'll never catch up. Fugetaboutit."

I know it's difficult getting to the computer or the legal pad. The process of actually getting there is often the hardest thing about writing. Once you've arrived, just start putting words on paper. Any words. Eventually the words will take on meaning and context. Page by page, day after day, you build your story, the characters take on life, you carry these thoughts into the rest of your day.

Don't worry about tomorrow, or how long it's going to take, or that you have to get it done by such and such a date.

It doesn't matter. It'll get done when it does. As long as you put in some work today, and some tomorrow. Five minutes, twenty minutes, whatever you have. Just promise yourself you'll do it every day. Keep the dream alive.

My Day

For seventy years, Somerset Maugham followed a rigid daily work schedule. Up early in the morning, he did some mild exercise and then wrote from 8:00 A.M. until noon, at which time he declared himself brain-dead. In the afternoon, at his Riviera villa, he wrote letters, and in the evenings, he entertained. He turned out some very good books that cut across all genres, and he found himself at the top of his form and on bestseller lists for most of his life.

He sat by himself at his desk every day, no matter what. He did not want to be disturbed, and wasn't. He knew what he had to do.

No matter where we go—an office, a classroom—we have to put the time in. No matter who pays us. If we quit, we starve. If we don't show up, we're fired.

That's working for somebody else. Writers usually work for themselves. I'm convinced that one of the main reasons I became a writer is that I can't stand working for somebody else. It's one of the main reasons anybody becomes a writer. Self-motivation. I don't wait for the muse. I sit at my desk and summon the muse to me, and eventually, the muse shows up. The muse doesn't show up when I'm sleeping, when I'm walking the dog, or when I'm playing basketball.

Like just about every other writer, I searched a long time for the right work schedule. I've tried eight-hour stretches and one-hour bursts. I've written on trains, in hotel lobbies, in bed, at various desks, on the floor, at the beach, in coffee shops. On this book, I worked two to three hours every morning, seven days a week, for a year, cranking out three to five pages a day.

The one constant in my schedule is that I work every day. I get up early, around 5:00 A.M. and work for two to three hours. I love the mornings. They're vital. By doing as much as I can early, anything I do afterwards is a gift. When I'm done, my reward is going back to bed. I love my bed. Personally, I need that reward system in just about everything I do. It's the Yankee work ethic, I suppose, or Catholic guilt. I've learned that I don't have to kill myself every day. I do what I do, day by day, and the project eventually gets done.

I used to badger myself about getting a certain amount completed every day—the minimum—and then ridicule myself for not having done it. I would count what I hadn't done, and punish myself for not living up to it. This practice does absolutely nothing except haul more guilt into the warehouse. I'm kinder to myself these days. "What's the big rush?" I say to myself. As long as I show up for at least a couple of hours every day, the work will get done.

With this attitude, the work has become better. I am not rushing, or anguishing about how much I'll complete in the next week, month, or year. Instead, I concentrate on the day's work; and when the day's work is done, I get up from the desk and go back to bed.

Do yourself a favor and pick the time of day when you work the best, or when you can find the time. If you have twenty minutes, take them. If, before your regular job, you can find a half hour, take it. At that rate, in about four months, you'll have the first draft of a screenplay. On the other hand, if you keep telling yourself that you need bigger blocks of time, or that you have too many other obligations, or you're too tired, in four months you'll have no pages, but a lot of excuses.

If you have the willingness, you'll make the time. I have a friend who works a hard eight-hour day and spends two hours each night writing. On this schedule, in three years, he has written two published novels and two optioned screenplays. He and his family live a full life. He's done what it takes to satisfy his urge to write. This, as far as I'm concerned, is what it's all about.

My friend started with twenty minutes in the evening. The further he got into each project, the more time he spent. He did not bury himself under an avalanche of expectations. If you exercise your will to write on a daily basis, neither will you.

It's now around 7:30 A.M. I've been working for two hours. It's time to snuggle with my wife Susan for about an hour, and then we'll both get up. Susan goes to bed much later than I do. As a literary agent, she does much of her reading after she says goodnight to her clients and film agents on the West Coast.

The next part of my day begins at 10:00 A.M. I'm out of bed and scribbling on a yellow pad, writing scenes for the new screenplay. I spend a couple hours each day at this. Writing longhand serves me well. I write fast and messily, and I often pay the price later when I can't read my own writing. After two hours of this, I put down the pad and pick up a novel or the morning paper.

Around 1:00 P.M., I go downstairs, where Susan and I talk about this or that, and then, depending upon chores, I'll read in bed, take a nap, hop on my bike, hit golf balls, play basketball at the Y. When I return, I take a shower, sit at the computer and record what I've written on the yellow pad. This becomes a mini-rewrite or a polish.

In the evening, I may go out to a movie, see friends, read, or do more work. Even when I'm traveling or giving lectures, the work schedule remains more or less the same. You take the work, and yourself, with you wherever you go.

You also take your fears and excuses with you. I always have to beware of the saboteur who sits on my shoulder, offering up reasons for not writing. That voice has ruined lives, prevented destinies, persuaded talented people that they can't cut it as writers. It's fear talking. Each day you have to remember to put a muzzle on your saboteur and get to work.

Exercise

Recommended Viewing

In the following pages, I'll discuss the movies below in some detail. Before you continue with the rest of the book, you should become familiar with the following. Chances are you've already seen most of them, but take another look.

- *Who's Afraid of Virginia Woolf?*
- *Secrets and Lies*
- *Tootsie*
- *Kramer vs. Kramer*
- *Welcome to the Dollhouse*
- *Blue Velvet*
- *Witness*
- *The Verdict*
- *Breaking Away*
- *Norma Rae*
- *Lethal Weapon*
- *Fargo*
- *Ordinary People*
- *Midnight Cowboy*

2
The Story

A writer is the priest of the invisible.

> Wallace Stevens, poet and author
> of *The Blue Guitar* and *The
> Necessary Angel*

You must remember that a writer is a simple-minded person to begin with and go on that basis. He's not a great mind, he's not a great thinker, he's not a great philosopher, he's a storyteller.

> Erskine Caldwell, novelist and author of
> *Afternoon in Mid-America* and *Miss Mamma Aimee*

Novels, Plays, and Screenplays

One of the crucial questions in the writing of a screenplay comes right at the beginning. *Is my story best as a movie, a play, a book, or a short story?* You must ask yourself this question—and answer it—before going on. Below you'll find some general rules on making this decision. Remember that these rules are not hard-and-fast, but you ought to at least pay attention to them. They will save you a lot of time and effort.

Plays are talky affairs with very little physical movement. They take place generally in one location, and rely for much of their power on performances before live audiences. Plays depend mostly on words and character and are more cerebral than physical. Some plays successfully make the journey into films. *Who's Afraid of Virginia Woolf?*, arguably among the top ten plays of the past fifty years, made the transition. *Sling Blade* made the cut from stage to film, along with *Driving Miss Daisy* and *The Crucible*. In these cases the original writers wrote the screenplays. Strong visual stories and compelling characters made the difference. *Lost in Yonkers* didn't make it.

If your story is very talky and basically stays in one location, it may work better as a play.

Novels move freely from exterior locations to interior monologue. They are often filled with reflection and memory and emotion. Novels can take place on Mars one moment, through a keyhole from a boy's point of view the next, and finally from the remembrance of an Indian grandfather's fearful epiphany outside Tucson. You get the picture. Novels have no limitations. They can be all thought or interior monologue, while in movies, you can't see thought. Central to good novels is the writer's voice, or style, which is almost impossible to capture on the screen. Witness the disaster of Tom Wolfe's *Bonfire of the Vanities* when it made the transfer. Why do you think that J. D. Salinger has never allowed a movie version of *The Catcher in the Rye?*

In **screenplays,** everything is visual or visible. Dialogue is at a minimum. You should not need words to explain the story. Pictures should do that work. Movies, by definition, are moving pictures. Pictures that move.

If your story is overly cerebral, it may work better as a novel. If it is talky, you might think about the stage, or television.

If it is limited in terms of scope and character, it might serve best as a short story. If you're not sure, tell the story to friends and ask their opinion.

Then ask yourself: in what form would *I* most like to experience this story? In other words, let your instinct, backed up by a few pointers, be your guide.

One other thing, I ask my novel students this question: When you're in a bookstore where do you go? What section pulls you to it, mystery, romance, historical novels, literary fiction? I ask my screenwriting students: When you look in the paper to see what's playing, what kind of movie gives you a thrill? Romantic comedy, action, low-budget character pieces? Think about that. Whatever draws you means that you have an affinity to this type of movie and probably should be writing in that area.

I made a big mistake once. My agent suggested that I write a big saga that takes place over many generations, with dozens of characters and exotic locations. He even suggested the subject, the fur industry, and a title, MINK! I labored for three years and failed miserably. One day a friend asked me a crucial question that in the beginning I should have asked myself: "Chris," the friend said, "do you even like to read this kind of book?"

"No," I replied, astounded by the avalanche of thought this question produced. "I can't stand them."

Get the picture?

The Story of *The Crossing*

FADE IN:
EXT. FLORIDA GULF COAST—DUSK
Glorious sunset. Wide beach. Seagulls perched on a fishing pier that stretches into a calm sea.

EXT. WIDE BEACH
Couples stroll along the sand. A house, with a deck, faces out. Inside there's the SOUND of men talking, loudly. CLOSER we hear the sounds of a POKER GAME.

INT. HOUSE
A living room. Five MEN, middle-aged, sit at a round table, engaged in a hand of poker. A YOUNG BOY watches, listens.

The hand ends. A tall, gregarious MAN, the boy's father, is at the head seat. He rakes in the money.

MAN
In the words of my Grampa Jake, I ain't had so much fun since the hogs ate Gramma.

MAN II
Where do you find these old sayings?

MAN III
I think they're disgusting.

The boy, sitting near his father, looks up.

BOY
You never had a Grampa Jake, Dad, did you?

DAD
No, but Charlie Buck did.

BOY
Who?

DAD
The man who almost won the biggest poker game of World War II.

This gets the others' attention.

>   MAN II
>   What was that?

>   DAD
>   When a member of the British Parliament
>   and a Spanish beauty cooked up the
>   million-dollar game on a liberty ship
>   traveling from Antwerp to New York in the
>   summer of 1945. Five men, a million
>   dollars, murder, and a big sting in the
>   end.

The boy leans forward in his chair, ready to hear this tale.

I was that boy. That night my father told the most perfect story I had ever heard.

At the table: the five top poker players of the European and North African theaters of operation. At stake: one million dollars, winner takes all. The audience: 250 soldiers coming home from war. The mystery: Who was killing off the players, one by one, and why? Agatha Christie meets *The Cincinnati Kid*.

The story mesmerized me. I said to my father, "How did you hear about this, Dad?" and he replied, "I was the Special Services officer on the ship. I ran the game." The story came out of the blue, out of my own family. I wasn't looking for it; it simply materialized. Over the years I never forgot it. When I started writing, the story surfaced in my memory. What a great tale, I thought. A murder mystery, a wham-bang ending, and it was based on truth. I would have been an idiot not to have seen the elements of good storytelling here. I wondered about these five characters and what winning, or losing, meant to them. As time passed, I would ask myself a crucial question that writers should always ask when faced with the possibility of writing a story: Would I read this book? Or: Would I see this movie? To which I answered a resounding yes.

I had to write this story. I also had to forget for the moment about being a writer or an author. Instead, I had to think about telling a story, weaving a tapestry, spinning a yarn. I was given a gift, this story. Now, how was I going to put it down on paper? The story stayed with me. Many years later—when I was playing a game of poker with my father and his cronies, some of whom had not heard this story before—I urged him to repeat it.

When my father finished, I asked if he would take time to sit down with me so I could record him telling the story. He agreed. As a result, I wrote a book entitled *The Crossing*. It was published and got good reviews. A Hollywood producer optioned it as a movie. That was fourteen years ago. Since then it's been optioned at least a dozen times, though it's never been made. It's still on that never-ending ride through Hollywood called "Development Hell."

The point here is that, like a photographer who is always looking for the startling image, as a writer you learn how to spot raw material. You take it and turn it into your own story, hoping to reach the movie screen. But how do you get it there, how do you turn raw material into workable material? Tools. Called the Craft of Screenwriting. Learn how to use the tools and the job gets easier.

Some people say you can't teach anyone to write. I agree. Artistically. Craftwise, I don't. Art needs a home, which is craft. Craft is a place where art can live, and grow, find its natural structure, a foundation, a world. You need a story, because without a story you have no screenplay; without a screenplay, you have no movie.

Fundamental Elements of Storytelling

As a kid, I was profoundly affected by two movies. The first was *Portrait of Jenny*, starring Jennifer Jones, about a woman discovering her identity. It takes place on the dark, brooding Maine coast. It fascinated and scared the hell out of me. Dreams of that movie still haunt me. In them, I see Jennifer Jones peering into a pool and suddenly seeing her own reflection staring back at her. I see the terror on her face—the shocking realization of self. She plays a tortured character discovering her dark inner self. As I think about this now, I can see myself looking into my own childhood pool, shocked by the distorted faces staring back at me.

The second picture, *The Crimson Pirate*, starring Burt Lancaster, exploded on the screen. A high-seas action-adventure with swashbucklers, treasure chests of gold, and exotic South Sea paradises, it had death and mayhem, island girls, cruel pirates, heroes, villains, and lots of fun. *The Crimson Pirate* had it all. For a young boy, this was better than tree houses, baseball, or TV. These two movies were very different in subject matter and mood, but they both had in common one essential thing—a good story that grabbed me.

In Hollywood, the story gets you in the door. The first question a producer asks is not *who* the movie's about but *what* it's about. A compelling story gets you into the room, strong characters keep you there. Without a strong story to guide them, your characters, though they may be fully developed, will wander aimlessly around until the producer yawns and thanks you for your time.

With this in mind, I am going to lead you through the door and into that room. In the chapters following, we'll learn how to build a screenplay together. We'll set aside the author and the writer hats, and put on the storyteller's hat. In that role, we'll learn to keep the reader fascinated and on the edge of his seat, wanting more.

The ultimate goal of all screenwriting is to create an emotional response, first in the reader and then in the audience who will pay good money to see your movie.

In the Steve McQueen movie *The Hunter*, my goal was to figure out how I could transform the book I wrote into something that audiences would want to see on the screen. I sat in my room and said to myself, "I've got a central character, a modern day bounty hunter, that I've got to get through Acts I, II, and III, and finally to a climax."

Just because I had written the book didn't mean that I could bypass the fundamental elements of storytelling in screenplay format.

A short list of the fundamental elements of storytelling:

1. Your story should take place at the most crucial time in your main character's life. Which means you can never make life too easy on your main character.
Like the card players in *The Crossing*, for whom winning and losing means everything, in *The Hunter* a bounty hunter has to bring back the most nasty desperadoes he has ever faced. His wife is pregnant (with a child that, despite his protests, she decided to have anyway) and being stalked by a madman. His best friend, a cop, is under indictment for drug smuggling. His finances and health are in shambles. In other words, the main character is going through emotional and physical hell.

A hundred and fifty years ago, novelist Henry James wrote that if a main character is not put through the most critical time of his life, the story is *not worth telling*. That is just as true today.

Put your main character in lots of trouble. Otherwise, the story is not worth telling. If your character has been through these trials in the past, he'll know how to deal with them. He must be challenged constantly.* Throw only the most surprising and difficult obstacles into his path. Make him sweat. Keep tension and unpredictability alive on every

---

* As standard practice, and for practical reasons, I'll sometimes use the masculine "he" rather than the feminine "she" when referring to a generic character. I do not mean to offend, but to simplify.

page. You've got to be hard on your protagonist so that he will be forced to change in a significant way during the course of the story.

2. Your main character wants to reach his objective more than anything he has ever wanted before, and he *must be willing to do anything* to get there.

Make it nearly impossible for him to get what he wants, and let's see how he handles it. It's said that in the best stories the main character reaches a point near the end of Act II where he can never hope to reach his objective, and then, because he reaches down inside one last time for the strength to do it, in Act III he gets the job done.

3. The story's focus should be on how your character faces these hurdles and whether or not he overcomes them.

What choices does he encounter? What failures does he endure? How does he grow through adversity? The journey of your main character is called the Spine of the story. Everything revolves around this spine. Every scene is written around it. The story stays on it, *is* it. The Spine keeps you focused and prevents you from wandering off somewhere and getting lost.

4. External Villains & Internal Demons

Nothing moves forward in any story except through physical or emotional conflict. Enter the villains and the demons.

External forces, villains, or antagonists, lurk in the shadows and strike when least expected. They can be bad guys, evil strangers who come to town, viruses, diseases, the next-door neighbor, a boyfriend, a wife, or even the kids. They are the things that come to get your main character in the middle of the night. Your reader needs to see them, be shocked or upset by them, feel them jumping off the page. Sometimes these forces are natural, like mountains to climb, or deserts to cross. Or maybe it's Jack Nicholson as a Marine commander whom Tom Cruise has to wear down in *A Few Good Men*. It's the million dollars and all it represents that Demi Moore has to face in *Indecent Proposal*. It's the river and gunboats in *The African Queen*. The nasty mother in *Welcome to the Dollhouse*, a Sundance winner and must-see picture.

Or it's the internal demons that make your characters really sweat, the ghosts of the past stalking them. Your characters' internal forces are the demons of their own worst fears, the emotional saboteurs we carry inside that prevent us from getting what we really want in life. Our obsessions. Our trepidations. Our personal terrors. The reasons we can't go the extra mile, or through a door, or get to the computer to write. Like Nicholson in *The Shining*. Look what happened to him.

Your character has established debilitating behavior patterns: picking the wrong lovers, getting in the same jams, having the same old arguments with the same old people. The character's life has been plagued by these behavior patterns/demons. By choosing this most critical moment in the life of your main character, you are testing him, and asking him to break the pattern once and for all and get on with his life. And it's not going to be easy. In fact, this will be the biggest test the character will have ever faced, beating back these demons. *Otherwise the story is not worth telling.*

Take a moment to think. What about your own internal demons? What is your greatest fear, that obsession, that thing you do too much of, or eat too much of, drink too much of? The one thing that, more than any other, has prevented you from getting what you have wanted all your life. You know what it is. The thing you don't want anymore because it's screwing your life up. Again. What would you like to shed, knowing that without it you'd be free? What's the emotional baggage you carry with you—the thing that says to you, "You'll never get that. Forget it. You don't deserve it. It's too difficult. You can't do it. Give it up!" What would you be willing to do to get rid of it? How far would you go?

You know what it is. Put this to good use and give it to your main character to carry around. See what he or she will do with it. You never know—in addition to writing a strong character, you might also figure out how to rid yourself of the demon.

In the course of the screenplay, your main character has to face each of these demons. I'm not talking about Sylvester Stallone wiping out the entire Laotian military to keep America free of yellow peril. I'm speaking of the dark interiors of our inner natures where fear thrives. Tap into that and you'll have a truly magnificent struggle for your character to overcome.

When the audience leaves the theater they take not the plot nor the scenery, nor the body count, but the main character's heroic struggle against his external villains and inner demons. For these reasons more than any others, *Casablanca* and *Citizen Kane* always appear on the "Ten Best Films of All Time" lists.

Where to Find Stories

A friend and fellow writer, the late Gary Provost, was looking through *USA Today* one morning and discovered an article about a Schenectady woman who tracks down missing persons by unusual means. He called her and set up a meeting. They struck a deal. Gary wrote a book, *Finder,* about her and her business, from which a TV movie was made. A writer has to actively pursue good ideas. Don't let laziness or fear hold you back when your instinct tells you that you've gotten hold of one.

Newspapers and magazines are excellent places to find stories of conflict and originality. I found one of my favorites in an Ann Landers column about a man who was in love with his own father-in-law, and the love, he suspected, was reciprocal. He wondered if he should tell his wife, or confront his father-in-law, who lived in the same house. Talk about family conflict.

One of the main reasons people go to the movies is to see people accomplish things they can't. Audience members identify with these struggles. They marvel at a character's dexterity, compassion, or how fear suddenly clamps down on someone. They get to *watch* the fear unfold and wrap the character in its snakelike grip. Then they root for the character to get out of the scrape. At the end the audience can then go home without having to deal with the consequences. The goal of writers is to choose critical moments in their characters' lives, compress them into a dramatic form, and see what their characters are made of when they face these dramatic times.

I have a writer friend whose grandfather was about to marry a woman thirty years his junior. The children went berserk. Inheritance issues came up. Some family members defended the old man, and others hired lawyers to prove his incompetence. My friend, who saw her family on a collision course, stepped forward, only to get run over by her crazed relatives. She pulled herself together, dusted herself off, and continued into the fray. She finally had to pull herself out or get run down for good. And she began doing the only constructive thing she could think of—turning the conflict into a screenplay. This crisis was terrible for family stability but made undeniably great drama.

A Dog Day Afternoon originated from a newspaper article about a guy who robbed a Brooklyn bank to get enough money for a sex change operation for his boyfriend.

Paul Schrader wrote *Taxi Driver* after traveling for months on the Silver Streak between Chicago and San Francisco doing research for a screenplay about a man who rides a train. He found the man, Travis

Bickle, all right, but he took him off the train and put him behind the wheel of a taxi. Schrader gave the train research to Colin Higgins, who wrote and directed *Silver Streak*.

By the time the story reaches you, the writer, the important thing to remember is how you can remake it into a tale to which the audience can respond. Good stories pass major litmus tests along the way. Each teller of the story uses a little tuck here, a pinch there, a turn of a phrase, a white lie, or a blatant falsehood. It's probably no longer even close to the original, but so what? Never let the truth get in the way of the good story.

One of my favorite movies started with a real-life situation, written by a writer who had never been published before. In a Chicago suburb, the writer had for some time been noticing strange goings-on at the next-door neighbors'. She saw a family of four: a seventeen-year-old boy, a fourteen-year-old boy, and their mother and father. The previous summer the older boy, an athlete-scholar, the smart kid, the one destined for fame and fortune, tragically died in a boating accident. His death sent shock waves through his family, from which they were not recovering. She learned that the younger brother blamed himself for the death. The mother turned rigid, cold, and stopped functioning altogether. The father tried, but without much success, to hold the family together.

Judith Guest, the observer and writer, saw an extraordinary story unfolding before her eyes. A simple story about a tragic moment in the life of a family.

Guest filed away the information; she changed events, altered characters, and made the story more palatable. She structured the story with a beginning, middle, and end. Then she wrote the book, *Ordinary People*, and sent it to a New York publisher where it ended up in a slush pile, the heap of unsolicited manuscripts that editors get to last.

By chance, an editor discovered and published it. This simple story about ordinary people at the most critical moment of their lives became a bestselling novel, and Robert Redford directed an Academy Award-winning movie from it.

Judith Guest did not have to go to faraway places to find her story. She did not even leave her own house. Good stories are right under your nose. You have to learn to recognize them. The best stories seem to be close at hand, at the writer's fingertips. The trick is being able to see them.

Ordinary People has two essential elements that all good stories should have: originality and familiarity. What Judith Guest saw across her window box was starkly original, an upper-middle-class family into which a bomb drops, the death of a favored son. The story is about how the family reacts to the bomb, how the fallout nearly destroys them, all the while pointing to our *familiarity* with the human tragedy these people suffered. We can identify with their pain and suffering, and with their hope. It's an original story with emotions familiar to us all. Most important, it moved Judith Guest. And she knew it would move others.

Look around your own neighborhood, inside your group of friends or family. What about the tragedy that struck your family members? A death, a divorce, a stranger who showed up unexpectedly. What consequences did the tragedy force them into, what hell did they endure? In these tragic moments you will find the seeds of human despair and human triumph, stories with which we can all identify. And you the writer know the people and the events. You have first-hand, on-the-scene knowledge. Or you can find out by asking a few questions.

Despite what you might think, filmmakers want original stories, told from a particular point of view, about real life situations.

Exercise

Do you have an idea for a story? Write it down here.

Exercise

Fill in the blanks:

"This is a story about _____
                          so-and-so

who wants _____
              such-and-such

and will do anything to get it!"

Put the above message over your computer and refer to it constantly. Everything you write must have something to do with this statement, as this is the spine of your story.
   For example:

- Tootsie changes genders in order to get what he wants—to work again.
- Lawrence of Arabia faces the trials and tribulations of a vast desert, thousands of miles from home, in order to right the world and discover himself.
- Billy Bob Thornton, in *Sling Blade*, kills the evil stepfather to free the boy and his mother, and to free himself from the world outside prison walls.
- Melanie Griffith, in *Working Girl*, takes over her boss's job and boyfriend in order to prove that she can realize her dreams.

Is your character willing to sacrifice everything, and do anything, in order to reach the goal? He had better be—otherwise you haven't got a story worth telling.

3
Character

Begin with an individual and you find that you have
created a type; begin with a type and you find that you
have created . . . nothing.

F. Scott Fitzgerald, novelist and
author of *The Great Gatsby*

Fuck structure and grab your characters by the balls.

Jack Kerouac, novelist and
author of *On the Road*

The definition of plot is character in action. Character is the flesh and
blood of every screenplay. Without well-defined characters you have no
chance of getting your movie made because no stars will agree to act in
it. Without a star saying yes, movies don't get made.

You may wonder, considering many of the flimsy films that have
made it to the big screen, how they get there? The truth is, many
screenplays bought by studios are quite good in their original form. In
the process of getting a movie made, a lot of character is washed out in
the development process. Look what happened to *Up Close and Personal*, a film originally based on the life of Jessica Savitch, which could
have been a true piece of art, that over nine years in development
became a true piece of junk.

Among the producers, directors, and market researchers, the good
stuff is often replaced with homogenized product. This is the failure of
"art by committee." That old saw—a camel is a horse made by a committee—found a home in the movie business. Moviemaking is a very
conservative business that takes few new directions or chances and
relies more on financial performance than artistic integrity when decid-
ing which movies to make.

This should not dissuade you from creating the very best characters you can. Many films work because the writer's original vision and characters are so strong that even the producers and directors cannot ruin it. The Coen brothers, Ethan and Joel—famous for creating original characters—write, produce, and direct their own pictures. In *Fargo* they pit a steadfast woman cop (played by Frances McDormand) who goes about her business with simple, clear-eyed vigor, against an out-of-control villain (played by William H. Macy), a weak-willed son-in-law whose only desire is to be his own man. Most Hollywood filmmakers know a good idea when they see it. What happens once the idea goes into development hell is another story. As a writer, you leave nothing for anyone else to do. You give to your characters an originality and complexity they don't want to screw around with because the characters are so damn good. That should be your goal.

Once you know *what* the story is about, you then have to concentrate on *who* it's about. Four types of characters generally populate movies. Once you get these in place, you can start to have fun. *The Hero or Heroine. The Villain. The Buddy. The Romantic Interest.*

The Hero or Heroine

Stories belong to *heroes and heroines*. They appear on almost every page of the screenplay. The camera focuses on them. They should be on screen about ninety percent of the time (in other words, don't lose them for long periods of time). The pacing of the movie depends upon the emotional and/or physical roller coaster you send them on. We as audience members depend on their rise and fall, and rise again, for our entertainment. It's why we go to the movies. We want to feel vicariously what these characters experience. Could we ever hope to survive what Scarlett O'Hara went through, or Lawrence of Arabia, or Rocky? The hero or heroine is who your story hinges upon.

Consider these guidelines

1. Never make your main characters too good up front because you'll have no place to go from there but down.
Don't make your main character too heroic or too wonderful in the beginning. You need a human being with vulnerabilities and problems. Give your character common dilemmas that we can identify with, because no one can identify with perfection.

Some characters are just awful people on the surface, but they still fascinate us. Look at Pacino's character in *Godfather II*. The protagonist is a Mafia don who sacrifices his wife and children to power. His is a case study of a diabolical, evil character, and yet, he captivates us.

In *The Last Seduction* the Linda Fiorentino character is a tough-talking, ball-busting woman that you wouldn't want as your best pal, but we can't take our eyes off her or stop wondering what she's going to do next.

In *Scent of a Woman,* Al Pacino plays a drunken, self-loathing, blind colonel who is so bitter that he tries to destroy everyone around him before attempting to take his own life. For some, this character is irredeemable. The writers take him so far out of our zone of sympathy that nothing can bring him back. I waited for the Pacino character to make a comeback and felt that the writers succeeded in locating within their character, if he stopped drinking, the potential for grace.

Henry Higgins, in *My Fair Lady,* is an intellectual know-it-all. In the beginning, you can't stand this officious snob. Through his relationship with Eliza Doolittle, he finds some humility. He faces up to his problems. He climbs down off his pedestal and finally becomes a human being.

The Laura Dern character, Rose, in *Rambling Rose* is saucy, flamboyant, troubled, emotionally needy, confused—character complexity at its very best. In creating this character, Calder Willingham was not afraid to mix it up. He struggled mightily to discover what made his character tick. You must do the same.

2. Pay attention to cause and effect.
Character should be the cause of everything and plot should be the effect, rather than the other way around. If you allow plot rather than character to drive your story, you end up with a series of contrived moments that will not engage the audience. Characters should be in charge. They are the engines running the story. You, as the writer, serve the story. "Characters have their own lives and their own logic," says Isaac Bashevis Singer, "and you [the writer] have to act accordingly."

The difference between a live screenplay and a dead one is that in the live one the characters take control. In the dead one, the writer depends upon plot to move the story forward because he cannot bear to relinquish his throne to his characters. In these ego-driven cases, the writer asks how *he, the writer,* would react to each situation, and not how his characters would.

3. Don't forget punks, deadbeats, and the common man.
Look at Peter Falk's character in *Columbo,* a schlemiel in a trench coat who can't do anything right. Underneath it all, however, he's a canny,

wily police lieutenant with a first-class brain. Notice that the writers always pit Columbo against suave, sophisticated, wealthy, driven women and men, outwardly successful, but inwardly unkempt and gnarly. The opposite of Columbo. Do you have elements in your story that suggest this kind of approach? What creature lies beneath the clothes?

4. Remember that your main character always wants something and will do anything to get it.

The main character's drive becomes the spine of the story. Your character sees something he wants. He goes after it. He's blocked. He tries another approach. That one's blocked. He knows he needs to get creative. He tries another. See how this works. The entire story is like the carrot on the stick. Character going after carrot is the main line. It keeps you focused on the story. I've read hundreds of screenplays in which the writer forgot about this and trailed off somewhere. These screenplays lost focus, forgot about the main character, and finally fell apart.

Two questions to ask yourself constantly:

What does my character want?

What will my character risk to get it?

Al Pacino's character in *Dog Day Afternoon* wants a sex change for his boyfriend. To get the money, he decides to rob a bank on a sunny Brooklyn afternoon. He's willing to break the law, even kill, for love. How much gumption does your character have, to what lengths will he go to get what he wants? That's your story.

5. Give your character a ruling passion.

A feverish dedication, a compulsion, a fear, a terror, an issue that drives your character or that has prevented him from getting just about everything he's ever wanted.

You've chosen this story, at this moment, for your main character to shed the thing that keeps him down. It's not going to be easy for him and that's why it's the most critical time in his life. Not only is your character going after something; in order to reach it he has to shed this THING, this monkey on his back that he's been carrying forever. The shedding of this THING is one of his options for reaching his objective. But it's not easy to shed old habits, old behaviors; like getting rid of a relationship you know is killing you, or cigarettes you know are eating away at your lungs, it takes a monumental effort. Your character needs a monumental effort to make your story work.

In *Taxi Driver*, ex-Vietnam Marine Travis Bickle is a mess of tangled obsessions. He obsesses over women he can't have and, even more, the men who can, and do, have them. The movie takes place inside his nightmarish head as we look at the world through his anger. It is in this story that he reaches his breaking point.

In *In The Line of Fire*, the Clint Eastwood character has his burden, a thirty-year-old wound inflicted on the day he failed to save President John F. Kennedy from a sniper's bullet. In this story, the opportunity arises to redeem himself. The present-day sniper, played by John Malkovich, has come to haunt him. Clint is much older, physically and emotionally, than he was thirty years ago. He wonders if he'll be able to meet the challenge. Facing the demons of his past, *and* a malevolent enemy in the present, he knows he must. He marches forward, reaching inside for courage and stamina that might not even be there anymore.

6. A character with a tragic flaw has to face up to it by the end.
A main character is transformed when he stands up to a crucial problem. In order to reach his full potential, your character has to resolve not only his external problems but also the fears and intolerance that have botched up his life. He reaches a *point of revelation* when he understands his problem and knows he must do something about it.

You have two conflicts for your main character to face: *Getting to the Point of Revelation* and *The Action of Resolution*. Both are difficult, painful journeys.

In *Guess Who's Coming to Dinner*, Spencer Tracy suffers from confused liberalism. He says, "Oh, I think black people are wonderful. I talk to them every day. They're fabulous, just like you and me." Then his daughter brings a black man to dinner, and suddenly Spencer Tracy has to face up to the truth of his intolerance.

In *Midnight Cowboy*, Jon Voight is a Texas boy who arrives in Manhattan with spangles and jangles, and the intention of seducing New York City women out of their money. He doesn't make a cent. The women laugh at him, call him a fool. He's a walking joystick in a ten-gallon hat. He has spent twenty years building an image, and in two days it self-destructs. Everything comes into question for him, especially his sexuality. Things happen. He reacts by engaging in a homosexual relationship. He gets beaten up. He ends up on the street. He hits bottom. Once there, stripped of all artifice, he opens his eyes and the light begins to shine. He finds something he doesn't expect at all— friendship. And he finds it with a very unlikely character, Ratso Rizzo, played by Dustin Hoffman. *Midnight Cowboy* is the painful story of a man who, through a series of shocking events, begins to unravel. All of the protective roles he has wrapped himself in—stud, lover, seducer—

peel away. When the objects of his obsession, women, laugh at him, he becomes undone. Now what's he going to do about it. Not what *you the writer* are going to do about it, but what your *character* is going to do about it. This is the question writer Waldo Salt asked of his character in *Midnight Cowboy,* and why he won the Oscar for his effort.

In *The Apartment* a reluctant bachelor, played by Jack Lemmon, gets caught up in his boss's love trysts, and as a result falls in love with one of the women. Even though he knows better, he's undeniably swept away by love for the boss's girl, played by Shirley MacLaine. The movie is about shedding fears and insecurities and accepting something that's right—and right in front of him—no matter how much he resists it.

7. Remember that a hero's/heroine's imperfections make him or her human.

A wonderful example of this is that most perfect-seeming of all characters in literature, Cyrano de Bergerac. But Cyrano does have one imperfection, and it is this imperfection that sabotages his chance for the one thing he desperately wants—love.

Cyrano has a nose, a gargantuan schnoz, and he is so ashamed of it that he hides behind other men's looks while offering his love to women.

Cyrano doesn't give women too much credit. He thinks they are more concerned with surface than substance. When in actuality, it's he, Cyrano, who's strapped by that notion. Until he realizes, through the lovely Rosalind, that it is not the nose but its owner that makes the man. Gérard Depardieu, in a dazzling performance, played the classic Cyrano, while Steve Martin in *Roxanne,* a contemporary adaptation of this story, made his "Cyrano" an engaging and very human character. They faced up to their demons. Your characters must face up to their demons, which they've been carrying around for a long time.

In his early movies, Woody Allen's big problem was never getting the girl. Never. This was his trademark—the poor intellectual schlub who's alone in the end.

At the time he was writing *Hannah and Her Sisters, The Purple Rose of Cairo,* my personal favorite of his films, came out to rave reviews. Woody Allen received such phenomenal notices for *Purple Rose* that he grew insecure. He had written and directed the picture, but not acted in it. So what did he do? He quickly wrote himself into *Hannah.* Until that time the movie had no role for Woody. So, into the script comes his old standard, the Jewish neurotic upon whom Woody Allen made his reputation. Even more shocking is that in the end, Woody Allen gets the girl! Here's an example of not only the character getting what he wants, but also the writer.

8. Watch out for clichés.
Writers, I among them, often see someone familiar coming their way— the dumb blonde, the mousy librarian, the stiff anal-retentive accountant—and feel a certain safety in this familiarity. False security. A cliché offers no safety. It points to laziness and lack of imagination. If you've seen it before, it's a cliché. Forget about the excuse that if it's been used before it must be okay, or paying homage to former characters of the same ilk. Strike out for something original, or against type. Recognize these hackneyed images, phrases, or characters for what they are. Cheap, lazy, and plagiaristic.

The Villain

"In most stories, villains provide the plot and make virtue interesting. Imagine the tedium of *Snow White* without the witch or *Little Red Riding Hood* without the wolf, the story of *Robin Hood* without the Sheriff of Nottingham or *Cinderella* without the Ugly Sisters. . . . The villains have always been the great entertainers, making the spectators feel safe in their comparative decency, enthralled by the wicked machinations on the stage and grateful that nothing like that is happening to them." So writes John Mortimer in his introduction to *The Oxford Book of Villains* (Oxford University Press). The villain is an essential piece of any story.

Consider these guidelines

1. The villain drives the story toward catastrophe.
The villain sabotages the intention of the main character and generally makes his life miserable. The stronger the villain, so the wisdom goes, the better the movie.

If you do not have a complex, well-written, dangerous adversary, your hero will not have to face the kind of competition that makes for riveting dramatic conflict. If your villain does not sorely test your hero, the reader falls asleep. Nothing moves forward in any screenplay except through conflict. If the villain is dull and the conflict is soft, the story suffers and the writer starts contriving plot devices in the absence of character.

On the other hand, if you have too many villains, as in *Batman*

Returns, you end up with a mishmash of unfocused writing and ultimately a scatter gun story. In that movie, one villain, the Christopher
Walken character, has nothing to do. He stands around waiting for
something to happen. Michelle Pfeiffer as Catwoman can't decide
whose side she's on, and is seized by the paralysis of ambivalence.
Danny DeVito is so repulsive and silly that he's never a villain except
to his own miserable self. If the people who made *Batman Returns* had
paid attention to The Joker's impact in the original *Batman* by using
one strong central villain the movie might have stood a chance.

2. Pay as much attention to developing your villain as you do to your main character.

Determine what in the villain's past brought about the evil. Ask how
these influences translate into present-day action. How will this wily,
treacherous villain sabotage the hero's intentions?

Hannibal Lechter, in *The Silence of the Lambs,* fascinates us. Hannibal puts Clarice through hell, because in his own sick way he sees her
as a challenge. They battle wits, one on one. We come to appreciate
both characters. At the end we even root for Hannibal as he prepares to
have the despicable psychiatrist for lunch. He is a complex and fascinating man, not simply an evil one, who plays havoc with our emotions.
How can we care about this guy after what he does? But we do. We fear
him and he mesmerizes us, and we can't wait to see what he'll do next.

3. In movies with institutions as villains, you must personify the evil by creating a character as complex and harrowing as the institution itself.

Movies like *The China Syndrome, The Verdict, Blade Runner,* and *Nine
to Five* are driven by strong villains who represent oppressive institu-
tions.

In movies where nature is the villain, in which man battles the
elements, the stories often begin with a quest like crossing a desert or
going on a weekend raft trip down a river with a bunch of pals. Nature
interrupts through storm, flood, quake, or by the creatures of nature
itself. *Jaws, Deliverance, The River,* and all the aptly-named disaster
movies fall into this category. *Twister. Titanic. Anaconda.*

4. The most critical conflict in almost all movies should be man against himself, the villain within.

Hamlet's indecision is his own worst enemy. *Dr. Jekyll and Mr. Hyde* is
the quintessential man-against-self story. Dr. Frankenstein created a
monster who turns on its own creator, the ultimate masochism. The Jack

Nicholson character in *Five Easy Pieces* searches for the past, only to find, at the end, his own misconception of it. Battling one's own demons comes into this. Nicholas Cage in *Leaving Las Vegas. Trainspotting.* Maggie Smith's riveting character in *The Lonely Passion of Judith Hearn.*

5. Never neglect the power of your villain.
What would Watergate have been without Richard Nixon? Or Irangate without Oliver North? The Three Little Pigs without the Big Bad Wolf? James Bond without Dr. No? We loathe Shylock, yet he says, "Hath not a Jew eyes? If you prick us, do we not bleed? If you poison us, do we not die? And if you wrong us, shall we not take revenge?" As much as we despise the man, we sympathize with him. This complexity makes him one of the immortals.

If the villain drives the story toward catastrophe, it stands to reason that he rules the story until the hero, beaten back at every turn, decides to stop running and take a stand. In this way, the villain controls the first two-thirds of the story. How does he do this?

The villain engineers the plot, through greed or fear, toward the achievement of his own goals. His goals eventually conflict with the hero's, creating the central conflict of the story.

What if *Casablanca* were told from the German commander's point of view? It was, in the writer's mind. The writer understands all points of view in order keep dramatic conflict alive. And the writer who knows what she is doing always treats the villain with at least as much respect and interest as she does the main character. Writing the villain is often a lot more fun. The Sheriff of Nottingham is a lot more interesting than that slug from the forest, Robin Hood, ever was.

As an exercise, list your five or six favorite movies and imagine the story from the villain's point of view. How, for instance, would *The Graduate* have been different if told from Mrs. Robinson's perspective?

6. Nothing progresses in a story except through conflict.
The greatest conflict in a story happens between the hero and the villain. Without a compelling antagonist, you don't have a story worth telling. Without a powerful Darth Vader, Luke Skywalker would have been a doe-eyed Huck Finn in space. Without the avaricious Mr. Potter in *It's a Wonderful Life,* hero George Bailey would never have exercised his nobility.

By concentrating on the villain, you'll be able to see your story from a new and original point of view. Always ask yourself: How does my villain see all this? What does he or she want? Most of the time your hero has no idea what is going on, but your villain does. Your villain knows just about everything; he's powerful, manipulative, and will do anything to get what he wants. Never make the villain some dumb, mindless adversary. He should be sly and cunning. The villain may be the lover in disguise or the best friend who plots behind the hero's back. The villain usually holds a secret that the hero must discover. Paint your villain so powerfully that your hero must go through hell to overthrow him in the end.

The Buddy

The buddy, or reflection character, takes the place of the main character's thoughts, which you find in novels. In movies everything must be visual; you can't see thought. The Buddy shares the hopes and dreams of the main character and allows him to talk to somebody instead of walking around the entire movie in soliloquy, or voice-over.

In movies, it's not a good idea to create a man alone in nature. You don't want your main character saying things like, "Oh, let me speak to my heart. . . ." Or worse, "Let my heart do all the speaking for me. . . ." Your main character needs someone to talk to, who shares his dreams and aspirations and will listen to his problems. Almost every movie has a buddy. In *Casablanca,* Humphrey Bogart and Claude Raines are buddies to the end. Without this relationship to help us along, we know very little about the story. Thelma is Louise's buddy in *Thelma and Louise,* and Louise is Thelma's buddy.

To shake things up, the buddy might also be the love interest, or could turn out to be the villain. This provides for irony and surprise and makes life much more interesting for your main character.

The Romantic Interest

The romantic interest tugs at the main character's heart, or breaks it. Movies always exploit love of some kind; bad love or good love, love gone awry, uplifting love, dysfunctional love, love that wanes.

When I lived in Hollywood, MGM bought my brain on an annual basis for a lot of money. This meant they got first crack at my ideas for movies. I was also required to watch *rough cuts* of films. Rough cuts are films without titles or music, patched-together footage to give the viewer—in this case studio people—some idea of what they paid for.

One of my favorite stories took place in a screening room at MGM.

From the back row, after viewing a director's rough cut, a studio executive yells out, "Where's the girl?"

"The girl?" says the director. "What girl?"

"The love interest. Where's the love interest?"

"There is no love interest."

"What!" the studio executive shouts. "I wanna see a love interest. Splice one in. Be back here in two weeks." At which point he rises and leaves the screening room.

The director scurries around half mad, getting his writer to write in a love story, casting a love interest, shooting the scenes, inserting the scenes into four or five places in the film, and returning to the screening room, two weeks later, with the horrible, patched-together results.

In most pictures, a romantic interest is a must. Sometimes the romantic interest shows up and then vanishes, as Robert DeNiro's wife does in *A Bronx Tale*. Or she gets killed off to show that the hero cares, as in the Rambo pictures.

In *Rambo IV*, which takes place in the Laos jungle, Rambo falls in love in record time with an Asian woman—in the midst of battle, no less. In the battle, the girl gets riddled with bullets. He holds her dying body in his arms, buries her in the river, and goes off to fight some more. In the early stages, somebody must have said, "He needs a love interest," and this is what he got.

Romantic interests work, at least strong ones do. Without a love interest, *Casablanca* becomes *Ishtar: A Prequel*. Love drives characters forward and acts as a prime motivating force in the creation of believable characters.

Exercise

In your story, identify your four types of characters:

Hero/heroine
Villain
Buddy/sidekick
Romantic interest

Remember that not all movies have all these elements, nor should they. But these elements show up in the vast majority because they provide drama and conflict.

Exercise: Once Again

Who is your main character and what is his or her journey?

4

Creating Characters

You can never know enough about your characters.

> W. Somerset Maugham, novelist
> and author of *Of Human Bondage*
> and *The Razor's Edge*

Consider the beginning of *The Crossing*, where we meet the central character:

FADE IN:

EXT. CENTURY HOTEL, ANTWERP, AUGUST 1945—EARLY AFTERNOON
A taxi pulls in front of the Century Hotel, Antwerp's finest.
Flags of Allied nations fly over the entrance. The war is over.
Soldiers and pedestrians walk the street.

PFC EDWARD "ANIMAL" PODBEROSKI, chunky, medium height, in his
mid-thirties, exits the taxi. He wears a sloppy, wrinkled Army
uniform, as if he has just climbed out of a trench. He carries a
bird cage, draped by an Army-issue rain poncho.

The TAXI DRIVER opens the trunk. Animal pays the driver. A
BELLHOP takes the duffel bag, and goes for the bird cage.

> ANIMAL
> That's okay, pal. I'll carry this myself.

INT. HOTEL LOBBY—DAY
Lavish, with high ceilings and hand-carved moldings. Paintings
on the walls and Louis XIV furniture. Animal is at the front
desk.

> ANIMAL
> I'm Podberoski. You have a reservation
> for me?

                              CLERK
                Yes, sir. We've been expecting you.

The CLERK pulls a message from the slot, hands it to him.

                              CLERK
                Mr. Santini would like you to join him at
                the Cafe Lucarne at five o'clock.

The Bellhop takes the duffel bag, and Animal carries the bird
cage toward the elevator.

INT. HOTEL SUITE—DAY
Elegant. Murals on the walls, a magnificent view of the city.
Animal pulls the poncho off the bird cage, revealing a CANARY.

                              ANIMAL
                Hello, sweetheart, you look terrific.
                Hang on. I'll be right back.

He pulls out a wad of bills and hands the Bellhop a tip.

                              BELLHOP
                Ah, merci, monsieur. Merci.

                              ANIMAL
                You bet.

Animal spills the contents of the duffel bag onto the couch:
crumpled uniforms, crusty dirty clothes. He pulls out a bag of
bird feed.

INT. BEDROOM
Animal carries the bird cage in, places it on the window sill.
Opens the cage door.

                              ANIMAL
                Chow time, sweetheart.

He pinches bits of feed from the bag, and the Canary eats from
his hand. He pulls out the desk message and waving it at the
bird.

                              ANIMAL
                Right here, kiddo. Half a million
                bananas.

Inspecting himself in the mirror, splashing on cologne.

                    ANIMAL
        I'm heading downstairs now to meet a guy
        who's gonna make us rich. I get to pay off
        the family market and marry my beautiful
        Shirley. You get your gold cage and your
        ten stud canaries, the works.

He straightens his tie, gives a kiss-kiss to the bird.

                    ANIMAL
        Be a good girl. Papa's going to work.

What do we have here? A gruff looking soldier—a slob really, with a
wad of money and a pet canary—who takes a suite at the finest hotel in
the city and is meeting a man from whom he's going to get a half million
dollars. Not a bad beginning. In order to reach this starting point you
should do leg work, or research into character. Keeping in mind Somerset Maugham's comment that you can never know enough about your
characters, it pays to start with specific elementary aspects of character.
In this case I wanted to create enough contradictory impressions to
make the reader want to read on. Slob named Animal Podberoski stays
in the city's finest hotel. Talks to his pet bird. Is here about to collect a
half million dollars, by possibly nefarious means.

It's true that you should always plug anticipation into the text—the
lure of what will happen next—but the lure won't matter if your character is lifeless. Remember that story will get you through the door, and
character will carry you the rest of the way.

Some Character Considerations

1. Names

A name should fit your conception of the character. Names conjure up
images. Hollywood stars often use their names to suggest something.
Rock Hudson. Madonna. Ice-T. Your character may be named Lance
Stud or perhaps Harriet Bellefleur Wigginbotham.

Not long ago I wrote a script for Anthony Quinn, whose character was
a Ukrainian diplomat. What name, I wondered, would I give to him?
I've always liked the name Nikolai. To me it represents strength, dignity, and power. The first name was easy. But I could not come up with
a last name. I roamed through Chekhov's short stories searching for a
name that would somehow reflect on his job as diplomat. I found a
character in one of the stories whose last name is Danchenko. It fit.
Nikolai Danchenko. The name Danchenko has the sound of the word

"dance" in it. What does a diplomat/negotiator do? He dances around issues. He cajoles. He manipulates, he charms. But with strength and dignity, as a Nikolai would.

What about basing a character on a real person? In the beginning, go ahead and use the real name. At this point in the writing, the name conjures up the original source. In the end, if you're not comfortable using the real name, use the *find/change* function in your word processing program to change the name wherever it appears.

Remember Joe Galvin, the Paul Newman character in *The Verdict?* Joe Galvin, as in "galvanize." What about Harrison Ford's character, John Book, in *Witness,* the straight arrow who does everything by the book.

2. Photographs

When I start a project, I leaf through magazines looking for photographs of people who approximate my characters' looks. I cut the photos out and tack this rogues' gallery on the wall.

Each time I sit down to work, I stare at the photos, drawing the characters closer to me. They now have faces. Away from my desk, when I think about them, I can see them. I see in their expressions pain, anger, love, fear, obsession. They take on lives of their own, which all characters should do. I notice expressions in their eyes, mannerisms, even fears. By visiting these people every day, I grow closer to them.

Perhaps your character reminds you of a popular actor. Put up his or her photo. You are the creator. You must see them. Too often I hear about writers wondering about their creations—who they are, what they look like. Having an idea what they look like starts the process. How can you know them if you can't even see them? In movies, what you see is what you get.

3. Age

How old is your character? And why? Why twenty-nine instead of eighteen? In *The Graduate,* Ben Braddock, at a crucial point in his life, turns twenty-one. People about to turn a certain age—thirty, forty, fifty—may worry about it, lie about it, or fear what it will mean. People lie about their ages for many reasons. Would your character lie about his or her age, and why?

4. Height and weight

Short people have problems; tall people have problems. Wafer-thin people and people who carry extra weight may have problems. Health problems, self-image problems. Use these to establish characters. At one time or another most of us have problems with weight, posture. Use these problems if you can to define your characters and make them vulnerable, and human.

In *The Hunter,* the main character, modern-day bounty hunter Ralph Thorson, weighed nearly three hundred pounds. A man has to worry about carrying that much bulk around, especially a bounty hunter who at this size becomes a big moving target to his enemies. To stay alive, he has to rely that much more on his wits. When Steve McQueen decided to play the part, that aspect of character, which was reflected significantly in the life of Ralph Thorson and in the book, no longer mattered.

In the movie, McQueen performed stunts that Ralph Thorson, in real life, would never have been able to do. In real life, Thorson used his brain to capture his prey. But since you can't see thought in action movies, the wiry McQueen refashioned the role to fit his own persona. To be fair, McQueen kept Ralph Thorson's vulnerability in key ways— through his lousy driving, his confusion over women, and his refusal to bring a child into his dangerous world.

5. Eye and hair color

Unless you have a specific reason for using hair or eye color, don't bother. You don't want to limit casting potential. I've been in casting sessions where an actor says, "I'm not thirty-seven years old, with blond hair and blue eyes," and wouldn't take the part. You don't want to do that to yourself.

Sometimes, however, these physical characteristics matter. In *Chinatown,* for example, Jake Gittes notices something in Mrs. Mulwray's eye, an imperfection that fascinates him. The imperfection points to a flaw in her character, something dangerous, as it turns out. This is where the color of an eye works. If for instance you have a character who constantly changes her hair color, this shows something about the way the character feels about herself, or why she disguises herself.

6. Scars and handicaps

A character with a small half-moon-shaped scar on her right cheek has a story to tell. The scar, and the story behind it, can reveal worlds about the character, or a mysterious past. Piper Laurie in *The Hustler* has mental and physical handicaps. Tattoos cover Bruce Dern's entire body in *Tattoo.* In *The Wild Bunch,* William Holden limps, as does Ratso Rizzo in *Midnight Cowboy.* These defects, problems, or conditions define characters.

7. Educational background

Education, whether it's a Ph.D. in chemistry or in life, reveals a character's point of view, prejudices, biases, fears, down to the very words he uses in a sentence. In *My Fair Lady* and *Educating Rita,* the subject matter was education itself.

8. What do they listen to?

What kind of music does your character turn on when he gets into the car? When she walks into her apartment, what does she put on the stereo? Country? Classical? New Age? Rock? What do *you* listen to, and why? Give your musical preferences to your character if they fit.

The effect of this is to start asking your character what other habits and preferences he or she has—art, music, literature. Likes and dislikes. Though you may never use some of this in the script, the information serves the creation of the character. If you don't know who this person is, how are we going to know?

9. A room of one's own

Everyone has a special room, a place to hide or think. What's yours? It could be a bedroom filled with mementos, or a kitchen where you like to eat and read. Where does your main character go? What does the room look like? What do we learn about the character from the paintings on the wall, the colors, the knickknacks, the absence or presence of things—fuzzy bears piled up on the bed, golf clubs in the corner? Is the room tidy or a mess? Stark or well lit?

After *The China Syndrome* had been completed and just weeks away from distribution, someone asked the director, James Bridges, who the Jane Fonda character was. We only saw Fonda at work as a reporter, shoving microphones into people's faces, asking them questions. We saw no personal side.

In reply to the question, Bridges shot a three-minute scene in which Fonda goes home to her small colorful apartment—the paintings, the books, the things dearest to her. The phone rings. Who is it? Her mother. She now has a family. They have a conversation. In three minutes we learn a lifetime about this character, all because someone was canny enough to ask a question about the character's personal life.

Past World/Present World

Your characters live in two worlds, the past and the present. The *Past World* begins at the moment of birth and continues up until we first meet the character in the screenplay. The *Present World* is the world of the screenplay itself. If you don't develop the past, you cannot hope to understand your characters in the present.

The Past World

If writing is asking questions and answering them, ask yourself simple straightforward questions. To jump-start this process, ask these questions of your own past. After each question, close your eyes, and concentrate. This exercise will get you thinking about things to ask your characters.

- Where were you born?
- In affluence or poverty, or in between?
- Who was the most influential person (positive/negative) in your young life?
- Did your parents argue and fight?
- Was there a divorce, deaths of loved ones? What were the moments—good and bad—that you remember most?
- Would you say you had a happy childhood? Why, why not? Be specific.
- Who brought you up?
- How did you feel about them?
- How do you feel about them now?
- Were you an obedient child, or a difficult one?
- Were you closer to your mother, or your father? Why?
- Did you move a lot, or did you stay put in one house?
- Brothers, sisters?
- Were you an only child?
- Did you have many friends, real or imaginary?
- Did you spend a lot of time alone?
- What are your most poignant memories?
- Was your family nurturing?
- Was there alcoholism, addictions, anger, arguments?
- What kind of trouble, if any, upset the family?
- In your group of friends were you a leader? A follower?
- Did you fit in? Or in order to fit in, did you do things you should not have—like drink or take drugs—to be accepted?

Remember, these details may not show up in the script per se, but they create a past from which to draw the character now. Your characters have a past, just as you do. Build it well. It becomes the foundation for what comes later. You started behavior patterns, good and bad, back then; so did your character. Be truthful; the truth spills over to your characters and makes them real.

Let's move forward, into your adolescence, into your teens.

- How did you get along with your peers, or not get along?
- What about sex? Was it difficult, nonexistent? Frustrating?
- Love? Perhaps you were filled with love but had no one to give it to.
- Or perhaps you needed love, but no one was offering it. How did you react to this? What did you do?
- What were your most poignant moments in adolescence?

In adulthood your character is good at something. The childhood influences take form and shape. Perhaps a good work ethic emerges, or a poor one. Pay attention to influences. Mom's business acumen, Dad's artistic talent. Your character is influenced by events in the past. Draw the lines between then and now.

- In the present do you have trouble getting along with people; does your character? Or do people have a difficult time getting along with you? Why?
- What don't you want the world to see? How do you hide it?
- What do you do to compensate for it?
- What does your character do?
- Are you impetuous, overeager, impatient?
- Do you rush into things, into relationships or love affairs?
- Or do you hesitate? Are you conservative, cautious, do you look before you leap? Has this created problems, like not acting fast enough?

In my earlier writing, I didn't bother exploring my characters' pasts. I wanted to get to the first page and start writing! I suffered for it, and my characters did, too. I still have to remind myself to hold the horses back and build slowly.

Ask yourself these character bio questions. You'll get to know your creations. You'll also get to understand and appreciate them a lot more because the truth is you've got to like, or be fascinated by, your characters. If you're not, we're not.

Not examining your characters is like saying to someone you've just met, "It's great spending time with you, but I don't want to know anything about you before the moment we met." Develop a strong relationship with your characters' pasts. Take your character from childhood up until the moment the screen story begins, and beyond.

The Present World

Once you've got your characters' Past World worked out, the Present World becomes clearer. In the Present World, your characters live in three basic environments: the job, the home, the private self. Let's take a look at what you can do with these.

1. The job

This is where the character works, has professional relationships, and makes money. Ask yourself: How does your character look at the world in general, through what kind of eyes? A musician's, a stock trader's, a housewife's, a fashion designer's? What does your character's profession mean to him or her? How far will they go to protect it, to keep it, to rid themselves of it? Is your character obsessed with the job? In most movies you'll notice the main character spending a great deal of time on the job.

For Stevens the butler in *The Remains of the Day*, his job takes precedence over everything, including his chance to love. He is a slave to his job; it controls his life. And, as he comes to realize (too late, in fact), this obsession finally destroys any capacity to love.

In *Fargo* jobs mean everything. These are hard-working, often driven people, up there in the frozen northland, who have to battle not only numbing inevitability but also the elements. The William Macy character's only need was to make a few extra bucks of his own. The story is how this simple need spiraled out of control and ended in murder. And what about our heroine—played by Frances McDormand, who won the Oscar for her performance—the small-town cop, pregnant, with a loving husband with whom she spent a great deal of her marriage in bed watching TV? Wasn't it her clear-eyed, no-frills approach to work—and to life, for that matter—that enabled her to cut through all the chicanery, untangle the evil web, and nab the culprit?

2. The home

With whom does your character live—a wife, husband, dog, lover? Are there kids? If they're married, do they have affairs on the side? Why? Is there harmony or strife at home? Do your characters spend time alone, or surround themselves with people? I once had a friend who could not stand to be alone and paid people ten to twenty dollars to hang around until he fell asleep. Do the characters find stability at home?

As the writer, ask yourself how you can upset the home order by hurling chaos into it. What kind of emotional bomb can you drop into this stable place?

"What if " are the two big Hollywood words. What if a young beautiful woman walks into the home of a respected British physician and MP, who falls madly, hopelessly, passionately in lust with her. What if the woman is his son's fiancée? What kind of *Damage* will that do? Always think in terms of upping the stakes. By throwing a big wrench into the works you automatically up the stakes.

What could you do to make life much more difficult for your characters? Can you destroy a home life seemingly beyond repair? Consider *Fatal Attraction.* How do your characters try to restore order in their shattered universe?

Home means stability and love, security. If I were going to upset my main character I'd go after the home and the work. Depending how much each means to my target, I would then choose which to attack first.

3. The private self

In the private life of a character, you discover strange little habits, hobbies, idiosyncrasies, things he does alone or beyond the home and the job. What does your character do when he is alone? Schopenhauer once wrote that the best way to tell what a person is like is to watch him when he thinks he's alone. Watch his eyes and hands, the small gestures, the habits, and you will discover worlds about this person you would never see when he wears his public clothes.

In the movie *Power,* which hardly anybody saw and fewer remember, Richard Gere has the annoying habit of banging a drumstick on whatever happens to be in front of him—airplane seats on the way to a power meeting, on tables, desks. This is supposed to represent his drumbeat of power. It gave me a migraine, but they had the right idea.

The Main Character

Every scene in the screenplay reinforces the main character's need, drive, or goal. Every scene either promotes the main character's well-being or tries to thwart it. Test your main character. Never let up. These tests bring out your main character's strengths and weaknesses, some of which he didn't know he possessed. The character's revelation creates change in the form of self-awareness—yet another reason why the story you tell must be about the most critical moment in the character's life.

The writer's challenge is to make these tests so difficult that the character literally breaks out of himself.

Things to Consider

1. A dull main character needs help.

A boring main character shows no vulnerability, doesn't act upon his or her convictions, and generally stands around while everybody else takes over the story. Sound familiar? It does to me. I've brought characters into the world with the constitutions of dishrags who, despite my best intentions, were so dull they nearly disappeared. Never allow your character to become passive. Vulnerable, yes. Wrong-thinking, absolutely. Confused, you bet. But never passive.

In Kevin Costner's *Robin Hood*, I wondered, who *is* this marshmallow, Mr. Hood, who supposedly runs the forest? Do we care about this lug who wears designer leaves and looks as if he's nodding out most of the time? And how vapid is Maid Marian to have fallen in love with this piece of toast? As played by Errol Flynn, Robin Hood had a life; as played by Kevin Costner, he needed to get a life. This is why, without the goofy Sheriff of Nottingham, Costner's Hood would have died an even faster box-office death.

Remember, your character wants something. This goal propels the character forward. He may make wrong turns or go through wrong doors, but he is in pursuit of something that will save his life, or get him out of a jam. At this, the most critical moment of your main character's life, you cannot afford to put him, or us, to sleep.

2. Define your main character's need.

Movies are about characters who want something and, in their pursuit of it, get into much greater trouble. A simple need becomes a holy terror. The essence of character is action. Your character is what your character does. Not what he thinks, not what he supposes he'll do, not what he did, what he *does*. Movies consist of scenes with characters in action.

In *One Flew Over the Cuckoo's Nest*, the main character wants one thing, which motivates everything he does—to get out. Everything the Jack Nicholson character does in that movie has to do with breaking out of the cuckoo's nest.

Nicholson in *Chinatown* starts out trying to determine if a man is cheating on his wife and ends up accused of murder with his own life in danger, trying to salvage his reputation.

In *The English Patient* the Ralph Fiennes character combs through what's left of his memory trying to disentangle the key to his past. We, the audience, get to peek into the mind of a petty, petulant adulterer and spy.

In *Shampoo,* Warren Beatty wants one thing: his own beauty shop. This need stands behind everything he does, and look at the problems he encounters.

In *Thelma and Louise,* Thelma wants a couple of days away from her miserable husband—a little freedom, that's all. Look at the trouble she and Louise get into! Their original need becomes a need to escape, on a far more terrifying level.

3. Watch out for autobiographical characters.

Autobiographical characters create problems because often the writer is afraid to reveal too much about him or herself. The writer hedges, gives us half-truths, falsehoods, or puzzling themes on how the character could be, not how the character is. The writer ultimately creates a cardboard character who ruins what might have been a compelling piece of work. In these cases the writer soft-pedals the main character and looks elsewhere, to secondary characters, for drama. These secondary characters grab the focus, leaving the main character in the wings. Beware of this; it's a story killer.

Even Shakespeare seems to have had this problem. In *Romeo and Juliet,* he starts out with star-crossed lovers and warring families. Into the fray he brings Mercutio, one of the most dynamic minor characters in his canon, who delivers the wondrously enigmatic soliloquy, the Queen Mab speech. All of a sudden, Mercutio, Romeo's best friend, is taking over the play. This eloquent wild man chews the scenery. Shakespeare wonders if he should rename the play *Mercutio.* But Shakespeare, being no fool, says to himself, "Wait a minute. What have I got here? Romeo and Juliet. A big family tragedy is brewing and now I've got this dancing poet, whom I adore, taking over my play. What am I going to do?" Shakespeare makes a decision. He certainly doesn't want to eliminate this mercurial character. Neither can he keep him, because Mercutio is now ruining his original conception. In order to get back to his story at hand, Shakespeare creates a sword, places it in Tybalt's hand, and tells Tybalt to run it through Mercutio—thus allowing Shakespeare to return to the story of Romeo and Juliet.

In the writing process, when the main characters falter, startling secondary characters step forward and take charge. At this point, your question as the writer becomes twofold: Is the secondary character necessary to the story you want to tell, and has this character taken over so thoroughly that the story is galloping off in another direction? You cannot leave your main character alone for too long.

What are your options? Remove this secondary usurper from the script or follow Shakespeare's lead and kill him off. Or give the story to this wild emerging creation of yours and forget about your original idea.

4. Make certain your characters act.

Characters have goals and move toward them. Along the way they act strangely (as anyone would who is at the most critical point in life), they make mistakes, they take wrong turns, but they are always in pursuit. The stakes are high and the character believes that reaching the objective is the only alternative for reducing the pain.

Even in so-called buddy movies, one character leads, the other follows; one makes things happen or gets them into more trouble. In *Butch Cassidy and the Sundance Kid,* Butch leads. In *Thelma and Louise,* Louise urges Thelma to break away from her husband and gets them on the road.

5. Herd mentality—too many main characters usually spoil ensemble movies.

Ensemble movies, which have four or five main characters, don't ordinarily work. *The Big Chill, The Breakfast Club,* and *Short Cuts* are exceptions. Ensemble movies aren't often made for a couple of reasons.

In two hours it is hard enough to develop one character, much less four or five.

Secondly, getting five actors of equal status to agree to do a picture at the same time is nearly impossible. At one time Hollywood's Brat Pack held the franchise on this type of picture, but look at the results: *Young Guns* and *The Three Musketeers.* You wonder why they bothered.

If you want to write a good movie, take your five bland characters and turn them into two dynamic characters. It's far more satisfying to follow the fortunes of two believable creations than five cardboard cutouts.

6. Build sympathy in your main character.

How deeply can we identify with the main character? How do you create sympathy for this creation of yours? One way is to make your hero a victim of some undeserved misfortune.

In *Mrs. Doubtfire,* Robin Williams, kicked out by his wife, desperately wants to see his kids, so he disguises himself as a woman and applies for a job as nanny in his own home. We, the audience, root for him. The entire movie is about the Robin Williams character trying to get back with his kids.

In *Tootsie,* Dustin Hoffman can't get work because his talent isn't recognized as it should be. We automatically like this character because the directors for whom he auditions neither pay attention to him nor recognize real talent when they see it.

Let's say, in an opening sequence, we have a kid running through a neighborhood with a blow torch in one hand and a straight razor in another. With the blow torch he sets fire to neighborhood cats, and with the razor he scrapes away paint jobs on new cars. We can't stand this little creep; he's the worst kid we've ever seen. Done with his day's nastiness, the kid runs home. He hurries through the front door, and there we meet his parents, the ogres who brought him up. Set against these two, the kid demands our pity.

This is precisely what *Silence of the Lambs* writers were able to do. By the end, they had made the psychiatrist in the story so despicable that we wanted Hannibal to have him for lunch.

Mario Puzo did the same thing in *The Godfather.* Yes, Don Corleone is a power-mad murderer, but the writers were smart enough to make all the other bad guys in the movie worse than the Don, thus making the Brando character sympathetic.

Sympathy also comes from putting your character in jeopardy. Maybe he loses a job, or faces a life-threatening situation. Or you make your character pleasant, or funny. In a word, ingratiating. Give your character a sense of humor. Engage us.

7. Let the character go.
Your characters will do things you don't expect them to. They'll start ordering you, the writer, around. If a character does something you don't expect, good, let him do it. If a character takes off in a different direction, let him go. If he goes too far, stop him and bring him back. But if he's acting within the world of the story you've created, he's free to roam because he's growing. This is a wonderful thing to watch. What a shame it would be to let your manipulative sticky fingers try to control your creation all the time.

That's unfortunately what Oliver Stone did in *Wall Street.* For two-thirds of that movie the characters lived believable lives. Gekko and the kid moved forward on separate but gradually fusing tracks. Then, at the beginning of Act III, Stone decided to turn *Wall Street* into Wal-Mart, predictable and safe, good guys versus bad guys, sappy and sentimental; and the movie became an American morality play.

Character Summary

1. *Nothing moves forward in a story except through conflict.*
2. *Your main character must be put at the most critical moment of his life, or the story is not worth telling.*
3. *The main character confronts forces that are far more powerful than he is.*
4. *The character cannot be alone; give him someone with whom to share his dreams and aspirations, someone to talk to.*
5. *He will probably find the love of his life, or stand the chance of losing her if he doesn't get his act together.*
6. *The character will be forced to confront his internal demons to discover why he has been unable to resolve the problems of the past.*
7. *Build your characters from the moment they are born until we meet them on page one of the story. They have been preparing for this moment all their lives.*
8. *The ultimate collaboration in film is between you and your main character.*

Exercise

Take Schopenhauer's advice: Watch someone when he thinks he's alone. Study him as if he were under a microscope. Then go back and, like a scientist, write down your findings.

Exercise

Make a list of tragedies family members or friends have encountered over the past few years. How did they react? What consequences did they face? Who faltered and who showed heroic mettle? In these tragic tales a great story lurks. Find it. Make notes. Draw up characters. Dig. You might find gold.

Exercise

Take three people you know and write three pages of a life story on each of them. Brainstorm. You will be shocked, and fascinated, by what you discover about them. Then use this technique in creating your main characters.

Exercise

Make a list of your leading and supporting characters and write their bios.

Exercise

Make a list of all the disasters your main character could face, given the context of the story. This becomes a master list from which to pick and choose the obstacles that best fit your story. Remember that as the story progresses, the obstacles should grow in intensity and danger. ***Never make it too easy on your main character.*** The more he or she has to overcome, the more tension and drama your story possesses. Movies are about the rapid acceleration of events your main character faces.

Exercise

Movies to Watch

The following movies illustrate many of the points in this chapter. Each year (while always adding to the list) I rent these movies to see how the writers created memorable characters. They are strong within the genres they represent. These are not the best movies ever made, but they intrigue me for various reasons. Next time you're at the video store, you might want to take a look:

Breaking Away
In *Breaking Away,* we have Mom, Dad, and Dave. Mom comes from a big family; she's a homemaker and performs the household duties. Two things about her particularly strike me. One of them is what's termed an echoing device.

An echoing device is an object or a line of dialogue that's repeated throughout the course of a movie. Echoing devices are anchors that hold the movie to its foundation. They're markers to indicate the passage of time or a change in events. For instance, in *Kramer vs. Kramer,* each time we see the boy and his father having breakfast, the story has progressed, the characters have moved forward, their relationship has changed. As another example of echoing devices, in *Out of Africa,* when we see the cuckoo clock and a pair of white gloves, the Meryl Streep character's fortunes have changed or her love affair with the Robert Redford character has taken a new twist.

In *Breaking Away,* Mom's echoing device is a book. Every time we see the novel, she's on a different page, and events have changed. The book is *Valley of the Dolls.* This book establishes Mom's dream world. She's a hausfrau whose family comes first, but she also has an active fantasy world.

The other item the writer, the late Steve Tesich, gives her is a passport she has never used. What do these two items show us about Mom? While taking care of a family, Mom reads a book about a life she'll never lead and owns a passport that allows her to visit places she'll most likely never go. This is not disheartening, though, because Mom knows herself, and she has accepted this and is grateful for her dreams.

Dad has a heart condition. He's been a hard worker all of his life. We learn that he bought a home when he was not yet twenty-one. He wears horrible clip-on ties. He owns a used car lot—his bit of larceny. We learn that he never went to college and that he somewhat envies his son.

Breaking Away is about their son, Dave, whom we find in a period of transition. He's a cyclist, obsessed with European cyclists. He studies them. He wants to be like them. He's won a batch of trophies from his cycling triumphs. He's preparing to take a college entrance exam. During this period of significant transition, he's even renamed his cat. Dave is at the most critical time of his life, getting ready for the next stage. His character is on the cusp.

Sling Blade

I wonder why people took to this story of a simpleton who gets out of an asylum after twenty five years (for murdering his mother and her lover) and ends up in the same Southern town for a command performance. Was it Forrest Gump reinvented as a killer? Did American audiences love Forrest so much that they wanted to see him in another guise. What will he show up as next?

The story, like Billy Bob Thornton's character, is simple, tightly drawn. There are no deep subterranean yearnings here, or even subtleties. Despite some major plot problems (why does the mother so easily accept this ex-killer as her son's playmate?), everybody is whom everybody says he or she is. Is the movie showing off our love of watching a character trundle along as a passive observer until he sees something that's not right, and then takes the law into his own hands? Maybe. If we go to the movies to vicariously experience the world through the main character—to do what he does, feel his pain, but not have to suffer his consequences—then this movie *is* indeed *Forrest Gump: Portrait of a Serial Killer.*

The characters are strong. The story is simple. But it's the relationships among the characters that pulled me in. Small town. Stranger with a past enters. Meets mother-son, abusive boyfriend. A gay pal. Things start to change through Billy Bob's seemingly blank perspective. Ah, but not blank for long. The sleeping giant inside, dormant for many years, awakens and all hell breaks loose.

The Crying Game

In this one, a seemingly dull IRA operative finds out what he's really made of when he confronts the death of his captive and the love of his (and the captive's) life. This is a movie about what's behind the mask, below the surface.

The main character shows hidden talents brought forth by sudden, dramatic change. *The Crying Game* is, in addition to its many assets, a study in patient writing. The writer waits for situations to bring out his characters' hidden talents and agendas, instead of driving us from plot point to plot point.

The message here: Be diligent. Bide your time. Let the story, along with the characters, tell itself. Don't divulge secrets, character traits, or agendas until the reader is ready to learn them. I read too many scripts where the writer is too eager at the beginning to let us in on all there is to know about the characters and the story. We are buried under a pile of details, with no context to make them worthwhile, and no interest to read on.

Norma Rae

This is a story about two very different characters who team up to unionize an old-time southern mill whose management is being unfair to its workers. Norma Rae, a rebellious woman, is one of these characters. We learn during the course of the movie that she was married to a man who was killed in a barroom fight and that she has an illegitimate child. She dates a lot of men; one of them is married. In this conventional small southern town, she does not play by the rules. In her fight against the mill, she hooks up with a New York Jewish union organizer, Ruben Warschovsky. Warschovsky is a book reader, an ex-Marine. He's artistic. His girlfriend is a Harvard-educated labor lawyer.

In a classic David-and-Goliath confrontation, these polar opposites battle the town's life blood, the powerful mill. The lesson in this movie: Norma Rae and Ruben Warschovsky have the same objective, which is to remove the mill's stranglehold on its workers, yet they come from totally opposite belief systems.

When you have a team going after the same objective, you must endow each character with individuality. Give them reasons to argue about method, lifestyle, everything. In this way you've established outer conflict—in this case, the battle against the mill—and the smaller central conflict between the characters. They both want the same thing, using different approaches; this leads to conflicts.

Norma Rae is a buddy love story, on a David-versus-Goliath battlefield, extremely well written, and a true original.

Lethal Weapon

In *Lethal Weapon,* Danny Glover is a family man, about to retire, who teams up with Mel Gibson, a younger cop with a skewed outlook and no personal ties except to the police force. Yet they have the same objective: to solve the crime. They never agree on anything, which keeps the conflict and tension alive. Their relationship holds our interest. Solving the crime is the structural engine that holds the plot in place. This breezy, very likable couple battles a treacherous villain, but the real story is the relationship between the two men.

The Verdict

This is another David-and-Goliath legal thriller. A down-and-out lawyer, Frank Galvin, takes on the Catholic church, always a favorite target. Galvin's adversary is Eddie Concannon, attorney for the archdiocese. He's rich, tough, connected, and the judge is his good friend. Frank Galvin, once a successful attorney, had been in jail for jury tampering and nearly lost his license. Galvin keeps a photo of his ex-wife on his bed stand and cries himself to sleep at night.

The story: A little guy goes against a power establishment and wins. During his course of action, Galvin faces and exorcises his demons, alcoholism, and his own insecurities.

You might be able to tell from this list that I'm a sucker for good underdog stories—single vulnerable characters pulling themselves out of their sad situations to take on a giant. These are stories of the human spirit prevailing against seemingly insurmountable odds. We go to the movies to see people do things that we, for our own reasons or the lack of opportunities, do not have to do. These stories uplift us, they give us hope, we root for these little guys, which is very satisfying, especially when they prevail in the end.

Big Night

Here's a movie I watched four times because I didn't get what all the hoopla was about. Even people whom I almost always agreed with about movies liked—hell, *loved*—this dog, and I couldn't understand why. After watching it the fourth time I got it. It was the script. It was unfinished. Somewhere in the mish-mosh that became *Big Night* the movie, there was a good idea worth developing: restaurateur brothers in exile, one the commercial maven, the other the artist/chef; a rival restaurant down the street; lovers wondering if the brothers would stay or go; the imminent arrival of Louie Prima on this Big Night, a make or break moment for the restaurant. And of course, the food.

Just because I have an eating disorder, is that—as a couple of people have suggested—why I hated the movie? Roger Ebert gave it a rave review. Maybe *Big Night's* untidiness had to do with one man—star, editor, writer, director Stanley Tucci—wearing too many hats. There was nobody on the set to say no to him.

The script needed about two rewrites to bring together its wayward elements. "What's wrong with it being a work in progress?" one of my friends (who cooks) protested. "It has the tone of a meal, this unfinished thing becoming a masterpiece."

"This is not a meal in progress, it's a finished movie."

"You're too rigid."

This unalloyed dedication to—and devout pigheadedness for—this movie eludes me. I got the same reaction when I walked out of a theater a few years ago and announced that the Kevin Costner baseball-field-in-Iowa picture was a manipulative piece of junk. They mercilessly attacked because I failed to see something that was obvious to them. What? Movie magic? I don't know. Maybe it's in those first ten minutes—they've either got you or they don't. Like meeting someone for the first time, there's something that draws you in or pushes you away.

Big Night appealed to urban people who liked to eat and/or cook good food, to members of warring families, to romantics that saw in these relationships mirrors of their own lives. Who knows?

I saw a half-thought-out story that went in ten directions, with scenes that went on forever, detours that went nowhere, and characters who appeared and then disappeared for God only knows what reasons. Call it *Waiting for Louie*.

It bothers me when ninety-nine percent of the people in the world like a movie and I don't. More than ever, people are saying, behind my back and to my face, "If Chris doesn't like it, it must be good."

Exercise

Compile a list of your five favorite films and their most memorable characters. Why do you respond to this list? Why do you feel the characters are memorable? Think about that. These characters possess certain traits that excite you for various reasons. If you can pinpoint these reasons you'll probably be able to carry them over into your own creations.

Exercise

What about recent movies you've seen. In which ones have the main characters been generally unchanged at the end? Is this one reason the movie didn't thrill you?

I've pitched stories to Paramount, Universal, Fox, Warners, and MGM, and each time the studio executive asked the question, "So, how's this character change?"

Make a list of traits your main characters possess at the beginning of your story. Then make another list of how you would like to see them changed by the end. This will help you set up each character's arc.

5
Building Your Story

You don't start with any aesthetic manifesto, you just do
what works.

> E. L. Doctorow, novelist and
> author of *The Waterworks, The Book
> of Daniel, Billy Bathgate*

After you've decided upon a story and have established the major characters, you will be ready to ask yourself some **Crucial Story and
Character Questions:**

1. Is my story compelling enough to watch for nearly two hours?
Do I have enough story to last for two hours? Is there a story to keep *me*
interested?

**2. Are these characters intriguing enough to spend a couple of
hours with?**
Or are they dull, boring? Do they fascinate *me?*

3. Can I see the story?
Screenplays are about character and action, told visually. You cannot
see thought.

4. Where should I begin the story?
Start your story at the last possible minute. Know what the story is,
establish essential information the audience needs to know, and begin.
Too often, stories wade through months and sometimes years of boring
backstory before getting to the point. By the time the real story starts,
you're halfway through the script. I often read scripts—well written,
with strong characters—that don't really begin until page fifty. In the
margins, I write, "What's the story? I'm already on page fifty, what's
going on here?"

For example, *Kramer vs. Kramer* was adapted from a novel written by Avery Corman. In the novel, Mr. Kramer meets the future Mrs. Kramer. They have a wonderful love affair, courtship, marriage, and their child is born. After a few years, Mrs. Kramer wants out of the marriage and she takes off, leaving her husband alone to care for their son.

The movie's writer-director, Robert Benton, said, "I can't make a movie out of this entire story. It'll take twenty-eight hours. I've got to get to the heart of what the story is about." So he asked himself the essential question, "What is the movie about?"

He came up with this: *Kramer vs. Kramer* is the story of a man who is suddenly forced into single parenthood and how he barely manages in this new role.

Robert Benton backed up just a few frames before Mrs. Kramer takes off, showing Kramer (Dustin Hoffman) at his job, which he is in jeopardy of losing. Then he establishes Mrs. Kramer (Meryl Streep) wanting her freedom. We see her go off to find herself in the first few minutes, neatly setting up the conflict.

5. Is my story yesterday's news?
Natural disasters, riots, summit meetings, stories about breaking news don't usually make good movies because the news media takes all the immediacy out of them. If, however, you have a unique angle on a victim of one of these newsworthy events, you might have something. In these cases, the characters must take precedence over the event.

In general, stay away from these kinds of newsworthy backgrounds. I've seen producers' faces when a writer says something like, "This is about a couple who went through the L.A. riots." Or: "This is about Norman and Maybelle, who lost their home farm during the Fargo floods."

When I was in California a while back, Mount St. Helens erupted. Remember all those great movies about the Mount St. Helens disaster? There must have been four dozen scripts in development around that time. Why weren't any of them made? After the media saturated us with news of the eruption, we lost interest. Yesterday's news. Make sure your concept will be accessible for a number of years.

6. Will the audience root for my main characters?
Main characters have to face big problems and hopefully triumph over them. The characters will falter, be wracked by self-doubt, but they keep going, despite all the warnings to stop. In this way, the audience pulls for them. Nobody likes a quitter.

7. Is my story appropriate for the big screen?

It's essential to understand this up front. If you're writing a movie-movie, choose subject matter suited to the big screen. Use material and characters who are visible and visual. The story should not take place in the minds of the characters, or in hazy memory, but should have the scope that movies demand. Characters shouldn't spend big chunks of time sitting around philosophizing. Remember that a movie is a motion picture, a picture that moves.

Ironweed is a wonderful book that never should have been made into a picture. All the talented people involved could not solve the inherent problems in the adaptation from page to screen. In Hector Babenco's movie, the ghosts from the book turn into gauzy Day-Glo apparitions, and the characters' inner thoughts become tedious dialogue, not components of a watchable movie.

Look what happened to *Dune,* which also should never have made the transition from book to film. Or *The English Patient.* I know, you loved *The English Patient* and bridle at someone calling it a prettied-up story about a guy in bed remembering his crummy life.

The point here is that some stories belong as novels and others as TV movies and still others as short stories. Before devoting six months to a year of your life on this project, you should take a good look at this aspect.

8. Can the audience identify with the story's setting?

You can have a location we've seen before, but it should be rendered in a new way. In *Witness,* we've never seen wheat fields in that context. In *The Grifters,* we've never seen the California locations reflect that particular grittiness. We have never seen Los Angeles as we did in *Blade Runner.* I've seen plane crashes on the news but never like the one in *Fearless.* Or Texas as it's portrayed in *Blood Simple.* Or a medical school as it is in *Flatliners.* Or Scotland as it is in *Trainspotting,* the future in *The Fifth Element,* or that hotel in *The Shining.*

It's important when you look at your story's location to give us the familiar signs but make it look and feel original, as these moviemakers have.

9. Do I have passion for this story? Or am I just mildly interested because the topic is currently hot?

If your interest starts to flag halfway into the screenplay, or if you feel that the story is a mess and there's no reason to go on, your passion for the subject should be enough to drive you on. Individual passion for the story will probably make the difference between its becoming a movie or not. If you get scared, or bored, or try to refit the story into somebody else's idea of what's hot in the market place, kiss it good-bye. Passion redeems. It makes up for momentary lapses of confidence. Go back to your initial thoughts about your story, to those points that sparked your interest in the first place. There you'll find the faith to go on.

A student of mine at Emerson College in Boston kept writing about a relationship between a young boy and his father. Initially the writing wasn't great, but the boy's fear, coupled with his need to get closer to his dad, made it obvious that something compelling was going on here—if only the student himself could just get to it. After a few weeks, he was still frustrated.

"I'm on the verge here," he told me, "but I can't get inside the character."

What he meant was that he couldn't get inside himself. I told him to go home and write down two of the most dramatic encounters he had had with his own father.

He returned with some of the most dramatically intense scenes I have ever read, gut-wrenching moments filled with anguish, hatred, longing, and tears. This was the breakthrough he had been searching for. In these two scenes, he had tapped into himself and found the terrible loneliness of a son who cannot reach his father. His work began to take on substance and importance, and drama. Once he discovered this link, it was as if somebody else had started writing—this inner voice.

Stay with your own individual passion for your work, or if you lose it, go back and retrieve it. Backing away from a screenplay is easy. Staying with it is the hard part. Forget about what's currently hot. If you run away from what you're doing to hop onto someone else's bandwagon— what the trend-followers say is currently popular in the movies—after the year or so it'll take for this derivative movie to get written and shown around, the bandwagon will be long gone. Stick with your original vision. D. H. Lawrence once said that a writer's greatest injustice to himself is to deny his own integrity.

10. Your movie will cost how much to make?!

You don't want your characters eating lunch in Madrid, having dinner in Buenos Aires and breakfast the next morning in Hong Kong. By the end of Act I, you'll have spent the budget. Just because you might have hang glided or played paint ball or eaten at a particular restaurant in Harper's Ferry doesn't give you the license to write a scene about it.

I have read scripts in which the lovers suddenly want to go off somewhere to spend a weekend. You know within two seconds that the writer has probably spent a romantic weekend in this same place. Fine, but do you have to take the two of them to Arizona to discover what they could just as easily find in their backyard or down the block, at a fraction of the cost? Characters, not locations, make good movies. You can take dull characters to the great locations of the world, and you'll still end up with dull characters.

Watch out for monstrously costly special effects. If you need special effects, by all means use them. But a thirty-million-dollar great movie is going to be picked up a lot faster than a eighty-million-dollar great movie.

11. How do my main characters change?

It's not a matter of *if* your characters change. After the hell and high water you put them through, they had better. It's *how* they change that matters, that keeps an audience interested. The simple exercise of checking how your characters are at the end as against how they were in the beginning will get you started. If they haven't made any significant movement, you had better take another look.

Make a list, one through five. How they were against what they've become. Emotionally, financially, mentally, physically, spiritually.

12. Why would your character go through all this misery in the first place?

Some characters might take a look at what they have to face and walk away. "Who, me?" they laugh. "Forget it." This is why you must establish *the character's need.* And raise The Stakes. Make sure your characters can do nothing *but* go on. What's Lawrence of Arabia going to do, quit when the desert gets too hot? What's Ben Braddock in *The Graduate* going to do, go back across the yard to his own house because Mrs. Robinson smokes too much?

The character has to go forward because his physical and emotional self depends upon it, literally. One method is to make it so your character must go forward because he cannot go back. Once again: Are the stakes high enough? Have you put him in a position so that the only thing he *can* do is to push ahead?

Could Jack Nicholson in *Chinatown,* once in motion, wash his hands of the whole affair? Absolutely not. Robert Towne, the screenwriter, piqued Jake Gittes's curiosity and threatened to sully his reputation. There was no way Gittes wouldn't follow the story to its end.

13. Is my story plausible?

This is a big one. If your premise has major flaws, your chances of getting the movie made are nil. Spend a lot of time asking yourself if there are holes in the logic of your story. Could this or that *really* happen?

You have to be honest with yourself. Don't let that second voice of yours say, "Oh, it's just a movie; they'll never notice." Or, "If they can get away with that in the Tom Cruise movie, I can do it in mine." Or one of my favorites: "You're supposed to suspend your disbelief in movies." Wrong.

Every once in a while a massive hole in the story appears during shooting. At this point, with millions already committed, there's no turning back. This happened in *The River,* starring Mel Gibson. We know from the beginning that there was no way in hell he could have saved his farm from the raging river. But the filmmakers went forward, trying to build a case for the farm's being saved. What a mess. You might ask how a movie like this could be made. Mel Gibson, who probably didn't see the hole either, said yes to it, and with his star power anything goes.

What about the logic, or lack thereof, in *Mission Impossible.* That movie got so fuzzy that two-thirds of the way through they gave the Tom Cruise character a dream he had to explain, hoping that the audience would understand what the filmmakers had lost control over—logic and clarity.

As a screenwriter, one of your tasks is to plug these holes in the story treatment stage, *before* you write the screenplay. You don't want to get through the first draft and suddenly discover gaping problems.

Mrs. Doubtfire and *The Piano* had plausibility problems. In *Mrs. Doubtfire,* the Sally Field character, a successful San Francisco interior designer, places an ad in a newspaper for someone to look after her three kids. What? In the local newspaper? With all the child-molesters and pederasts around these days? With bonded child-care services all over the place? Give me a break. This is a contrivance. The premise is flawed, leaving the rest of the story in question.

And what about the three kids who don't have a clue that this is their father when he walks in dressed as a woman? If your mother kicked your father out of the house and he showed up in a dress, looking for work, would you recognize him? Who *are* these kids in *Mrs. Doubtfire?* Yes, you have to suspend disbelief, but c'mon! The movie also borrows shamelessly from dozens of other movies. Go back and see *Tootsie,* which is a wonderful example of what *Mrs. Doubtfire* might have been with another dozen rewrites.

In *The Piano*, why did Holly Hunter remove a piano key and write a message on it for Harvey Keitel, whose character could not read? Duh. Why would she ruin the one instrument she loved by doing this? Where did Holly and Harvey get all the money in the end to be living on that estate? How come Holly's little girl suddenly runs to the nasty stepfather with news of her mother's infidelity? In many ways *The Piano* is a wonderful film, but plausibility-wise?

These problems are failures in screenplay execution. As screenwriters, you can't afford to overlook implausibility.

Have you seen *The Saint?* You could drive fleets of trucks through the tunnels of logic in that picture.

14. What's your logline?

A logline is a punchy one-or-two-sentence description of your story. The reason for having a logline is that you have to sell the idea to an agent, who has to convince a producer to look at it, who in turn has to sell it to the financing organization (the studio), and so on up the line until the idea reaches someone who can say yes to it. In your local newspaper or *TV Guide,* look for these short enticements designed to convince you to watch the movie. You have to do the same thing for your screenplay.

For instance:

At Play in the Fields of The Lord:
Mismatched Americans are caught in a web of deceit in brutal Brazilian jungles.

The Untouchables:
Eliot Ness and his G-Men battle Mafia kingpin Al Capone in Prohibition Chicago.

The Secret of Santa Vittoria:
An Italian town and its drunken mayor hide a million bottles of wine from the Nazis.

The Piano:
In the late 1800s, a Scottish mail-order bride lands on a raging New Zealand coast to discover a world of dark primitive passions.

Emma: A proper Victorian girl meets an emotion.

Sling Blade: Portrait of Forrest Gump, Serial Killer.

Finding the Right Logline for Your Story

In the following movie descriptions, I've scattered around a few pieces of information. Somewhere in there is a logline for you to find. This will give you practice toward working on your own.

1. If you're on cocaine when you see *The Boost,* you probably won't do it any more. Or if you haven't done it, you won't want to start. *The Boost,* starring James Woods and Sean Young, points to what a drug can do to prosperity. In a meeting with a West Coast businessman, Lenny Brown and his wife find wealth beyond their dreams. To maintain their energy and drive they resort to taking drugs. Their fall from grace begins. Powerful stuff here. How would you make this dramatic in one or two strong sentences?

2. We are on the French Riviera. A sophisticated American, Laurence Jameson, bilks women out of their money. He's very successful at it and has carved a valuable niche in this world. A stranger comes to town, in the person of a rough-hewn young con man who wants to horn in on Jameson's territory. The young con man challenges Jameson at his own game. The story concentrates on two very different people with conflicting styles working toward the same end—the ultimate con—in *Dirty Rotten Scoundrels.*

3. In *The Devil's Own* a veteran New York City cop, a straight-arrow family man, and a young IRA rebel whose father had been killed by British soldiers are thrown together in Manhattan against a background of arms smuggling, big-time politics, and the Irish question. Betrayal of principles and friendship hound them until a bitter end.

4. A small-town sheriff faces big problems. On his retirement day, he is getting married. A killer he once sent away returns on the noon train for revenge. And his soon-to-be wife is a Quaker. If you think you've put too much conflict in your main character's life, remember what Gary Cooper has to face in *High Noon.* The stakes must be high.

5. We're in German East Africa on *The African Queen.* It's World War I and we've got a rugged steamer captain who takes a missionary's sister downriver. They battle gunboats, leeches, malaria, bloodsuckers, and a German battleship, and they fall in love. I think I've done this one for you.

6. How about three secretaries who have had it with their chauvinistic boss? Everything in *Nine to Five* has to do with one thing, their goal—to get rid of the bastard. They plan, they fail, they plan again, they fail again, and so on. We root for them, and so on. Notice how clean-cut the story is, and how the characters are left to carry the story.

7. Remember the four middle-class guys from Georgia who go white-water rafting one weekend? They're having a wonderful time until they run into some people on the river they don't understand. At which point their lives become a living hell. Look what happens to these men in *Deliverance:* a test of manhood, a rite of passage, death, cowardice, courage. The evil they face makes them confront the essence of their own mortality. The order of their universe is destroyed, corrupted, defiled by events that compel them to reach down into themselves to find something—anything—that will get them out of this terrible mess. Some of them make it, some of them don't.

8. It's invaluable to see motion pictures that fail. *Batman Returns* is a great-looking piece of junk. The movie has too many villains. It's over-acted, poorly written and conceived, and it has no clear purpose. As I watched the movie, I kept asking myself, "Who *are* these people and what is going on?" There must have been a logline at the beginning of this dog. What do you think it was?

9. In *Flesh and Bone,* a thoroughly forgettable movie, Meg Ryan and Dennis Quaid, both decent actors, play out their crummy lives on a vast Texas wasteland. We have a slaughtered family, a mean father (played by a mumbling James Caan), and a huge contrivance that ruins what's left of this mess. For those of you who saw this strange, storyless picture, try a logline.

10. Sam Peckinpah's *Straw Dogs* got to me. Loaded with raw gut-wrenching violence, we watch unfold an eye-for-an-eye revenge tragedy in which a mathematician and his wife return to her hometown in England. Townie boys from the old days taunt the couple and rape her. The mathematician (played by Dustin Hoffman) discovers a creature within as he pursues the men, moving inexorably toward a riveting final confrontation. On one level, *Straw Dogs* is a family story about a man whose life and love have been violated, and what he does about it. How would you gather these pieces of information to create a logline?

11. In *The Graduate*, Ben Braddock comes home to parents who give him sports cars instead of love. He's unhappy but he's stuck, so he has an affair. Not with a woman down the street or in the next town, but with his older, next-door neighbor, the alcoholic, chain-smoking Mrs. Robinson. This is called keeping the dramatic intensity physically close. He also falls in love, not with a girl down the street or in the next town but with Mrs. Robinson's daughter. Again, the writer keeps the pressure up.

Never let your characters off the hook. Never take the drama out of town, or in this case out of the neighborhood, if you can help it. The best way for characters to confront one another is to shut them in a closet and lock the door. In *The Graduate*, the closet becomes the two houses, next door to one another, forcing the characters into confrontation.

12. In *Who's Afraid of Virginia Woolf?*, originally a play, the characters are all tightly wound together, even though they're not wound too tightly themselves. They cannot—will not—break away from each other, yet they try all the time. It's academia. A college professor has been married to the university president's daughter. They like to play mind games with each other and with whomever they can entice into their mentally twisted little world. Enter Nick and Holly, a new teacher and his wife, who are about to go on the ride of their young lives.

13. In *Dead Ringers*, twin gynecologists get involved in a weird love triangle. Beverly and Elliot Mantle, both played by Jeremy Irons, are twin gynecologists with some odd obsessions that surface when an actress falls in love with one of them. This logline just sprang out of me. If you do these long enough, you can cut through all the crap and find the nugget.

14. What about an ambitious assistant district attorney and a free-spirited waitress going into battle against the legal system after the waitress is gang-raped? In *The Accused*, two strong yet very different women go up against a male-dominated legal system and a society that refuses to believe that rape victims are not somehow responsible for their own fates.

15. In *Tequila Sunrise*, two friends from high school, a retired drug dealer and a cop, from two different worlds, clash when the cop is assigned to put the former dealer, his old buddy, behind bars. Caught in the middle is a woman they both love. Even bad films must have loglines. But remember that the movie was sold up the line. Michelle

Pfeiffer, Mel Gibson, and Raul Julia all said yes to something. And so did Robert Towne, the writer/director.

16. In *Working Girl*, a classic David-and-Goliath story, we find a young ambitious woman, who, sabotaged by self-doubt, can't seem to move up the corporate ladder. She finally gets the picture, however, by understanding how her boss, the tyrannical Sigourney Weaver, lies and cheats to further her own ends.

Exercise

Write loglines for the following films:

Casablanca
The Joy Luck Club
Thelma and Louise
Fargo
Raging Bull
The Age of Innocence
Four Weddings and a Funeral
Jerry Maguire
E.T.

Or make a list of five movies you've recently seen and write loglines for them. Don't worry whether you liked them or not. At this point, you're interested only in selling them.

Practice writing a logline for your story:

The logline keeps you focused on your story. If your focus on your story fuzzes over or if you find yourself trailing off, use your logline to refocus. It'll get you back on track. *Star Trek*, for instance, was sold as *"Wagon Train* in the sky." *The Car*, a terrible horror movie about a car that eats people, was sold as *"Jaws* on wheels."

You've got to make Hollywood people salivate to read your script. A good logline can do it. Don't wait until you finish the screenplay; start now. Develop the logline and hone it. Make it riveting, so that by the time you finish the script and are ready to send it out, your logline is so powerful it will sell your movie. In addition to writing the screenplay, you also have to peddle it.

6
Plot & Structure

The three most important aspects of screenwriting: structure, structure, and structure.

> William Goldman, Oscar-winning screenwriter of *All the President's Men* and *Butch Cassidy and the Sundance Kid.*

How often have you hit upon a brilliant idea for a movie, but you couldn't find a way to tell the story? You couldn't establish the context, give it a home, establish a world for the story to live in. This is where structure comes in. Structure is the flagship in the craft of writing. Without it, to paraphrase William Goldman, you have nothing more than an idea. Ideas are cheap; execution is everything. Structure gives you the ability to execute.

The Basic Elements of Plot Structure

1. The basic idea
The idea of the story reduced to a sentence or two. The idea must be short and concise so that it can be easily told through the studio ranks until it reaches someone who can say yes to it. Long, wordy, confused ideas will get bogged down and come to a screeching halt. The basic idea of *Indecent Proposal* is a man who offers a million dollars to a young couple so he can spend one night with the wife. Simple, straightforward, high concept, and it makes you think. You want a strong basic idea that can quickly climb Hollywood's corporate ladder until it reaches someone who can give it a green light.

2. Backstory
Information about the characters' past so that the audience will understand what the main story is all about. Backstory information should be

delivered the same way you deliver thought: through characters' action and dialogue. In *Intersection,* a movie with Richard Gere and Sharon Stone, the story is told through a series of flashbacks in order to explain why Gere is about to get crushed to death at an intersection. Most of the time you don't need or want flashbacks. Snippets of dialogue placed strategically throughout the story will do to explain what has gone on. A strong opening sequence can also establish the information you need to prepare your audience.

Don't confuse backstory with story. Determine the story of your movie and then sprinkle backstory throughout it.

Watch out for spending too much time in the opening pages on backstory. I have read too many scripts in which by page 40 I still didn't know what the story was.

3. Exposition
Information in the main story that the audience needs to fully comprehend. This information should be dramatically laid out, not just handed to us. Dramatize information; show it, don't tell it. Nothing moves forward in the story except through conflict. Alfred Hitchcock refused to make movies in which the characters stand around explaining the plot to each other. Go rent any Hitchcock movie and turn the sound off. You will need no dialogue to explain the story.

If you need to have one character deliver information to another character, put the exchange in a dramatic context, through argument or by using an emotional outburst of some kind. Don't just hand it over. That's when a scene is called flat. Information must be dramatized, through character.

4. Pace
Or rising dramatic action. The story must escalate in intensity the further it goes along. In *JFK,* the closer Jim Garrison gets to discovering the terrible truth, the shorter the scenes become, the greater the obstacles, the more intense the revelations, and the more accelerated the pace. One of the strongest elements of *Schindler's List* is pacing. Steven Spielberg juxtaposes scenes with high intensity against scenes of stark humanity. In Brian DePalma's *Scarface,* starring Al Pacino, 170 minutes felt like 45 minutes chiefly because DePalma knew how to place moments of raw street action next to Pacino's drive for power, indecision, and addiction.

When movies crawl along at a snail's pace, the audience gets fidgety, wants to leave, grows bored. The beginning of Bertolucci's *The Sheltering Sky* bogs down in superficial chatter and languid camera shots and never recovers. Through confusion and dull characterization, *Ironweed* crawls to a halt ten minutes into the picture and dies.

The more dangerous it gets for your protagonist, the shorter the scenes and the higher the tension, until by the end he or she is in the midst of a choking density.

5. Plot or turning points

Events or moments in the plot that significantly move the action forward. Turning points grab hold of the action and/or characters and spin them into a new direction. These often violent upheavals result from a bomb being dropped into the action, or the sudden appearance of a significant stranger, a tragedy. In *Lawrence of Arabia,* every time Peter O'Toole turns around he's being thrust deeper into Arabia and, consequently, into his own soul. A significant turning point occurs when Lawrence meets in the desert with Ali, fusing the two worlds. In *Indiana Jones and the Last Crusade,* as the father (Sean Connery) and son (Harrison Ford) meet for the first time, the story takes on the crucial emotional appeal that propels the movie to the end.

6. Hurdles

Problems or obstacles (situations or characters) the main character faces and overcomes in order to get on with the story. Indiana Jones must deal with dozens of external hurdles thrown in his way just as Joanne Woodward must face a battery of internal demons in *The Three Faces of Eve* in order to climb back toward sanity.

7. Dramatic irony

When the audience knows something the character does not. How many times have you seen a character on screen and wanted to shout, "Don't go through that door!" Or, "Don't fall in love with him, he'll leave you!"

8. Climax

The biggest scene in the movie, where all the loose ends are tied up and where the main character fights his final (emotional and/or physical) battle. This is where Luke Skywalker faces Darth Vader.

9. Resolution

The end of the movie, the last scene. When the Lone Ranger rides off into the sunset.

The Three-Act Structure

Stories have beginnings, middles, and ends. Act I is the beginning; Act II, the middle; and Act III, the end.

Screenplays run from 100 to 120 pages. The reason for this is economic. The number of pages represents the number of minutes the movie runs. One hundred pages represents about 100 minutes of screen time, 110 pages equal 110 minutes, 120 pages take 120 minutes. Some pages have a lot of action, which may take 5 minutes of screen time; other pages may be all dialogue, which may take 20 seconds of screen time. It all averages out. A 100-page screenplay can show maybe five to six times in a theater per day, whereas a 150-page screenplay may run only two or three times.

When someone sends me a screenplay to critique, the first thing I do is turn to the last page to see how long it is. It's a habit I share with just about everybody who reads screenplays. There's an unwritten rule that states: If the screenplay has fewer than 100 pages, the writer does not have enough material to tell the story. If it runs over 120 pages, the material is too unwieldy and the writer has let it get out of hand.

You don't want the reader to think like this before he reads your material. Bring it in between 100 and 120 pages. Break the screenplay into three acts. Act I is roughly one-quarter of the screenplay; Act II is half; Act III is one-quarter. Let's take a 120 page screenplay. Act I is 30 pages; Act II is 60 pages; Act III is 30 pages. Act One runs between pages 1 and 30; Act II runs between pages 31 and 90; Act III runs between pages 91 and 120.

The inciting incident takes place around pages 10–15; Plot Point I takes place around pages 20–25; the Midpoint takes place on page 60; Plot Point II takes place around pages 75–80; and the Climax takes place around pages 110–115.

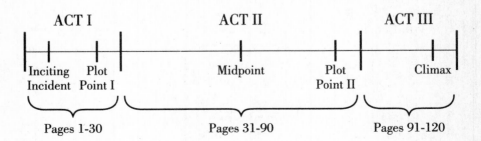

Act I: The Setup

In Act I you begin the story, establish characters, clarify the movie's premise, location, and genre. In other words, you start with a main character whose entire world is about to be shattered, who is going to be more severely tested than ever before, and whose way of looking at life is going to be changed forever.

The First Ten Pages

The first ten pages of any screenplay are the most important, and should be delivered with authority and originality. If you don't grab the reader in the first ten pages, you might as well forget about it. The reader will toss the script or muddle through it because he or she is paid by the agency or studio to read and write a report on it.

If the first ten pages aren't strong, it won't matter how good the rest of the script is. You've got to dazzle us in the opening sequence. Spend a lot of time on these first ten pages. Use them as a standard below which you will not sink during the rest of the script.

A strong opening is in demand in any business. Hollywood readers give you ten pages. New York book editors give you twenty pages. A poetry magazine editor once told me that she gives poets one line in her poetry quarterly. I don't know what that would have done to T. S. Eliot, Ezra Pound, and company, but today you have to grab people quickly and effectively; otherwise they're gone.

Elements of the First Ten Pages

The first ten pages should include:

1. The main character
Who he is. What does he do for a living? What does he lack: some vulnerability. The kind of life he lives, a life that is about to be over-turned. For instance, in *Splash* we learn that Tom Hanks knows his fish business but hasn't a clue about having a relationship with a woman. He's got a problem brother, John Candy, and he longs for love.

2. A strong sense of location and mood
In *Carlito's Way*, we're in the drug world of Spanish Harlem. In *The Remains of the Day*, we're in pre–World War II upper-crust England. In François Truffaut's *The Story of Adele H.* we're in Halifax, 1863, at the high point in Adele's life, which is about to take a big turn. In *The*

Piano we get the wild New Zealand coast. In *Tootsie* we're on the New York stage. In *Witness* we're in the traditional world of northern Pennsylvanian Amish country. In *Alien* we're on a garbage scow in space. In *Shine* we're in an Australian pub with a rather eccentric character.

3. A clear sense of which genre your screenplay fits
Is it an action/adventure, a romantic comedy, or a psychological thriller?

4. The premise
For instance, *Mrs. Doubtfire* is a story of a wacky, irresponsible husband kicked out by his wife. He will do anything to be with his kids. The story becomes how or if he'll be able to retrieve what he so desperately wants.

Beginnings & Endings

I always know the ending; that's where I start.
  —Toni Morrison, Nobel Prize–winning
      novelist and author of *Beloved, Song of
      Solomon, Jazz, Tar Baby*

Screenplays are road maps. They head forward in a conscious direction. The old romantic notion of "I'll find my ending when I get there" is for writers who think that writing is nothing more than creating wonderful images on the page. These people have no idea what it means to write; they will never be screen craftsmen. There is the art of screenwriting and the craft of screenwriting. And you must know both.

A couple of years ago I received an imaginative script from a man in Illinois. The story began with a camera angle. Let me see if I can recreate the scene, using script technique. Note that this writer was not afraid to try a creative approach. It's obvious that he considered many different avenues before he landed on this one. You should exercise your creativity in order to grab the reader in the opening sequence.

FADE IN

INT. DARKNESS
A sense of forward movement. Light appears ahead. We are in a cave of some kind.

A sea of red sinewy plasma moves above and below, lined by rows of white picket-shaped objects. Where in the hell are we?

Moving toward a hole of light at the end of a tunnel. The plasma
seas undulate. Gusts of wind howl by.

Ahead, the white picket-shaped objects open and shut. It's as
if we're on a small raft heading for the opening, into an
increasingly bright light.

A silver iron shaft with a hook attachment slips in between the
pickets.

The hook snares a piece of dark stringy material—LOUD SOUND OF
SCRAPING—and draws it out between the picket rows.

We move toward the opening. SOUND of loud breathing.
SOUND of a machine, a drill of some kind.
We pass between the rows of pickets into unbearable light and
find ourselves staring up into the huge face of a MAN, 40s, in
glasses, a white coat, and plastic gloves.

He smiles down at us. His voice is hollow.

                         MAN
              Don't you worry, Mrs. Galthwait, we'll
              have that tooth out in a jiffy.

It was the first script I'd read that entered a dentist's office through a
patient's mouth. It got my attention. You have to grab your audience,
make them want more. Trick them, surprise them, mesmerize them.
Somehow you must make them react. Otherwise, you've lost them. You
should rent *Housekeeping; Ramblin' Rose; Passion Fish; Raising Arizona; Olivier, Olivier; Carlito's Way; The Piano.* From the opening sequence I wanted to know what happened to the characters in these
films. The writers knew how to draw the audience right in, from the
beginning.

   How do you begin a picture? One way is to start with an image, or an
emblem. Movies that start with dialogue throw audiences off. Movies
are motion pictures. Give us a picture that moves, and that moves us in
some way.

   Sometimes a specific image does the trick. A pool table begins and
ends *The Hustler.* Water in *Splash.* A highway in Spielberg's *Sugarland
Express.* A local political/promotional rally kicks *Dave* into gear. *All the
President's Men* begins with, what else, the Watergate break-in. *An Un-
married Woman* starts with an argument and, soon after, when her husband leaves her for a younger woman, the protagonist becomes an un-
married woman. *Fearless* begins with Jeff Bridges walking out of a plane
crash.

Kinds of Openings

How do you lead into a movie? How do you set us up with the right image or mood or character to tell the story you want us to see? There are ways. Here are some of them:

1. The blatant approach
When we know within the first few moments exactly what and who the movie is about. *Rambo, The Terminator, CON-AIR, Cliffhanger, Volcano, Last Action Hero, Air Force One.* All the James Bond movies. We know immediately who the hero is and how clever he is, and also how dangerous the villain will be in the story to come.

Opening action sequences leave little doubt about the nature of the film. A main character who does one thing well, in a new brutal way. Fifty-five percent of all movies made nowadays are action-oriented because they rely on simple dialogue and lots of visual pyrotechnics— which are big sellers here and translate easily to the foreign markets.

2. A regular day
Here we get a sense of place, of serenity perhaps, of life bumbling along at its own pace, and *then* we meet the main character in some sort of turmoil.

In *Ordinary People* we're in an upper-middle-class Chicago suburb. It's autumn, leaves fall, we're taken to a town green, a church, a choir. Now we're inside the church. We hear singing. We see the faces of the choir members. One of them belongs to Timothy Hutton. Then there's a shock cut to him in bed, vaulting up out of a nightmare. Sweating. We know something is very wrong.

In *Blue Velvet* we get red, red roses, a white picket fence, and blue, blue velvet. We're in lovely, serene Lumberton, N.C., prototypical American small town. A fire engine passes by. The fireman waves to us. A green lawn, a shady street, a man waters his flowers. The man suddenly has a heart attack, and he falls. The camera goes down with him and continues, underground, to pick up lawn creatures gnawing away below the surface of the earth. This is the metaphor for the movie— what looks undisturbed and pristine on the outside is eroding at an alarming rate beneath the surface. This is exactly what Dennis Hopper and his gang of hoods are doing to Lumberton itself.

3. Dramatic irony
This one opens with a scene excluding the main character. In *dramatic irony,* the audience knows something the hero does not, which will soon change the course of the hero's life.

In *Jaws*, young lovers stroll the beach at night. The girl goes for a swim, the shark gobbles her up. Then we cut to the ordinary life of the town, all the while knowing that as soon as the girl's death is reported all hell will break loose. Roy Scheider, the sheriff, gets the word, and all hell *does* break loose. Sharks are bad for summer business, not to mention life expectancy. This type of opening puts the audience in a superior position and also sets up tension and anticipation.

4. Foreshadowing

This is an opening sequence that takes place long before the main story begins and anticipates what happens later.

The Omen begins centuries before, in the Dark Ages, when dogs howl in a monastery and the Antichrist is born to rule the earth. After this satanic moment we move forward to the present, to London, where the modern-day Antichrist, a kid named Damien, walks down a street holding his father's hand. Damien has come to rule the modern world. We know it, but nobody else does.

Again the audience is in a superior position—another example of dramatic irony. This is a favorite for end-of-the world flicks and horror movies. Something born out of time comes to wreak havoc on a peaceful suburban community.

5. Narrator

Sometimes the narrator is the hero, or sometimes just a storyteller reading a tale. The narrator tells somebody (often the audience) a story that happens at the most crucial moment of the hero's life. Examples: *Princess Bride, Annie Hall, Edward Scissorhands, Ramblin' Rose, Stand By Me.*

6. Flashforward

This type of opening has two stories running simultaneously, the *A* story and the *B* story. The *B* story has a narrator, who tells the main story, which happens in the past, usually about himself. At various times we flash forward to the narrator who continues his tale. The difference between the flashforward opening and the narrator opening is that in the flashforward the narrator has his own story going on as he relates the other one. Is this confusing? Let me offer some examples.

In *Amadeus*, Salieri, now an old man, tells the story of how he battled with Wolfgang Amadeus Mozart for musical superiority in the Vienna court. The *A* story occupies the main chunk of the picture, the relationship between Salieri and Mozart in the Vienna court. The *B* story shows

Salieri as an old man going through his decrepit, bitter life, reliving the past.

In *The Last Emperor,* the Emperor, now an old man, reflects back to a time when he was child ruler of China. He tells a multilayered adventure story of his childhood, escape, the war, adulthood. The *A* story, the past, occupies the bulk of the picture; the *B* story, in this case, is the story of the old man as he looks back. The interesting thing about the flashforward approach in the case of *The Last Emperor* is how the old man gets to where he is now, as the old narrator. We are also curious about what will happen once the *A* story, which moves rapidly through time, intersects with the *B* story.

This is not as complex as you may think, but be sure to study this form before using it.

7. Shotgun/montage

This is an opening that should be used more often because of the wildly dramatic effect of compressing time. In the shotgun/montage opening, a cluster of short scenes or clips accelerates the pace of the story until it reaches the main story, at which point it slows down to a regular pace.

In *Raising Arizona,* the writers, the Coen Brothers, needed to show how Holly Hunter and Nicholas Cage got together. They could have used flashback, but wisely decided against it. They also could have referred to the relationship through dialogue during the main story, but didn't. Instead, they chose the montage approach, which was perfect for the movie's comedic pace while telling the story in a dramatic way.

This approach answers a question many of us run into in our stories: "How do the characters get here?" This opening is good for comedy, but to my thinking it's also an excellent way to show what happens in the weeks or months, or even the years, preceding the main action.

8. True beginning

This is where the audience experiences a brand new adventure with the main character. A plane lands. A boat pulls up on the shore. Someone meets someone for the first time. A stranger comes to town. And the movie begins. Examples: *Children of a Lesser God, Red Rock West, The Karate Kid, The Piano, Alien, E.T., Star Wars, Boogie Nights.*

The Inciting Incident

The inciting incident, a big turning point that takes place about fifteen minutes into the script, kicks the story into gear. We are hurled, as we should be by all good stories, from order into chaos. All movies start with a kind of status quo. The first ten pages tell us that this is the world, crazy as it may be, where our main character lives. It can be war or peace, a family battle, or the lovely beach resort in *Jaws*. The story unfolds, characters establish themselves. We fall into the pace. Then something happens. A big problem arises which *must be resolved* by the main character by the movie's end. This is the inciting incident. The inciting incident begins the trail of glue that binds the story together. You establish it during the first fifteen minutes, you bring it to fruition by movie's end. These are the vertebrae in the spine of your story. Call it linkage. It holds the story together, gives it direction.

Until the train-station murder occurs in *Witness*, we have no idea what the movie's about. We see Amish country, a death, the bereaved widow and her son going to visit a sister in Baltimore. No story there. We are waiting for something to happen. Enter the train-station murder witnessed by a young boy: the inciting incident.

Now we know what kind of movie this is going to be: a murder mystery. A boy witnesses a murder, and you know the killer or killers will soon go after him. The inciting incident now focuses us on the movie's chief problem, the murder, which becomes the engine that drives the story forward.

In *Tootsie*, the inciting incident has the Dustin Hoffman character learning from his agent that he'll never get another acting job because of his bad attitude. We know that he has integrity and that the directors are jerks.

But now he's finished. He's had it on Broadway unless he does something drastic. This inciting incident establishes the main character's big problem, which in *Tootsie*'s case is that he'll never work again. This in turn establishes his need to work more than ever. But how? By using his actor's imagination. Sure, he gets work—but in the soaps, and as a woman. His stint as Tootsie is a Band-Aid. He has to work as *himself* again. In other words, find himself, find out what's kept him from the big time all these years. The inciting incident starts this process of self-discovery.

The inciting incident establishes the problem and the motivation for the main character to go forward in his quest, taking big risks and facing grave danger in this most crucial moment of his life.

Plot Point I

At the end of Act I, around page 25, another big moment happens: Plot Point I. The story is going along in one direction when suddenly a giant hook drops out of the sky, grabs hold of the story, and yanks it in a totally different direction.

What is your character willing to do, ready to risk, to get what he wants? Every movie is about someone wanting something more than he has ever wanted anything in his entire life—and willing to do anything to get it. Remember that sentence you wrote on a card and put above your desk, the one that reads, "This is a movie about so-and-so who wants such and such." This need becomes the movie's spine. Everything must feed the need of your main character.

Every story is told through a series of plot or turning points because they move the story forward. They anchor the script. The two big plot points are Plot Point I, at the end of Act I, and Plot Point II, at the end of Act II. Plot Point I forces your character to take a big risk. Not only do the fortunes of the characters change, the location can, too.

In *Witness,* Harrison Ford, learning that corruption goes to the top of the Philadelphia police force, takes Kelly McGillis and the kid to hide out in Amish country.

In *Tootsie,* the moment comes when Tootsie dresses in women's clothes and prances down Fifth Avenue. This character wants so much to work as an actor that he is willing to change his gender to do it.

Plot Point I is not only a single scene or moment but is often a small bundle of moments that lead up to a bigger moment of recognition. For instance, in *Witness,* the progression begins with the Amish boy recognizing a photo of Danny Glover as the one who killed the man in the train station. This leads Harrison Ford to the police captain to whom he tells this information. The captain says he'll take care of it. Next we find Harrison Ford in his underground parking garage. A shot rings out. He is hit, he looks up and sees the assailant—the Danny Glover character. Ford now knows that the corruption goes all the way to his captain's office, which leads him to the conclusion that he must get the Amish woman and her son out of town.

Act II: The Confrontation

In Act II, the character faces a series of obstacles. These confrontations come fast and furious, in greater numbers and intensity as the story moves forward. As your main character moves ahead, trying to reach this goal, everything—the protagonists, the inner demons—seems to be in his way. Your character has to reach down and call up reserves that will enable him to overcome these obstacles. This is called *dramatic conflict,* which establishes the action and tension for the rest of the story.

If your story starts roaming all over the place, if you're unclear where your character is going, if you've got twenty characters you're trying to keep an eye on, you'll lose control and, out of frustration, probably give up. If your plot is simple and you leave complexity to character, you will be able to follow a straightforward line. Think about your main character and what he wants. Then make it nearly impossible for him to get it. There's your story.

The complexity comes from the choices your character makes. Your character will face high hurdles and daunting obstacles, both emotional and physical. The hurdles and obstacles are in direct proportion to how much the character wants what he's after.

You've got to throw the kitchen sink at the main character. Never make it too easy on him. Otherwise the journey becomes a breeze, and there's no dramatic conflict. If he gets what he wants too easily, no one will care.

Raging Bull is the story of Jake LaMotta, who came out of the slums to become middleweight champion. LaMotta has a problem with women. He wants to possess a woman but once he does, he assumes she'll leave him for another man. On the outside he struggles to become champion; on the inside he is riddled with jealous insecurity. The movie explores how jealousy can be transformed into violence in and out of the ring. In Act II, LaMotta is tormented, his self-esteem hits bottom. He turns to violence in the ring, but he's defeated and loses everything. He becomes a second-rate stand-up comedian with nothing left but memories. Act II is also where most movies run out of fuel and lie down to die. Your main character's need to reach his objective keeps him going. Give him big emotional and physical hurdles to keep him occupied.

In *Awakenings* we're treated to a wonderful setup. Robin Williams, who can't stand to be with people, is forced to take over a ward full of them, including Robert De Niro, who is saddled with an unknown afflic-tion. At the beginning of Act II, De Niro gets well and the movie goes into cardiac arrest. The screenwriters had nothing to do for an hour, so they fabricated De Niro's love interest, they gave him a mother, they trucked out a bunch of boring patients. They inched across Act II's desert, blinded, exhausted, and lost. In Act III, De Niro gets sick again and the movie gets well, picking up where it had left off in Act I. The filmmakers bought a good idea with a cancerous second act. They had nowhere to go until De Niro got sick again, so they jerry-rigged Act II and dragged the thing along.

As screenwriters, you can't afford these gaping holes, because studio executives, agents, and directors will see them and pass. The same condition sabotages other big movies—movies that have star casts and directors, stories that looked good on paper—with second acts that Atlas himself couldn't have supported.

In *A Perfect World,* Act II is taken up by Kevin Costner on the run with a kid he's abducted, while lawman Clint Eastwood searches for him. We flip back and forth from Costner, trying to be a nice guy/big brother to this kid he's just abducted, to Clint Eastwood, running his search from a trailer. Costner and Eastwood never meet, so the filmmakers are stuck with trying to create some tension when there is none to be had. The only thing we have to look forward to is Costner's predictable capture in the end.

In *The Devil's Own,* the Harrison Ford character and the Brad Pitt character never really connect because the entire relationship is built on a lie, so that when Ford discovers the lie, the movie, coming off a weak second act, tries to keep up the charade with a pseudo father-son relationship. The premise is flawed from the beginning, with no chance of these characters, operating on separate tracks throughout, making a legitimate connection.

In *Sleepless in Seattle,* the main characters, Meg Ryan and Tom Hanks, don't meet until the end. Cowriter and director Nora Ephron made up for this by focusing endlessly on the too-cute kid, slow-motion schmaltzy songs, and other business, most of which was interchangeable. There is no real movement until the two main characters—one in Baltimore, one in Seattle—actually start off to meet each other.

The reason these pictures were made had to do with things over which a writer has no control. *Sleepless in Seattle* got made because Nora Ephron wanted it to and got Meg Ryan and Tom Hanks to say yes. *A Perfect World* was shot because Clint liked the story and got Kevin Costner to costar. These are called *element pictures,* meaning that the right elements (director or stars) come together out of a mutual love of the material, or love of money. You don't have the luxury of Ryan/Hanks or Eastwood/Costner waiting for your pages. You have to make sure that Act II spins on strong turning points, catapults toward the end, driven by a main character we root for and a villain who makes it nearly impossible for the hero to go on.

The definition of drama is character in relentless, perpetual conflict. Nowhere should this be more evident than in Act II.

The Subplot

Plot drives the action. Subplot carries the theme. In *Witness,* the plot shows John Book trying to save Rachel and her son, the witness, from the clutches of corrupt cops. The subplot explores the relationship between Rachel and John Book. In *Field of Dreams,* the plot focuses on the building of the ball field, the field of dreams itself. The subplot explores the lost relationship between father and son.

If you ask almost any writer what his story's about, he will tell you about the subplot, usually having to do with the theme of love, or loss, or finding one's way through this crucial moment in time. The subplot aims at what films are really about—relationships. The function of a subplot is to expand the story in a more human way, to give it dimension. Like plots, subplots have beginnings, middles, and ends. Often in a script you find a number of subplots. But watch out: Too many subplots often expose a weak, flimsy plot. Subplots should support the story's main spine.

Things to watch out for

1. At times a subplot will occupy a major portion of the story.
In *Witness,* the love story between Rachel and John Book occupies the entire Act II and flows into Act III before it's resolved in the end.

2. Make sure that your subplots intersect the main plot.
Don't leave the subplot floating out there with no conclusion. Watch out for sloppy, rambling structure.

3. Sometimes a subplot begins a movie and plays itself out before getting to the main action.
In the beginning of *Out of Africa,* we see a lot of Meryl Streep and her relationship with her husband. It seems to take forever to get to the Robert Redford character—the main story line. Why? The writer and director fell in love with their subplot.

In *The Graduate,* Ben Braddock, wandering aimlessly, has an affair with Mrs. Robinson in Act I. It's not until Act II that Ben meets and falls in love with Elaine (Mrs. Robinson's daughter), at which point the main plot begins, the character finds a direction, and goes after something.

4. Dislodge your subplots from your main story.
Look at them, see if they have a beginning, middle, and end. Ask yourself: Do they hold together? Do they intersect the main plot at

crucial junctures? Subplots that don't intersect the main plot are called *parallel plots,* which are television, not motion-picture, devices. There's nothing like a bunch of subplots to move the action forward at a good clip. Farce, with its crazy slamming-door, wham-bang action, is almost all made up of subplots. Action-adventure films, on the other hand, have few subplots. The focus should be on the main plot, where the central character goes on one big mission.

5. Remember that the main story and the subplot show us two different perspectives of the circumstances: the hero's and the villain's.
For instance, in *Thelma and Louise,* the main plot gives us the two women on the run. Subplots include Geena Davis having a brief affair with a drifter who robs her, another with the cops who chase them down, and a third with Geena's husband.

6. In films, the main plot must command central focus.
Think of the main plot as a noun—with subplots, as adjectives, modifying it.

The Midpoint

To the screenwriter, the *midpoint* is the structural lifeline in the vastness of Act II. The midpoint is a turning point halfway through the screenplay, often as the introduction to a new character that forces the main character to redefine and sharpen his central need. The midpoint also enables the writer to get through this section.

   In *Tootsie,* the midpoint occurs when Jessica Lange comes on the scene. Dustin Hoffman falls for her, and now he wants more than just to work—he wants to work as a male actor again. Why? Because if Jessica Lange wants to fall in love, it's with a man, not a Tootsie. Jessica Lange's entrance at the midpoint shifts the action. And to make Tootsie's dilemma even more interesting, Lange's father falls in love with Tootsie. Lange's introduction leads to Hoffman's decision to shed his clothes on national television, revealing his true gender. This resolves three things. He shows the world that he can act after all, he gets to pursue Lange, and he can return to his true self, a wiser male.

Plot Point II

At the end of Act II and the beginning of Act III, we arrive at a critical juncture, Plot Point II.

Plot Point II is when the main character says, "Enough! I can't stand this anymore. I need to resolve this problem." By this time, your character is about to lose it. His world is shattered, dark. Yet the faint light of salvation shows his path. He must decide how to bring this disaster to a close. Plot Point II should satisfy certain plot elements. It should:

1. Demand that the character take action in trying to resolve his chief problem, the problem created by the inciting incident.

2. Raise the stakes for the main character, whose time is running out though the job must still be done.

3. Focus the character on his objective.
Since Harrison Ford in *Witness* cannot go to Philadelphia, he will bring Philadelphia (in the person of the cops) to him. Harrison Ford has just discovered that his partner has been killed. He calls the corrupt police captain and threatens to track him down. It's an empty threat because there is no way Ford can go to Philadelphia; he'll be shot on sight. His emotions churning, Ford goes out into the small Pennsylvania village and beats up a local tough kid. The word gets back to the Philadelphia cops, who have been searching for him.

What a brilliantly conceived plot point. The Harrison Ford character commits this violent act instinctively, without conscious forethought. He can't go to Philadelphia, but he can bring Philadelphia to him, the only ground on which his character has a chance to stand.

Act III: The Resolution

Act III is the working out of the decision made by the main character at Plot Point II. Here, time is almost always a factor—known as the ticking clock. The hero has to untie the heroine from the track before the train runs her over—in five minutes. In Act II the main character finds himself in a thicket of emotions and actions. By now, moments of tension no longer share space with moments of relaxation. The pace drives forward, fast-forward. The main character sees his objective—if only he can reach it. He's so close, but ahead he sees obstacles. Should he turn back now? No, he's committed.

In *The African Queen*, if Humphrey Bogart and Katharine Hepburn decided to park their boat on the shore and take a nap, what would that have done to the story? In *Casablanca*, what if Bogart and Ingrid Bergman crept off somewhere and decided that love could conquer all, and, in the end, Paul Henreid flew off alone? What if Rocky didn't want to fight and instead went home to be with his family, knowing that a simple life was the one for him after all?

I have read scripts where the main character decides it's not worth the effort and walks away. What a disappointment. Make sure your character is driven to reach his goal, no matter what. You don't have to have a happy ending, but you can show some kind of hope, or promise of it. A torch being passed. Wisdom carried over. Something satisfying for the audience.

In *Carlito's Way*, Al Pacino dies, a victim of having broken his own code of the street. But he leaves a legacy with the Penelope Anne Miller character: a child, money to take care of them both, and love. In *Broadcast News*, the three main characters go their separate ways, and though we might have wanted Holly Hunter to end up with either Albert Brooks or William Hurt, we believe they all made the right decisions.

Movies are about problems being solved, stories that are resolved at the end. Ambiguous endings are not a possibility. Watch out for the yellow-ribbon ending where all the strands are tied neatly into a little package of contrivance. How many times have you walked away from a theater, thinking, "How nice and tidy, and false." Tidy endings broadcast themselves early in the movie; they're flat and predictable and dissatisfying except for those who want to live in tidy, predictable worlds. So much for reality.

The Climax

The climax should be the biggest scene in the movie, where good confronts evil and where the final battle is waged.

1. Make sure your main character is here.
I have read many scripts where the main character is nowhere to be found at the climax. Or standing around on the sidelines watching the cavalry gallop in to save the day.

2. The climax is the scene in which the main character's problems are resolved.
Your main character must resolve his own problems. It's hard to imagine putting your hero through all this hell and then, at the last minute, shipping him off somewhere, or bailing him out with the help of a convenient savior. These types of endings are too easy and not fulfilling to the audience, who deserve more.

After I saw *The Joy Luck Club*, I stood outside in the rain, thinking,

"She took a boat?" The main character had told her aunt that she couldn't write to her cousins about her mother dying because they wouldn't get it before she got to China herself. Logic sets in. And she takes a boat? Boats travel faster than air mail? Obviously the writers and director thought a boat would be a more romantic way to arrive in China. They should have made no reference to the letter.

I stayed for the end of *A Perfect World*, which must hold the record for the longest death scene in cinematic history. Kevin Costner came back from certain death, by my count, five times. This is a movie that didn't want to end, or which the filmmakers didn't know how to end.

3. Don't do sloppy work. That voice you hear that says something's not right—pay attention to it.
You've probably heard stories about shooting four or five alternative endings and then testing them before audiences. This is a more expensive way of doing what we, as writers, attempt in the seclusion of our rooms. Your aim should be to deliver the ending that is most satisfying for the audience. Ask yourself what you have already given them in the story, and from that you determine what's satisfying. The effective main character solves his own problem by clever means, using tools from his own personal kit.

Breaking Your Story Down

In order to see your story in its entirety, you have to break it down into acts. In order to understand it, and then write it, I recommend going through the following two steps: *The Mini Treatment* and *The Scene Breakdown*.

So far we've discussed the overall, overreaching idea. You've thought about who your characters may be, where your script will take place, the genre in which you'll be writing.

You have a general idea where the story begins, and ends. But you haven't worked out the in-between, the blow-by-blow drama of what happens to whom, and when. You will probably go through the following two steps—*The Mini Treatment* and *The Scene Breakdown*—at least twice during the course of the creation of your screenplay. These steps will guide and refocus you on the story at hand.

The Mini Treatment

The Mini Treatment is a three-to-five-page story of the movie, in prose. Pretend you're telling the story to someone with a short attention span—you want to keep them interested. Tell them only the essential parts, using strong, active verbs, and lively, visual descriptions.

The Mini Treatment will become an outline of the story. Don't get bogged down in details, or in long-winded renditions of scenes. Use the "once upon a time" approach. Once upon a time a moo cow met an aardvark, and they went off to the Brazilian rain forest, where they met a group of Carmelite nuns. And then show what happened to them all.

Break the Mini Treatment into three acts: Act I—the setup; Act II—the confrontation; Act III—the resolution.

Below you'll find a good example of a Mini Treatment by Pam Tien, a student of mine at the Rhode Island School of Design (RISD), in Providence, Rhode Island.

The Mini Treatment of Alabama Story
by P.L.P. Tien

ACT I

San Francisco after WWII. A young, handsome Chinese man, Walker Chang, works for a baby photographer by day and as an airplane mechanic by night. He meets a beautiful red-headed white girl, Meg Wilde, who works at Woolworth's now that she is no longer needed for the war effort. They defy convention by going on one date, falling in love, and getting married. They spend their honeymoon in a movie theater watching *The Barefoot Contessa*. He buys an old biplane, and they move to her hometown, Holly Springs, Alabama. Population, 93.

Ten years pass. Walker now lives with his ten-year-old daughter Ava Gardner Chang. In the meantime, Meg has fallen in love with a man named E. G. Arnold and has run away with him to Panama.

Despite Walker's cultural difference, he seems almost a southern gentleman, an aristocratic crop duster. He has hired a black woman, Josephine Moore, also thirtyish, to help take care of Ava while he works. Ava, a Chinese-American mix, is not allowed to go to the white school, or a black school. She takes private lessons every Sunday at the home of a Chinese woman, Mrs. Chow, a sixty-five-year-old widow who taught at a university in China before the revolution. She now lives in the nearby city of Huntsville.

Ava enjoys going to Goodenough's general store for Coca-Cola, peanuts, and comic books. On her way home, she pretends that she is flying. Flying is her passion, and every morning she asks her father to take her up in his crop duster, but he feel that it is too dangerous for little girls.

PLOT POINT I

On Sunday when she is to go to church and to Mrs. Chow's, she says she is not feeling well and stays home. Her father leaves and goes to church. While he is away, a mysterious woman drives up to the house. She is thirtyish and, to Ava, looks like movie star. The woman knows Ava's name, but does not reveal her own. During conversation she asks for some lemonade. When Ava returns, the woman and Cadillac have vanished. The father comes home. Ava tells him about the woman. He seems disturbed by the news.

ACT II

A knock on Josephine's door. Josephine opens the door and sees Meg Wilde, Ava's mother. Josephine's feelings are mixed. She is happy to see Meg, but she does not want to see Walker and Ava get hurt again.

Josephine and Meg are old friends. They grew up together. Meg asks to stay the night. Josephine says yes, even though she does not approve of her past actions. They eat dinner and talk about Ava, Walker, E. G. Arnold, old times, and why Meg left. Josephine reveals that Walker still loves her. Meg doesn't understand; she thinks he ought to hate her. Meg listens to a record, "their" song.

The next morning Walker, up all night, arrives at Josephine's, knowing Meg is there. Josephine goes to work. Meg and Walker talk. They go for a drive. He asks why she is back. She wants to be forgiven and come home. She knows what she did was wrong. They embrace. He says he will always love her no matter what happens, but he doesn't want to hurt Ava. If Ava says it is OK, she can stay.

They return to the house. Josephine and Ava are in the garden, talking, laughing. Walker introduces Meg to Ava. Ava is stunned. She looks at her father. He explains that Meg will stay only if Ava agrees. Ava sees that her father wants her to say yes. Josephine gets ready to leave but Ava won't let her go.

Finally Ava says if Meg wants to stay she can; then she turns and goes back to work in the garden. Walker and Meg return to her car. Josephine knows that Ava is upset and comforts her with homemade ice cream.

The next day, Ava is silent and distant. She greets Walker's attempts at interaction with indifference. Walker decides to talk with Ava alone. He understands that it must be hard for her. She asks why Meg has come back now. Walker explains that we all must learn to forgive. Ava feels that Meg left because of her.

Ava was tortured by her absence and now is tortured by her presence. Walker explains that Meg wants to make up for her past. Ava is struck by her father's completeness now.

Walker suggests that Meg take Ava to town with her, shopping. During their drive, Meg asks about Ava's life. Ava refuses to respond. Meg talks about childhood with Josephine and the troubles she got Josephine into. In town, people whisper about Meg's return. Ava is surprised that Meg shows no discomfort. Instead she warmly greets all.

Ava is embarrassed and scared as Meg takes her hand. Strangely, Ava feels a sense of admiration for Meg's strength. They buy the groceries and leave for home.

During the drive home, Meg says the town hasn't changed a bit. She reveals that she never felt that she belonged anywhere. She is unlike Josephine who has always felt at home here, even though she is black.

Meg says she didn't leave because of Ava, but because she felt trapped by the place. She had to get out. She felt that if she disgraced herself she could never be tempted to return; so she ran off with E. G. Arnold. Ava begins to understand and relate to her mother.

Meg settles in. Ava relaxes toward her, but not completely. After church on Sunday, they head to Mrs. Chow's for Ava's lessons.

While Ava studies, Walker and Meg work in Mrs. Chow's yard. Afterward, they decide to go to a movie. At the theater, the manager insists that Ava and Walker sit in the colored section, but Meg can't sit with them.

Irate, Meg confronts the manager and wins. After the film, they find "Jap Lover" written on the Caddy's windshield. Meg storms back into the theater, takes soap and water from the restroom, and washes it off. With her lipstick, she writes, "*Chink* lover, you moron!" They all dissolve into laughter. On the way home, Ava and Meg lie across the car seats and look up at the stars.

PLOT POINT II

Late afternoon, Ava goes to Mr. Goodenough's. Mr. Goodenough gives the message to Ava that her father has had engine trouble and may not get home tonight. While she is there, reading the comics, a stranger, late 20s, handsome but mean-looking, enters and buys a pack of cigarettes. Goodenough recognizes him and seems worried. After the man leaves, Mr. Goodenough tells Ava to hurry home and tell her mother that E. G. is back in town.

ACT III

Ava runs home and tells Meg. Meg is concerned. She takes Ava and they drive off. Ava asks where they are going. Meg doesn't know. She seems worried now, but not frightened. Meg says they'll drive around until Walker gets home. Ava remembers that he may not be home tonight. When Meg hears this, she decides to ask Josephine if she will come and stay the night.

When she tells Josephine that E. G. is back in town, Josephine worries about her safety. She seems to know what E. G. is capable of doing. Arriving home, they are relieved to see no one and enter the house. They decide to make dinner and go about their normal routine. A car arrives. E. G. calls for Meg to come out; he wants to take her back to Panama.

Josephine and Ava beg her not to go out. She goes out to confront him rather than let him come in. Outside, E. G. seems drunk, and is vicious. Meg threatens to call the sheriff, but E. G. knows they don't have a phone. She turns to go back into the house. E. G. leaps onto the porch. They struggle violently. He strangles her.

Ava jumps on him; Josephine follows. In the struggle, he knocks them away, freeing Meg. She lands a hard right to his jaw knocking him backwards and off the porch. He falls, hits his head on a rock, and dies.

Walker arrives home, discovers what has happened. He goes to town to tell the sheriff. The next morning the sheriff and the ambulance arrive. The sheriff has known Meg since birth. He questions her and declares that E. G.'s death is an accident, Meg is free to go.

Early fall, late afternoon. Meg and Ava are in the garden harvesting, talking, and laughing. They finish and have some lemonade on the swing. Ava wants to go to Goodenough's. When she comes back, Meg's Caddy is gone. She is confused. Josephine looks at her; they know Meg has gone for good.

She hears her father's plane land and runs to meet him across the field in the twilight. She leaps into the air. He catches her and asks her what she is doing. "I'm flying, papa, I'm flying," is all she says.

When you break your story down into this form, you'll notice the broad sweep of events. You'll also notice the three-act structure at work, with the two main plot points. Your intention is to create a world in which your story can be dramatically told.

These are the four most difficult pages you will ever write for any screenplay. At the International Film & Television Workshops in Rockport, Maine, where I teach each summer, the students have one night to do this. This is a crucial step. Without it, you have no chance of building a successful screenplay.

The Scene Breakdown

Once you commit the Mini Treatment to paper, get comments and fix it on the second go-round.

Do the Scene Breakdown. A Scene Breakdown is, as it states, a scene-by-scene delineation of the story. You break down the story into scenes. On the average, screenplays have approximately 60 main scenes. Looking at the three-act structure, Act I (a quarter of the screenplay) holds 15 scenes. Act II (half the screenplay) has approximately 30 scenes. Act III (a quarter of the screenplay) holds the remaining 15. I generalize with these numbers. You may have 10 scenes in Act I, 30 in Act II, and 15 in Act III.

The important thing to remember is to look at your story from this new perspective. The Scene Breakdown will give you focus and enable you to look specifically at how your story unfolds, scene by scene.

The purpose of the Scene Breakdown is to render each scene in minimalist detail. Location, character, situation. Notice how the story moves along in this new format. Notice how you need to put in scenes you hadn't thought about including, remove scenes that don't work, bring to life characters you need to perform certain functions, and eliminate or diminish characters who earlier seemed more significant.

The 3 × 5 Cards

The pattern of the thing precedes the thing. I fill in the gap of the crossword at any spot I happen to choose. These bits I write on index cards until the work is done.
—Vladimir Nabokov, novelist and
author of *Lolita*

Once you write the four-page Mini Treatment and are ready to do the step outline or scene breakdown, there is one more invaluable step you can take. Write details of each scene on a 3 × 5 index card. I, along with thousands of other produced screenwriters, do this with every story. When I expand the scenes, I place each on a card—details, characters, motivations—anything I might need for a better sense of each scene.

I use white cards for the scenes in Act I, yellow for Act II, and pink for Act III. I then tack the cards on a cork board against a wall in my office. This gives me the ability to see the entire screenplay, via cards, right in front of me. The cards provide a total visual picture of the story from beginning to end. I roam back and forth, studying these cards, fine-tuning. I look for pacing, character development from one scene to the next, and rising dramatic action. I change some scenes, eliminate others. I move cards around. I can see where I need to set up something in Act I, reinforce it in Act II, and pay it off in Act III.

Remember to put only salient details on the cards: location, characters, central issue or issues of the scene. I sometimes write a snatch of dialogue or add a detail here or there. If you have to write on the back of each index card, do it, or if necessary, use two or more cards, tacked together. Use the cards. They sharpen focus and give you, in one large picture before your eyes, the elements of story and structure.

Examples

Act I/Scene 8
Sally and Beau in bedroom.
Sally crying.
Beau guilty over his affair with Kit, Sally's friend.
They fight. Beau, anguished, storms out.

Act I/Scene 9
Beau outside house/hops in car.
Won't start/ ripping mad.
Gets out/ it starts to rain.
Bangs on car/goes wild/uncontrolled.
Collapses on ground/on one knee/ he cries.
A hand touches him/it's Sally.
She's there for him, even now.
Just a look/ a tease/ no verbal reconciliation.

I asked Pam Tien to do a breakdown of her *Alabama Story* to give you an idea of how this is done.

The Scene Breakdown of Alabama Story
by P. L. P. Tien

ACT I

1: North Alabama, summer, late 1950s, POV from plane over small rural town; as plane comes closer to ground, we see a young girl, Ava Gardner Chang, running.

2: Begin voice-over intro/setup as: plane flies over Ava, she waves, runs up porch steps and into house.

3: Inside the house Ava, Chinese/Caucasian, approx. 10, greets housekeeper, Josephine Moore, black, 30s, preparing supper.

4: Ava sets the table as she and Josephine talk.

5: The sound of the plane landing filters into the kitchen. Ava runs out through screen door to greet the pilot, while Josephine watches.

6: At the plane Ava's father, Walker Chang, picks her up and spins her around in the air. They return to the house.

7: Inside house Ava and Walker greet Josephine, who tells him to get cleaned up for supper.

8: At supper table the three finish eating. Walker says they will leave the dishes for later. They drive Josephine home.

9: They arrive at Josephine's house, and Walker asks if she remembered to take some of the vegetables from the garden. She says they are in the back of the truck; she will see Ava and Walker Monday.

10: Ava asks her father if she can ride in the back of the pickup; he agrees.

11: On the way home Ava stands behind cab, arms out, flying in the twilight.

12: In her bedroom, Ava tells her father she does not feel well and asks to stay home from church and her private lessons at Mrs. Chow's in Huntsville.

13: Walker leaves for church. Asks Ava if it is okay with her if he goes on to Mrs. Chow's to fix her back step, as he promised the week before.

14: In the early afternoon, Ava rises and goes to Goodenough's and buys a Coke from the machine.

15: Ava returns home and lies on the porch swing, drinking the Coke. A Cadillac comes up the road, and Ava goes into the house.

16: A stranger gets out and calls to the house, but Ava does not answer. A woman approaches the house, Meg Wilde. Ava is unaware that Meg is her mother.

17: Ava and Meg talk, but Meg does not reveal her identity; while Ava makes lemonade, Meg disappears.

18: Walker comes home, and Ava tells him about the woman who disappeared; he seems disturbed.

19: Later, Walker puts Ava to bed and goes out and sits on the porch swing in the night.

ACT II

1: Meg knocks on Josephine's door. Josephine is shocked to see her. Meg asks to spend the night.

2: Int. Josephine's house, the two women and Josephine's daughter, Rena, eat and talk. After supper the three lie outside and look at the stars.

3: Walker, who has been up all night, goes to Josephine's to see Meg, knowing that she will be there.

4: Josephine comes out of her house and talks to Walker, asks him what he's going to do. He doesn't know.

5: Walker knocks on Meg's door. When she opens up, he asks her if she would like to dance.

6: Pickup truck. They drive to river and talk. Meg asks to be forgiven, she wants to come home. Walker says it is up to Ava, not him.

7: At their house they find Ava and Josephine working in the garden. Ava is shocked that Meg is her mother and reluctantly agrees that she can stay.

8: The next day Ava is silent and withdrawn. Walker talks with her about forgiveness.

9: Walker suggests that Meg and Ava go to town together on Saturday for groceries.

10: On the way to town, Ava is silent and withdrawn. Meg tries to make conversation; no progress.

11: In the grocery store they have a run-in with Mrs. Killian, an openly hostile minister's wife.

12: Outside the grocery store Mrs. Killian intentionally knocks Ava down and refuses to apologize, until Meg forces her.

13: In the car Meg puts the top up for Ava to watch the sky. Meg tries to reach Ava by retelling why she left home in the first place.

14: At home, Meg tells Walker and Josephine about the incident. Walker reminds Ava about her homework.

15: Sunday, the family leaves church services and drives to Mrs. Chow's in Huntsville, for Ava's lessons. Meg and Walker do yard work while Ava studies.

16: Leaving Mrs. Chow's, they decide to go to movies because the night is so hot.

17: At the theater Meg argues over Walker and Ava's having to sit in the colored section: she wins.

18: After the movie, they find "JAP LOVER" written on Meg's car. Furious, she goes back into the theater.

19: Coming back out with soap and water, Meg washes the words off the windshield. In lipstick, she writes "CHINK LOVER, YOU REDNECK PECKERHEAD." Walker laughs, which melts Meg's fury. She joins in.

20: On the way home with the top down, Meg and Ava lie back looking up at millions of stars. Walker drives. The radio plays.

21: At his store. Mr. Goodenough gives Ava a message that her father may not make it home tonight because of trouble with the plane.

22: Outside the store, a man drives up, gets out of his car, and comes in.

23: Inside he doesn't notice Ava and asks for cigarettes; Mr. Goodenough recognizes him but doesn't let on. The man pays and leaves.

24: Mr. Goodenough tells Ava to run home and tell her mother that E. G. Arnold, the man from Panama, is back in town.

ACT III

1: Home. Ava arrives, tells Meg about E. G.

2: They leave in the car, Meg saying they will come home after Walker does. Ava remembers that her father may not be coming home.

3: Meg decides to go to Josephine's, where she explains the situation and asks Josephine to stay the night with them.

4: At home all seems safe. They cook and go about their business, though an air of nervousness overshadows them.

5: As they clear up dinner they hear a car and hope it is Walker. E. G.'s voice calls Meg out.

6: Ava and Josephine beg Meg not to go, but she is determined to keep him from coming in.

7: Outside, E. G. is drunk and mean, and knowing they have no phone, calls Meg's bluff when she threatens to call the sheriff. Meg tries to go back into house for shotgun, but he grabs her.

8: They struggle violently. E. G. is strangling Meg; Josephine and Ava join in, freeing Meg.

9: E. G. grabs Ava and pummels her. Meg frees her and with a right upper cut knocks E. G. off the porch.

10: E. G. lands on the ground, striking his head on a rock.

11: Meg comes down from the porch into the yard and finds that he is dead. She decides to go into town to call the sheriff in the morning.

12: Not wanting to leave the body in the yard or in the house, they load E. G. into his car.

13: Inside the house, Meg tries to get Ava ready for bed. Ava can't sleep. The women hear the sound of another car arriving.

14: A car door slams and the car leaves. The women hear footsteps on the porch.

15: Someone tries to open the door. They tense. Walker enters.

16: Walker tells them how he got a ride. They interrupt him and tell him about E. G.; he decides to walk toward town, to phone the sheriff.

17: Next day. At the house, the sheriff questions Meg and finally declares E. G.'s death an accident.

18: Fall, late afternoon. Meg and Ava harvest the garden.

19: At the house, they have lemonade on the porch. Meg talks to Ava about the problem of freedom and choosing. A look that Ava wonders about passes between her and Meg. Ava asks to go to Goodenough's and runs inside for her things.

20: When Ava returns, she finds Meg and the Cadillac gone.

21: Ava hears her father's plane. As he lands, she runs to meet him, leaping into his arms.

I expect that you've noticed things in the Mini Treatment and Scene Breakdown you would alter. Turn that critical eye to good use when you tackle your own story. When you finish the Scene Breakdown, the next step will be to expand each scene to include more detail, perhaps some snatches of conversation. Once the Mini Treatment and Scene Breakdown establish the world of the screenplay and the pacing, the characters begin to take shape. Ask yourself, "Who are these people, and how am I going to bring them to life?" The story gets you in the door. The characters carry you into the room.

Exercise

Go to any college library. In the drama or film section, you'll find copies of produced scripts. Choose ten of them and read the opening sequences—the first ten pages. See how the pros do it. Look for pacing, setup, format, and character establishment.

There is no better way to learn how to write movies than to read scripts. After reading these openings, analyze them, break them down, and then take your own idea for a movie and play with it, trying a number of these types of openings to see which might be best for your story.

Exercise

In the next few movies you watch, search for the midpoint. How does it function? How does it shift the action and reinforce the main character's primary goal?

Exercise

Write a Mini Treatment. Start with Act I, then Act II, then finally Act III.

Exercise

Do a Scene Breakdown. Start with Act I, then Act II, then finally Act III.

Exercise

Assuming that you have between 45 and 60 master scenes in your screenplay (the range in an average-length screenplay), break out your cards. Put only the essential details of each scene on each card.

Tack the cards to a cork board or other surface. Keep it simple. It'll take a couple of hours. When it's completed, stand back and take a look at the results.

7
The Scene

I believe more in the scissors than I do in the pencil.

> Truman Capote, novelist and
> author of *In Cold Blood*

The scene is the most important element in a screenplay. It is an event in a screenplay that occupies time and space. Each scene has a beginning, middle, and end. Treat every scene like a small screenplay. Without sharply focused scenes, you have no screenplay. Without knowing what to do with a scene—or what a scene can and should do—you have no chance to write a decent screenplay.

The main purposes of a scene are to move the story forward and to further character. If a scene doesn't satisfy these objectives, it doesn't belong in the screenplay.

Scene Elements

1. A scene can be a single shot or three pages of dialogue.
A scene possesses two elements: Space and Time. Here's an example:

INT. BEDROOM — NIGHT

Hortense rushes in, flips on the light. She gasps. On the bed she sees Rudolpho, a hatchet buried in his skull.

EXT. PARK — DAY

Rudolpho skateboards from out of the trees. He sees a lone WOMAN (Hortense) on a bench, reading. He angles toward her.

The woman looks up sharply. Rudolpho stands over her, leering.

                    RUDOLPHO
     Were you in my bedroom last night?

                    HORTENSE
     Hello, hatchet face. You're looking
     better.

2. *INT.* means *Interior.*

The scene takes place inside a building, a cave, or somewhere with walls around it, an enclosed space. In the first scene above, the interior is the BEDROOM, and the time is NIGHT.

3. *EXT.* means *Exterior.*

The scene takes place on location under the stars or in sunlight, in a field, on a busy city street. In the second scene, the space is an exterior, the PARK, and the time is DAY.

Every time you change locations, show the designations: INT. BEDROOM—NIGHT or EXT. PARK—DAY. A move from the bathroom to the kitchen is a change of scene. With each change of time, use a new designation. These designations inform the reader and establish continuity during shooting.

Nobody can afford to shoot a motion picture in sequence; the budget won't allow it. Consequently, if during the course of the movie you have five or ten scenes that take place in the same location, they are shot all at once. Later they're edited into their proper places. This makes you appreciate how complicated filming is. You wonder how actors can deliver great performances when the movie is shot out of sequence. Top actors know precisely what their characters' emotions are at any given time in the story.

4. Start each scene with CONTEXT.

Ask yourself what you need contextually in this part of the screenplay to keep telling the story well. Remember that every scene must have something to do with the spine of the story. The spine is the *main character's need.*

Let's say I need a scene where Hortense discovers Rudolpho's body. How can I make this scene as dramatic as possible? What if I have her drive along and spot his wrecked car down below in a ravine? But then I'd have to get Rudolpho into a car first. Where would he get a car? Whose car? This would mean I'd have to create another character, or incident. Forget it; too complicated.

I ask myself: In what other, equally dramatic way could she discover the body? Maybe she looks down the well in the backyard and sees him floating face up. Except that I've seen that before, it's a cliché.

If the movie is called *Hatchet!*, why not have one buried in Rudolpho's skull? In his own bed. And have Hortense shocked when she finds him.

5. A screenplay is made up of approximately 50–70 scenes, which should appear in the order that best explains the story.

6. Remember the rule: *simple plot* **and** *complex characters*, **rather than the other way around.**

7. Begin each scene at the last possible moment.
We don't want Hortense beginning her day and then going through a series of moments leading up to the discovery. Why not start her out in her own room, fretting about something? She is angry at Rudolpho about something and she wants to have it out with him. She leaves her room and storms down the hallway. She knocks. No answer. She tries the door. It's unlocked. She enters.

```
INT. BEDROOM — NIGHT

Hortense rushes in, flips on the light. She gasps. On the bed she
sees Rudolpho, a hatchet buried in his skull.
```

8. You first establish the need for or context of the scene.
You then fill it with the details, or content. Two elements appear in each scene: the visual and the spoken. Sometimes there's only the visual—a spaceship flying through the heavens.

9. Don't forget that the primary functions of the scene are to move the story forward and to enhance character.
Characters who sit around chit-chatting are deadly dull.

Questions to Ask Yourself About Each Scene

1. How does the scene add to the hero or heroine's chief goal?
Does the scene help him get what he wants, or prevent him from getting what he wants? Each scene must move the story forward, which means moving the main character toward his objective.

2. What does each character want in the scene?

Since nobody ever agrees with anybody in movies, each character in a scene wants something different. Determine what each character wants to accomplish in the scene before you start to write. Briefly outline the scene, set up a few points you want to cover. This preparation will contribute to the scene's tension and dramatic conflict.

3. Does the scene have its own beginning, middle, and end?

William Goldman, writer of *Butch Cassidy and the Sundance Kid* and *All the President's Men,* suggests that when you decide what the central issue of the scene is, back up a click or two and begin. If two characters head out from different places to meet somewhere, don't start them in bed that morning and move them simultaneously through the day to reach the meeting. Economize. Get them there without fuss. You don't want flat, dull "en route to" moments in which nothing happens. Always keep in mind the *purpose of the scene.*

4. How does each character feel?

Every character has just come from somewhere. Determine what just happened and the character's frame of mind. If a character's wife just died, you're not going to have him dancing around. I've read scripts where the character has just suffered some tragedy, but the writer somehow forgot about it and had the character doing something completely *out* of character in the following scene. Carry the character's emotional life from one scene to the next.

5. Is each character in the scene necessary?

Watch out for a secondary character, like a waiter in a restaurant, stealing the scene. This practice usually indicates that the writer, for some reason, wants to avoid the conflict between his principal characters and drags some other person in to grab the focus. Whatever it takes, stay with the conflict, work through it. Don't translate your fear on confrontation by introducing conflict-killing characters, when the real problem might be writing the conflict itself. No matter how colorful a waiter or some other character might make the scene, if the character doesn't move the scene forward in a significant way, get rid of him.

6. What does each character want?

All characters enter a scene with a purpose. They want something, and will usually do whatever they can to get it. They will be clever, mean; they will use blackmail, extortion, fear. Make sure you know each character's motivation in the scene.

Don't take just one side of the argument, either; take both or all sides. Look at the scene from the main character's point of view, and from the others'. Knowing each character's motives will make the scene clearer to you and will also allow you to find interesting ways for each character to go after what he or she wants. This, in turn, will give you a better understanding of what each character is capable of doing, and possibly a greater understanding of each character's need in the scene.

7. Does the scene show confrontation and/or anticipate it?

For instance, Rudolpho and Hortense are on the phone. Rudolpho tells Hortense to meet him under the Schopenhauer Bridge at midnight. Hortense says, "That's dangerous, Rudolpho!" They argue, then reluctantly agree to meet. This scene has confrontation, *and* it creates anticipation about the meeting under the bridge. The scene vaults us into the next scene. By creating anticipation, you move the story along.

8. Construct each scene through a series of beats.

A dramatic beat is any event in the scene that significantly spins the action forward. This is not to be confused with the word *beat* which turns up in a screenplay, in parentheses, as a pause. I am talking about a *dramatic beat*. Most scenes, like screenplays themselves, have turning points, called beats. Build the scene from beginning to end by using these dramatic beats. Consider the following:

```
INT. BEDROOM — DAY
Hortense sits on the bed, crying. Rudolpho rushes into the
room, stops, looks at her.

                    RUDOLPHO
          Hortense, honey, what's the matter?


                    HORTENSE
          Don't "Hortense, honey" me, you cheating
          bastard.


                    RUDOLPHO
          What do you mean?


                    HORTENSE
          Does the name Ludwig von Bee mean
          anything to you?


                    RUDOLPHO
          My God, you know about Ludwig!
```

                   HORTENSE
You and Ludwig, a *man*. I can't believe it.

Tears spew out of her.

                   RUDOLPHO
What do you mean?

                   HORTENSE
You know exactly what I mean.

Rudolpho sits on the bed beside her, touches her hand. She
recoils.

                   RUDOLPHO
I have been meaning to tell you
something.

                   HORTENSE
I'm sure you have.

                   RUDOLPHO
This is very difficult.

                   HORTENSE
How do you think it's been for me?

                   RUDOLPHO
Ludwig is my . . .

                   HORTENSE
Oh, I can't listen to this.

She gets up and takes her coat, heads for the door.

                   RUDOLPHO
       (profound sadness)
Ludwig is . . . my brother.

This stops her; she turns.

                   HORTENSE
Your brother! You're having an affair
with your own brother!

                   RUDOLPHO
Affair! It's *his* affair he's troubled
over.

                   HORTENSE
His affair? Oh, my goodness, no wonder.

                         RUDOLPHO
          What is it, Hortense?

                         HORTENSE
             (with tears)
          That affair he's having . . . is with me.

                         RUDOLPHO
          What!

                         HORTENSE
          That's right!

                         RUDOLPHO
          My own brother is having an affair with
          the woman I love?

                         HORTENSE
          You . . . love me?

                         RUDOLPHO
          From the moment we met, but now . . .

                         HORTENSE
             (in terror)
          My God . . .

Here we have a revelatory scene that builds through a series of dramatic, emotional shocks, or beats. Conflict and tension intensify after each turning point. We could leave Hortense and Rudolpho at this moment and go on to another scene, or we could search for some temporary resolution. The reason a scene seems flat is that the writer has forgotten to build it, beat by beat, toward a dramatic resolution.

9. Leave us wondering at the end of each scene.
Writers often feel the need to explain everything, to tell the reader too much, because they feel the reader needs to know it. Leave the reader hanging at the end of each scene. Don't tell the reader anything until you feel that he or she *needs to know it.*

The Sequence

There are three general ways by which to perceive a screenplay. The first is the grand overview itself: the beginning, middle, and end. From this perspective we stand on a cliff and see the entire valley of the screenplay laid out before us. On the smallest scale we view the screenplay through a microscope, at the moment by moment rendition of what happens within each scene. The third perspective falls between the two: it's called the Sequence.

A sequence is a series of scenes connected by a single idea. It's a unit or block of action that usually takes place in one general location. Remember the chase sequence in *Bullitt*, or the opening wedding sequence in *The Godfather*. The rape sequence in *The Accused*. The African sequence in Spielberg's *The Color Purple*. These sequences are strings of scenes held together by a central idea that moves the story forward. The entire third act in *Rocky* is a fight sequence. How about the brilliant escape sequence in *The Killing Fields*? Or the escape-through-the-forest sequence in *The Last of the Mohicans*? Or the opening sequence on the studio lot in *The Player*? It goes on and on.

Once again: A sequence is series of scenes stitched together, unified by a single thought or intention. Look at each sequence as a mini-version of a screenplay.

Each sequence has a beginning, middle, and end. It has *context* (where it belongs in the story) and *content* (the material itself). Without necessarily being aware of it, every screenwriter writes sequences. Look at your own work. You've probably got a sequence at the beginning of your story that takes place in the same location, has a beginning, middle, and end, and tells a compelling story that feeds the greater story of the screenplay itself.

Perhaps you place your main character in a sequence of events starting when she comes home from work one night, carrying over until the next morning, when she goes off to work. This night changes her life. This night could be the entire screenplay itself. Remember how Martin Scorsese did this very thing in *After Hours*? Or you can use five or six significant scenes, all of which take place at the character's home, to act as a turning or plot point.

It may take four or five scenes to get your point across. This block of actions is a sequence, chunks of the screenplay that move like glaciers across the sea of the screenplay. Stanley Kubrick, Steven Spielberg, Frank Pierson, and others create their pictures in terms of sequences. They view—and create—their stories in big blocks of action, the sum of which makes up the story. Pierson wrote *Dog Day Afternoon* in approximately twelve ten-minute sequences, equaling 120 pages.

Another method is to create a sequence of cross-cuts. An example of this follows: A plane is about to land with a human cargo. Cut to loved ones on the ground waiting. Cut back to the plane, drawing closer to the landing strip. Cut to the ground where terrorists wait. Cut to the plane where the main character tries to prevent the plane from landing. Cut to another part of the airport where the passenger's family or loved one waits. Cut to the terrorists, who see that the passenger is trying to divert the plane and rush to the control tower. Cut to the main character in the plane, etc.

In a cross-cutting sequence from *Marathon Man*, Dustin Hoffman runs along the park, while uptown on 86th Street two old codgers brawl in traffic. Later in the movie we discover what these two seemingly unrelated events have to do with each other.

No matter from what perspective you look at your screenplay, it all comes down to the group of brilliant nuggets called scenes. Ideas are cheap; execution is everything. Screenplays bear witness to the notions that unify them, but in the end what makes movies memorable is the individual scenes we remember, and the moments within them.

Exercise

Write a scene from your screenplay that doesn't require dialogue.

8
Dialogue

Character and thought are merely obscured by a diction that
is overbrilliant.

> Aristotle, author of
> *The Poetics*

Dialogue is, first and foremost, a function of character. It develops
gradually. You don't have to get it perfect right away because, like
everything else in character development, writing good dialogue takes
time. You usually have to wait until halfway through the screenplay for
your characters to begin speaking to you in their own voices.

I hear students say they can't write screenplays well because they're
not good at dialogue. First of all, great screenwriting is not about good
dialogue. It's about strong characters and stories. Unless of course
you're looking for an excuse—in which case bad dialogue is as good as
any. Don't be too hard on yourself, though. Strong, believable, character-driven dialogue will come. Just keep working. If you have to write
down what you want your character to say, write it literally, on the nose,
for the time being.

                    HORTENSE
          I feel anger.

                    RUDOLPHO
          Feel anger?

                    HORTENSE
          Misery, frustration. I have tons of
          anguish inside of me.

You can change it later. If you're scampering through a scene, don't
stop to find the right word. Keep going, you're on a roll, finish the scene.
Dialogue breeds conflict. In movies, nobody ever agrees with any-

body. Something as simple as what to do tonight could turn into a major disaster.

>   RUDOLPHO
>   Let's go see *Husbands and Wives*.
>
>   HORTENSE
>   I wanna see *Under Siege*. *You* see that
>   Woody Allen drivel.
>
>   RUDOLPHO
>   Drivel!? You see *Under Siege* and you'll
>   be incapacitated for a week.
>
>   HORTENSE
>   I like Steven Seagal.
>
>   RUDOLPHO
>   You'd spend seven bucks to see a little
>   muscle? In a mindless piece of dreck? I
>   thought I knew you better, Hortense.
>
>   HORTENSE
>   Pardon me for living, Rudolpho, but my
>   likes are not always your likes.
>
>   RUDOLPHO
>   I hate to go to see a movie alone.
>
>   HORTENSE
>   Then come see *Under Siege* with me.
>
>   RUDOLPHO
>   No thank you.
>
>   HORTENSE
>   And I don't wish to see Woody Allen
>   psychologically relieving himself on the
>   screen.
>
>   RUDOLPHO
>   And I don't wanna see Steven Seagal blow
>   up shit.
>
>   HORTENSE
>   One man's shit is another woman's
>   salvation, Rudolpho.
>
>   RUDOLPHO
>   So now I'm dating a philosopher.

> HORTENSE
> Not anymore, Rudolpho.

She grabs her coat and slams the door behind her.

> RUDOLPHO
> (shouting after her)
> You're cooked, Hortense; you'll never find
> anybody as good as me.
> (beat; opens the door)
> Hortense?

Get it down; get it right later.

Effective dialogue accomplishes many things

1. It communicates information, moving the story forward.

If dialogue impedes forward movement, get rid of it. Every word must mean something to the story or character.

This is how *not* to do it:

> HORTENSE
> Rudolpho, guess where I've been all day.

> RUDOLPHO
> Where, dear?

> HORTENSE
> At Jordan Marsh. I bought a dress and
> shoes, and a matching scarf, and they had
> a sale on coats. The coats at Jordan Marsh
> are so lovely. Here, let me show you four
> I bought, same style, different colors.

> RUDOLPHO
> I love it when you model your clothes for
> me, Hortense. I want to hear every detail
> of every moment you spent buying your
> lovely clothes.

Bored yet? I am. If you must write a scene like this, put some tension or conflict in it, minus the chit-chat—unless it means something. Another way you might try the same scene:

> HORTENSE
> Rudolpho, guess where I've been all day.

                         RUDOLPHO
          That's what I'd like to know.

                         HORTENSE
          At Jordan Marsh. I bought a dress and
          shoes.

                         RUDOLPHO
          That's not what Millie told me.

                         HORTENSE
             (not listening)
          . . . and a matching scarf, and they had a
          sale on coats. The coats at Jordan Marsh
          are so lovely. . . .

                         RUDOLPHO
          Millie said she saw you with Fred Bonano
          at the Sappho Grille.

                         HORTENSE
             (speaking faster)
          Here, let me show you four I bought, same
          style, different colors. . . .

                         RUDOLPHO
          We're finished, Hortense. It's over.

                         HORTENSE
          I thought you loved to hear about my
          shopping experiences.

                         RUDOLPHO
          Not when you're shopping for other men.

2. Dialogue reveals emotional stakes.

How do your characters speak during outbursts—slowly, quietly? In
measured voices? Or do they lose it. Do they shout, rail, intimidate? Do
they complete sentences, or do they flip around in half phrases, grunts,
wild scattered language?

3. It reveals quirks, moods, intelligence, education, temperament, attitude.

Let's say your character receives a phone call informing her that she's
just won a million dollars. How would she react? Would she throw
herself into a chair and scream? Would she collapse on the floor? Would
she run outside and tell the neighbors? Would she roll into a ball and

rock herself into oblivion? Would she not believe a word of it and hate whomever told her this terrible lie?

If she gets a phone call telling her that her best friend just had a bad accident, does she slump by the phone and cry? Does she run out into the street and rage toward heaven? Does she stand by the phone, stunned?

When your character finds ten thousand dollars in an envelope sitting in a lobby, does she turn it in to the desk clerk? Does she go out and spend it? Does she keep it for a few days, wavering between guilt and responsibility, then tell her best friend? What would she say to her friend? How would she say it?

When your character needs somebody to do something for her but needs a way to ask, would she lie? Would she be forthright? What words would she use?

When your character doesn't get her way, does she rant and rave? Is she petulant? Is she resentful? How do her words reflect this? Does a character talk in complete sentences, or in quick emotional bursts? Fast or slow? With expletives? Harsh or mild? With clear or muddled diction? With an accent? With a *phony* accent?

Take people you know and study their emotional relationships. How do they use verbal outbursts to reveal their emotional states?

4. Dialogue reveals conflicts between the characters.

If the definition of drama is character in perpetual conflict, is your dialogue riveting? When you enter a scene and find a point of conflict between your characters, work each one of them into a frenzy. Remember that one man's external frenzy may be another man's internal frenzy. That is, one character may let it all hang out, while the other hides it inside. It all comes down to character.

In movies, dialogue replaces much of the inner thought found in novels. You must show thought through dialogue. We have to see or hear it. Let nobody off the hook. The more conflict, the better the movie. And dialogue is "conflict heaven," if it's done well. The key question is always: How will your character act, or what will he say, under each given set of circumstances he or she faces?

In a scene, each character wants something different from the other characters. This provides conflict. If every character wants the same thing, the scene becomes flat. Or let's say each character ultimately wants the same thing—to rob a bank, for instance—but has a different idea how to go about it. This provides conflict.

In *Annie Hall*, the Woody Allen character wants to know why Annie Hall won't marry him. "I'm going to California," she says. "But, we're in love, aren't we?" he replies. "I'm not in love anymore," she says. "I'm going to California." "You can't do that!" He's beside himself with grief and anguish.

Before writing each scene, decide what each character wants, and what they'll do or say to get it. This will make the scene easier and more interesting to write.

5. It creates tension.

Tension should always be part of dialogue, either on the surface or in the subtext, below the surface. Hidden agendas lurk everywhere. Ask yourself the question: How does your character react to each situation he confronts during the course of the story? By consistently asking yourself this question, your character, often through dialogue, begins to emerge. A steady and consistent awareness of how your character reacts to every given set of circumstances leads the way to discovering who your character is. This is also called the *character arc*.

Exercise

Write a scene from your screenplay with dialogue.

Exercise

Start your screenplay. Begin by writing the first ten pages.

9

The Format

If it don't look right, it ain't right.

a student

Formatting is presentation. You want and need to make a good impression. Situation: You walk into a corporate boardroom to present a new idea to the hierarchy. This idea could make you a vast fortune. But you're hung over from last night's celebration, a little shaky, your suit or dress wears a couple of stains. Let's not mince words: You're a wreck. In your presentation, you're not sharp; in fact, you're disorganized. You forget key points. There's no real continuity or build, not the way you planned it, that's for sure. You are impolite, even surly. Somewhere in the midst of this mess, the great idea lurks, but the people in the room are wary of you. You, in this case, represent sloppy format. You may have the best screenplay ever written and maybe somebody will be able to wade through the slop to find it, but don't count on it.

I personally can't stand to read a poorly formatted screenplay. It's like reading a novel with a three-inch column of text running down the middle of each page, or a poem with one word on every other page. I throw them in the trash. When someone hands in a screenplay like that, I hand it back, saying, "I already have a bad attitude about this. Do you still want me to read it?"

If you screw up the format, the reader will figure your idea is probably no good either. It's like spelling mistakes. Readers will never get to the art if they have to wade through a field of blunders. Go ahead, send an agent a screenplay with misspellings and format problems. See how fast you get it back. Or don't get it back. I belabor this point because I get scripts all the time, and when the formatting is a mess, the script automatically loses credibility, whether it deserves it or not.

Formatting Tips

1. Use no camera angles.

You're the writer, not the director or cinematographer. You're a writer with a story to tell and nobody cares if you know what a medium close shot of a hand coming into frame is or what a registration dissolve looks like. Just tell the story.

You will notice some camera angles in certain scripts. These are the third, fifth, even tenth drafts of already bought screenplays that have been through many pairs of hands. They are called *shooting scripts.*

You are offering up a *presentation script.* You are not responsible for camera angles. If you need a close shot on something, simply say: Rudolpho wraps his fingers around the glass. Or Hortense watches the sun rise over the distant mountains.

2. When a character is introduced for the first time, capitalize his or her full name.

This is a signal to readers that they have not met this character before. An example:

```
INT. GRAND BALLROOM — NIGHT
Rudolpho waits. Couples dance by him. He watches their elegant
faces, their pleasure. Rudolpho finds no pleasure at being
alone.


The music crescendos. He looks up suddenly to the entrance. The
crowd parts, opening a wedge. He sees a FIGURE emerging, a
woman.


She approaches. Rudolpho knows who this is. He strides forward
to greet this most elegant of creatures, the inimitable
HORTENSE.
```

I sometimes find names capitalized in snatches of dialogue. Capitalize first-time appearances only in the narrative—when they show up live, in the story.

3. Do not number scenes.

Numbered scenes appear in later drafts, after the script is bought.

4. Watch out for too many details in your location or character descriptions.

Screenwriting is about essences and minimalist writing. When you enter a scene, look around, ask yourself what is essential to achieve a sense of the place.

Some good examples:
- A Victorian living room with enormous paintings of ancestors hanging on the walls.
- A dark cell. Light streams through a window high up and out of reach.
- A Florida neighborhood of blocky pastel-colored houses and sweltering summer heat.
- A short gruff man, mid-40s, well dressed, walks with a pronounced limp.
- A severe woman, late 30s, in dark clothes, hair in a tight bun, stumbles forward.
- A rainy East-Side Manhattan street at four in the morning.

The reader will get the picture. Convey the *essence* of the person or place. Then let the action do the rest.

A Bad Example:
EXT. VICTORIAN HOUSE — NIGHT
A Victorian house with great columns and a weedy front yard sits
on a street filled with nicer homes. The paint is chipped, and
the windows need washing. The front porch has steps missing,
and an old rusted swing stands on the front lawn, which hasn't
been mowed in years. It's a disgusting place, from years of
neglect, and a place badly in need of repair. The widow's walk
looks as if it will tumble down any minute, and you'd swear
there are bats flying around in the moonlight.

The Rewrite:
EXT. DILAPIDATED VICTORIAN MANSION — NIGHT
Once majestic, gone to seed, the house is bathed in eerie
moonlight.

A Bad Example:
RUDOLPHO, a tall skinny man with red hair and blue eyes,
slightly bald, and wearing fashionable clothing, carrying a
walking stick, struts into the room. On closer inspection his
clothing is worn, somewhat threadbare, even tattered. His shoes
are scuffed. Though he looks disheveled, he nonetheless smiles
confidently, as if his world, no matter what it looks like, is
always glorious.

The Rewrite:
RUDOLPHO, 38, thin, confident, in good but shabby clothing, with a
cane, struts into the room.

5. Watch out for blocky, chunky paragraphs.
Either cut back the description or break big paragraphs into two or
three short, pithy ones.

A Bad Example:
INT. BOWLING ALLEY — NIGHT
RUDOLPHO, a 45-year-old man in elegant evening clothes,
slightly worn and covered with mud and leaves, enters this
bowling alley. The alley has twenty lanes, and is sort of seedy
and grimy, a fifties kind of place. He looks around and down at
the end, beyond three or four alleys, where FAMILIES and
SINGLES bowl, he sees two tall MEN, and a WOMAN Rudolpho
recognizes as Hortense.

Rudolpho doesn't want to be spotted so he hides behind a potted
plant, looking at them. He wonders why Hortense looks as if she
is having such a good time when in fact she has just supposedly
been kidnapped by these two men.

Rudolpho sneaks along the ball racks, getting closer to where
they are. He feels inside of his jacket for the .38 Special he
carries there. He is feeling nervous and keeps looking around,
hoping not to be spotted. He hears a noise behind him and spins
around to see.

This is visual but windy. Remember that screenplays are read
down the page (not horizontally, as in a novel), in a shot-by-shot
rendition of the action. Think in short visual bursts when writing a
screenplay, as if you're reading a movie.

The Rewrite:
INT. SEEDY BOWLING ALLEY — NIGHT
Rudolpho, 45, in a mud-splattered tuxedo, enters.

He sees families and singles on the lanes. At the far end he
spots two tall MEN and Hortense.

He ducks behind a potted plant.

Hortense laughs and jokes with the men. Rudolpho, confused by
her behavior, reaches inside his jacket, pulls out the .38
Special, checks it.

He crouches low and moves along the ball racks.

He hears a SOUND behind him and spins around. Standing above him
is . . .

6. Convey intention through essence and movement only.
We can know Rudolpho's feelings only by the way he acts (he pulls out
the .38) and looks (confused). We cannot see thought. You are after one
sharp visual image after the other. No excess.

7. Please: no actors' names.
A Tom Cruise type. A Michelle Pfeiffer look. This is unprofessional. No
actor or actress wants to be a Tom Cruise or Michelle Pfeiffer type.
Agents will not send out a script with these references.

8. In sex scenes, do whatever you think conveys the essence of the scene in the best way without being pornographic.
Fewer, stronger words do the job. Some writers write, "They have sex,"
and let it go at that. Others go into graphic detail about heaving bodies
and sweat-drenched orgasmic verisimilitude.

9. Use strong nouns and active verbs.
Kill adverbs and most adjectives. Adverbs, like most adjectives, make
us lazy writers.

10. Never write "Special Effects."
Describe special effects in a few well-chosen, descriptive words. Otherwise, how will we know what we're supposed to see?

11. Follow these music guidelines.

- Don't send cassettes of recorded music along with the script.
- With original songs, don't write out the entire lyric. Include a stanza
  or two and describe the rest of the song in a sentence or two.
- Do not include soundtrack music. If the characters can't hear it,
  leave it out. Of course, you should mention what kind of music the
  character listens to when he gets in the car and turns on the radio.
  Pearl Jam, Chopin, or Emmylou Harris.

12. Make no reference to where movie credits should begin and end. That's not your job.

13. Observe these technical conventions.
- (O.S.) = off screen.

This is when somebody from the kitchen, off screen, yells, "Dinner is ready!"

> HORTENSE
> (O.S.)
> Dinner is ready!

- (V.O.) = voice-over.
  Heard by the audience, but not the other characters. In movies where the lead character gives us a running commentary or the narrator tells us a story (e.g., *Blade Runner, Amadeus*).

> RADIO ANNOUNCER
> (V.O.)
> Today in East Gambolaville, five ducks
> marched across Orange Street.

14. All scripts should be three-hole punched, on 8.5 × 11 white paper, one side only please.
What a shock it was the first time I received a thin little script, copied on both sides of the page.

15. Scripts should be bound together with ACCO clips, also called Chicago screws.
The reason for this binding is that readers, myself included, take the clips out and read the pages loose. The reading process is more enjoyable, easier, and goes faster.

16. Use a plain cover with no creative artwork on the front.
If I see a lot of doodads on the cover I get suspicious. "Is all this masking a real dog underneath?" I wonder. Let your script speak for itself. Leave the fancy stuff for some of your fancy characters.

Screenwriting Software

Over the years, screenwriting computer program companies have sent me their wares. I've tested them, used some of them, eliminated others. I am computer-stupid and need help, simple help. The more complicated the program, the faster I toss it away. I am a firm believer in anything that makes the screenwriting experience easier. Programs fall into two categories: Story Development Programs and Formatting Programs. I recommend the following:

Story Development Programs

Collaborator. Software for Mac, IBM, IBM clones.
This software, as its name suggests, helps you build story and character. It keeps you focused on story line, three-act structure, step-by-step story analysis. It does not format. I use this one more than the others, especially at the beginning of each story. Collaborator asks you questions and then asks you additional questions for your input. Invaluable. (800) 405-8344.

Writepro. Software for Mac and IBM.
Less expensive than Collaborator, WritePro helps you develop characters, establish conflict, and build structure. (914) 762-1255.

Formatting Programs

Scriptor
An excellent formatting program used by many studios and production houses. (818) 843-6557.

Script Thing
A formatting program for Windows and Mac. (800) 450-9450.

Superscript
A formatting program that works with WordPerfect. Superscript is the simplest and least expensive program. IBM only. (310) 559-3814.

Final Draft
The best formatting program for Macintosh only. (310) 395-4242.

Scriptware
A popular IBM-only program. (800) 788-7090.

10
After It's Written

At the end of it, one is empty, like a dry shell on the beach, waiting for the tide to come in again.

> Daphne du Maurier, novelist
> and author of *Rebecca* and
> *Don't Look Now*

This section is for those of you who have finished your screenplay. What a relief, what a joy! You write FADE OUT on the last page, you walk around the room carrying this 120-page manuscript, this dream child. For those of you who have finished, congratulations. Hooray! You've taken your screenplay as far as you think you can, and you need to go on to the next step.

What is the next step? Looking for an agent? Not yet. First you've got to shape up this masterpiece. This next step, a crucial one, is an intermediary step between finishing the draft and preparing to send it out into the world.

It's called *market research*. The question now becomes: What have you got here, this creation into which you've just poured time, talent, and energy? Before you send your bundle of artistic joy into the cruel commercial world, you ought to get some outside opinions.

After you've rewritten and polished the screenplay until you feel you can do no more, make eight copies. Keep the original or the floppy disk in a safe place. Don't take any chances by giving away your only copy.

Protecting the Baby

You can send Copy One to the Registrar of Copyright, Library of Congress, Washington, DC 20540, or call (202) 707-9100, if you feel the need to copyright what you do. For additional protection send Copy Two and a twenty dollar nonmember fee to Writers Guild of America, West, 7000 W. 3rd St. Los Angeles, CA 90048. Attention: Script Registration. Or call (310) 550-1000. Or to Writers Guild of America, East, at 555 West 57th Street NY, NY 10019. In your brief letter, identify the type of screenplay you have: feature length motion picture; made-for-television movie; documentary.

After you send off the package to the Writers Guild, a couple of weeks later you'll receive a registration number in the mail. This is good for five years and can be renewed for another five years. Or you can protect yourself with a Poor Man's Patent by sending Copy Three to yourself in the mail, registered. When it arrives, don't open it. The post office seal should not be broken. The Poor Man's Patent is the least effective way of protecting yourself.

If you've decided to protect your manuscript in any or all of these three ways, you'll have five copies of the original eight remaining. These you send to people who will be willing to critique the screenplay. I would recommend not sending it to your mother, who may love everything you do (or who may hate everything you do) and therefore will not often give you the best advice.

Send Copies Four through Eight to people who will give you a straight answer. People who read, who know what a story is, and who can tell you if your characters are interesting or not. This is a critical stage, and you need the best advice you can get. If you have to pay a few hundred dollars for a pro to read it, pay it. All this nonsense about it not being worth it if you have to pay is bunk. What's free these days? Does the plumber come over and fix your sink for free? Does a mechanic fix your car for free? I would rather shell out a few bucks for a professional who doesn't pull punches than give it to well-wishers with glad tidings, only to find out later on that real problems existed that could have been cleaned up with a more discerning read.

The best scenario, of course, is to get five good readings by smart people, for free.

The five opinions come back. Three of them are strong, positive. The other two have problems. There's a lot to think about here. One question is whether or not you want to follow certain advice. Watch out here. Listen to your instincts. Don't automatically defer to your internal saboteur who says, "Yeah, I know this advice is good but consider the source. He doesn't like me, he's jealous. He doesn't usually say anything positive about anything, blah, blah, blah. . . ." Put a muzzle on that saboteur. Listen to your gut.

Maybe the criticism is right on the nose. Maybe you don't want to listen because you don't want to spend more time working on this, you want to get it out there in the market place. This is called impatience overruling reason. Maybe you fear you can't do it, can't go that extra mile. Why not? You've gone *this* far. You *will* do whatever it takes to get this screenplay in the best shape possible. If you've worked this hard, for this long, and you know this is good advice, spend another few days following it. You can't allow that lazy saboteur inside to screw you up now!

The question is, does it work? If the advice is sound, do the work. Some advice is terrible. Hemingway said that all writers have built-in shit-detectors. The solid criticism stays; the rest of it slides on through. Taking criticism is not always easy. Two tenets to follow when receiving criticism—oral and written—are never defend your work, and don't pretend to listen.

If someone says, "I don't understand this," say thank you and ask them what precisely they don't understand. Don't get defensive. Don't let the short hairs on your neck rise. Don't try to explain what you meant to say. Just say thank you, ask a question or two. And either fix it, or don't. If the reader doesn't understand something without a long explanation from the writer—there's a problem and it should be addressed.

Don't pretend to listen. It's not easy hearing that your work is less than wonderful. The tendency is to shut down the receptors, ignore the criticism, smile, be polite, and pretend to listen. Don't. One piece of advice can solve many problems. I have seen it happen a thousand times. One tidbit of criticism someone delivers can be the vacuum cleaner in your story, clearing out all the rubble. The rule is, if you feel the suggestions work, use them. If you don't, don't. Do a rewrite based on the suggestions you get from these five people, and do a final polish.

11
The Rewrite

I have rewritten—often several times—every word I have
ever published. My pencils outlast their erasers.

Vladimir Nabokov, novelist
and author of *Lolita*

"Writing is rewriting."

"The first draft is labor, all the rest are management."

These old adages seem more important today than ever before. Yet
there are those who, by the completion of the first draft, feel they have it
all in hand. A pinch here, a tuck there, and the thing is done, ready to
be embraced by the world. When word comes back that the script is
less than perfect, in fact, *far* from perfect, the writer feels this great hole
in his gut, as if he has committed the greatest sin of all—deceit of self.
"How could I have been so stupid as to not have seen these flaws?" he
might ask. Or, in the case of the angry, defensive writer, "How can *they*
be so stupid as to not see the real genius of this masterpiece?" Then
everything settles down and the writer begins to revise, barreling forward into the rewrite.

Where do you start? What do you look for?

I finish the first draft, and then set it down for a week or two to get a
better perspective. During this time I give it to people who can read
screenplays and offer sound advice. Once I get my readers' suggestions,
I head back into the battle, armed with their advice and the two weeks
of my own thoughts and note-taking. Then I bring out the 3×5 index
cards and chart a rewrite course through the story.

I begin with character. I take aim at the main characters and draw a
line from the beginning to the end of the screenplay to see what has
occurred with each. This is the *character arc*: a scene-by-scene delineation of how each central character progresses through the story.

In the first draft, you already have the story laid out, at least the fundamentals of it. It's the characters who have eluded you. You have spent a lot of time laying down the story track, and the characters have suffered. Fine, no problem. That's the way it should happen.

The second step goes beyond character into what all stories are ultimately about: relationships. Trace the arc of the central relationships in your story. On the cards, write the essential elements of the scenes in which the main characters meet and what happens to them. Tack them to the wall and look at the progression. You'll discover fascinating things. The cards will give you a clear line from beginning to end. Once you see the progression, you'll be able to pinch here and tuck there and begin to build the relationships into the rewrite. You must take a very close look at these relationship arcs. They're the key to a successful screenplay.

How does the Romeo and Juliet relationship move from one point to the next? How do Thelma and Louise get along together so that, at the end, they can both agree that going over the cliff together is the only answer?

Some writers make two lists. The first is a list of the emotional and physical particulars of each main character at the beginning of the story. The second is a list of the emotional and physical particulars of the main characters at the end of the story, after you've put them through all this hell. The meat and potatoes of the story is what happens in between—the character arc.

Take a look at the wonderful independent film *Heavy* to see how through a series of emotional upheavals the main character changes. Or *Bent, Boogie Nights,* and *L.A. Confidential.* Or, conversely, how nothing but the cranky machinery of the picture changes in those pieces of fluff, *The Game, In & Out, Seven Years in Tibet,* and *U-Turn.*

Remember that everything leads to a conclusion, a catharsis, something earned after all the hell the characters go through. How the characters reach this end is the subject of the story. Like anything else, you have to *chart the progress.*

Once the fundamentals are established, most writers I know write a very fast first draft. They know they must so that they can get into the real meat of the work—the revisions. The rewrites bring out the surgeons in us. Of course, who wouldn't like to create a perfect first draft, but let's get realistic.

Okay, so you've done the first draft, sent it out to the readers, made the changes. Now you're ready for the next step, sending your masterpiece into the world of commerce.

The Players

Who are these movie players who will take your screenplay the rest of the way? William Goldman, in his wise and witty book *Adventures in the Screen Trade*, said that everybody has a shot at Hollywood because, as far as he can tell, nobody in Hollywood knows anything.

Hollywood is a business, but what kind of business is it when eight out of eleven products off the assembly line lose money? How many businesses can survive with this track record? Only Hollywood.

On its way to getting made into a movie, a screenplay finds its way into the hands of five different categories of people: the agent who sells it, the producer who develops it, the financing organization that funds it, the stars who act in it, and the director who shoots it. The script can go to any one of them first. Whichever way your script can get into the cycle, that's the right way. You may know a star or a director or you may have a money source. Through a friend, you may be introduced to a producer. You may have an aunt who's an agent, or who is represented by one. Your third cousin runs Fox.

The important thing is that you get the screenplay read.

I know a guy who every day for a week sent a dozen roses to an agent to get her to read the script. She did. She hated it, but that's not the point. The important thing is that she read it. You may have a great screenplay. Unless it gets into the proper hands, it means nothing.

Director-writer Colin Higgins was producer Robert Evans's pool boy when he asked Evans to look at a screenplay he had written for his UCLA master's thesis. It was *Harold and Maude*. The rest is history.

Exercise

Rewrite your first ten pages using the suggestions found in this chapter.

12
Finding an Agent

You need an agent, but to get one you have to sell something,
but you can't sell something unless you have an agent. You
get the picture.

General Wisdom

I got my first agent through divine ignorance. I was out of college and
living in New York. I had written a couple of newspaper features and
one unpublished book. I was twenty-four years old, and somebody told
me that if I wanted to get anywhere in this writing world, I needed an
agent. The only agency I had ever heard of was the William Morris
Agency.

I called and told the receptionist that I was a good writer and that
William Morris was the only agency I had ever heard of. The receptionist, either taken aback or amused, told me to wait a minute. A man
came on the line and said he understood that a very good writer was
looking for an agent. His name was Don Gold, and he was head of the
Morris literary department.

I told him about myself, he asked me some questions, and he made
an appointment for me to see Gary Cosay, a rising star in the agency. I
went up to see Gary and showed him a couple of pieces I had written,
and suddenly I was represented by the biggest, most prestigious talent
agency in the world.

There are more conventional, less romantic, and just as successful
ways of getting an agent. If you have no contacts, if you don't want to
send flowers or badger a receptionist, the first thing I recommend doing
is this: send the Writers Guild of America (West or East) $2.50, and ask
them to mail you a current agency list: WGA, 7000 West 3rd Street, Los
Angeles, CA 90048, Attn: Agency Dept.

The names you find on this list belong to signatories to the Writers

Guild, which means they signed the 1975 Basic Agreement signifying that as agents they will abide by Guild rules.

When you receive the list, you'll notice that some agents have an asterisk beside their names. This asterisk means they will read unsolicited screenplays. This does not mean, however, that they will accept full screenplays. You must query them, by phone or letter, before sending the script.

Another way to get names of agents takes more effort. Next time you go to a movie, watch the credits and jot down the name of the screenwriter. Next day call the Writers Guild, and ask for the name of the agent who represents the writer, and they'll give it to you.

Write to the agent, complimenting the picture and saying that you discovered that the writer is one of the agent's own clients. This would indicate to the agent that she is dealing with a clever and/or thorough person, both good qualities in a screenwriter. Tell the agent that you have a screenplay with the same fine qualities and would like to send it. Remember: getting it read is essential. All they can say is no, and you just try the next one.

If you don't make an effort, your screenplay may never get read. You've spent all that time writing it, don't stop now. Don't let FEAR (remember the False Events Appearing Real) get to you, not after you've come so far.

Do You Need an Agent?

Some of you may wonder why it's necessary to have an agent. Why should you dole out ten percent of your earnings when you may not need to? Good question. It's because an agent provides you with immediate credibility. The producers will ask, "Who represents you?" If you don't have an agent, the producer will say, "We don't accept scripts unless they're agent-sent." Producers don't want to read a bunch of potentially lousy scripts by people who couldn't get agents. Agents become filtering systems to weed out junk (if they want their credibility to remain intact) before sending good scripts to producers.

There is also a legal side to this issue. Producers do not want to see unsolicited scripts or non-agent-sent scripts because they may already have something in development on the boards similar to the script sent to them. If they look at it, and later on down the line their film is similar to your script, you could sue them and, if your case is strong, probably win at least a settlement.

An agent is essential because he or she knows what kinds of pictures certain producers, stars, and directors make or would like to make, and which of them are available. Why waste your time sending your work to somebody who has no interest in your subject matter, or who is booked solid for the next five years, or who gave up the business and now works on political campaigns?

The agent also protects you from plagiarism and other acts of larceny by those who might steal your idea. And finally, for a ten-percent fee (for every dollar the agent brings to you, you pay the agent a dime), you stand to make ten times what you would be able to make on your own.

The Query Letter

It's now time to write a query letter to the agent. This letter is crucial. I would recommend not making it more than a page long. Short and sensational. You want to hit them hard and make them salivate for this piece of work you've completed. If you send a long rambling letter, the agent is probably going to assume that you've got a long rambling screenplay and say no. If you write a sharp, concise query letter the agent will assume that you have written a sharp, concise screenplay.

Here's what you should include:

1. Why you're writing
I am writing because I have completed my *recent* (not first) screenplay and I am looking for representation. Be straightforward.

2. What category of screenplay it falls into
What is it? Feature-length movie. Movie of the week. TV series episode. A romantic comedy, a thriller, a western, sci-fi, or horror? Include a logline about your movie.

3. Your logline is crucial. It has to be fresh, incisive, and dynamic enough for the agent to want to see the script.
The idea behind your screenplay has to be sold on up the ladder: to producers, stars, directors, and studio executives. The logline is the transportation. The more vivid and dramatic and original the logline, the easier it is to sell. Your idea, fashioned into this sensational logline, has to catch the attention of people who hear fifty decent ideas a day. In other words, it has to make its way up from the gallows of creativity to the throne room of commercialism.

4. One paragraph on your background or achievements to date

If you have a special talent or area of expertise that you've brought to the screenplay, let them know. For instance, if your story is about a horse and you've broken in a few in your time, this lends credibility. If your story is a corporate thriller and you've been a corporate executive, tell them about it. Or if you've won filmmaking awards, mention them. Maybe you're a lawyer, a teacher, or have been through a harrowing experience that you've turned into a screenplay. Tell them about it, briefly.

5. Send no résumés.

6. Don't tell the agent about the social significance, or market viability, or infinite greatness of your idea.

The thing will speak for itself. Sell the product, not your ego or insecurity.

7. There is no limit to the number of agents to whom you can send this letter.

A woman from Cambridge, Massachusetts, who took my week-long class in Rockport, Maine, sent out two hundred letters. Thirty agents responded. She sent scripts to fifteen of them. Four agreed to represent her. She flew to California and talked with them. She chose one. She now has a deal. Her diligence paid off.

I wouldn't send out two hundred letters, but what do I know? Do whatever you feel is necessary. I'd recommend, however, that you start with ten or twenty query letters. If you get no response, there might be something wrong with the letter. Don't burn all your bridges right away. Show the query to a few people; ask them if it's strong enough. Maybe it's vague, or misleading, or not dramatic enough, or out of focus.

8. If you don't like to write letters or, more to the point, if you are good on the phone, there's an alternative.

Get some 3 × 5 cards and write the above information on them. Then call up the agencies and literally read the cards to whomever you reach. In this way you get an instant response, or you are told to write a letter to so-and-so, or you find out that the agency isn't looking for new scripts.

Try to convince the person you talk with to read the script. Almost all receptionists are agents-in-training. Say to them, "Hey, why don't I send *you* this phenomenal script of mine. Read it and, if you like it, pass it on to your boss. If it's optioned or bought, you'll be a real live agent a lot sooner than you thought." Or you can send the agent a dozen roses five days in a row.

9. Some people send postcards with their query letter.
On each (self-addressed, stamped) postcard draw two boxes. One reads: "Please send screenplay." The other: "Don't send screenplay." For those with the "Please send screenplay" box checked, return the postcard with the manuscript as a reminder.

These postcards make it easy for the agents to respond. If you decide to send query letters, in a few weeks you'll start getting responses. If the mailbox is empty, however, or the phone doesn't ring, it means they're just not interested. Don't expect letters thanking you for sending the query letter.

You may get phone calls from people asking to see the script, in which case, send it to anyone who wants it. You have worked very hard on your screenplay and you shouldn't have to wait for each response, unless, of course, an agent calls and asks for an exclusive for a few days. Why not? But stipulate a deadline. One week is plenty.

If after a week you haven't heard anything, call the agent. As nicely but as firmly as possible, inform him if you haven't heard from him by close of business, you'll assume he's not interested and you'll be sending it to the other agents who have asked for it. If he asks for another extension, decline. The agent is playing a game in which you don't want to get involved.

Send the screenplay to all agents who ask for it. The first one to say yes is the lucky one. That's how you should look at it. They're searching for good properties and you've given them one. Furthermore, agents send screenplays to any number of producers and directors at one time. Why then shouldn't you send it to agents who ask for it?

What Kind of an Agent Do You Need?

You need an agent who is genuinely interested in your career. That's the most important thing. He makes a commitment to you. He wants to nurture you. He wants to build you. He wants to turn you into a money-maker.

You want an agent who has power and clout in the industry. Ask an agent what he has accomplished and who his clients are. It will please him to mention his accomplishments in a town where everybody knows what everybody else has done. "Can you tell me some of the successes you've had?" This is a compliment. "Sure, I'd love to tell you," he'll probably say. Your business is to write the script, your agent's is to sell it. Sometimes this gets confusing, usually to the writer, who in a moment of inflated self-worth thinks he can do a better job.

During various negotiations a few years ago, when I was under the mistaken impression that I was indispensable to his doing a good job, my agent sent me plane tickets, to Mexico, to get me the hell out of town, out of his hair, away from a telephone and the calls I made to him every fifteen minutes. I was a royal pain in the ass.

Your main job is to write. Let the agent take care of the business end. That's why you hire an agent. He or she takes the heat off when you're supposed to be writing.

When a producer calls to bad-mouth your agent because the producer is not getting what he or she wants, you say, "My God, are you serious—my agent wants you to pay me more money! Gee, I'm sorry about that but I'm just the writer. Talk to him." You're the good guy. You're the one who is going to be working with the producers. The agent can be the bad guy; that's one of the reasons he or she is there.

The Contract

Most agents will not give you a contract until they sell something you've written or get an option deal for you. So don't worry about signing agency papers. Some people are contract-obsessed. They have to sign something before they do anything. That's not the way all agents operate. They want to see if your work is marketable before they bring you on the team. Can you blame them? After ninety days, by contractual agreement (which means you send them a letter), you can dissolve any agent-client relationship.

Most contracts basically say the same thing, but read them anyway because you never know. You might get an agent from Botsaloosa, Alabama, or Bear Feathers, Montana, who wants to sign you and your family up for twenty percent of your total earnings forever.

I've seen contractual horror shows in which the agent gets everything and the writer gets nothing. If you have doubts, show a lawyer the contract before signing it. In an effort to find the security a contract offers, writers sign anything. I understand the need, the feeling that there's somebody out there who believes in you, a link with the people who can buy your work and turn it into a movie. But sit back and think: You've labored long and hard on your work. Don't give it away and regret it forever after. Don't let impatience overrule reason. With established agencies you probably have little cause for concern. With unfamiliar agencies it's a good idea to check the fine print.

13
The Business of Hollywood

They don't make movies in Hollywood; they make deals.

> George Lucas, producer of
> *Star Wars* and *Raiders of the Lost Ark*

You have an agent. The agent has your script. The agent's periscope rises up over Beverly Hills and the surrounding communities, looking for the right producer to make a movie out of your script. The agent is also looking for stars, and a director. Who, the agent wonders, can get this movie made?

"Ah ha!" the agent exclaims. "There's so-and-so, a producer on the Universal lot who did well with such and such a movie, who is well thought of, who has money and a lucrative deal with the studio. Perhaps, I could marry the producer and a star, or even a director. I could package this deal and then bring the package to the money people at the studio."

Your agent could be a member of one of the big packaging agencies—CAA, William Morris, ICM, United Talent—which means that the agent will first look within the agency itself for producers, directors, stars, and writers whom they represent.

This is what happens:

Scenario A: The agent shops your script to people inside the agency, some outside. Before long, there's a bite. Let's say a producer on the Universal lot believes he can make a movie from your script. He calls your agent and makes an offer—an outright buy. Your agent calls you and says that the producer is willing to buy your script for $300,000 in a preemptive offer (which means: take it or leave it, now). Which means, if you accept the offer, they own the script. They may make it, they may put it on the shelf and leave it there. They own it.

Scenario B: What usually happens is that your agent sends your script to stars, then to directors, and, if there are no takers on those levels, finally to producers. Or in reverse order. Or to all of them at once.

Let's say a producer agrees to option your screenplay and pays you $25,000 for a one-year option against a purchase price of $250,000 if the picture is made. This means that for $25,000 you give the producer the exclusive right for one year to try to set up your script. During this time the producer will send it to actors, directors, and the studios. "Against a purchase price" means that if your script goes before the cameras, you will get the difference between whatever you've made so far on the project and, in this case, $250,000. This option agreement usually contains a clause granting the producer additional option time—for more money—if he or she needs it.

I know one man who has produced thirty-six pictures, twenty-five of which made no profit. Not on the initial run, anyway. Some made money later. You might say, "Why would this guy be hired to produce movies if they don't make money?" Well, first of all he produces movies because he gets them made, no easy task. He doesn't make the first movie on his wish list or sometimes even the fifth or the eighth. Sometimes he has to make his eleventh or fifteenth choice.

He makes element movies. He is a very nice guy who knows the business and is fun to work with, so stars and directors know this will be a hassle-free experience—a big plus in this ego-slathered business. This producer runs quiet sets, he makes his movies on time, and he brings them in under budget.

This producer also has the dubious distinction of having produced the first picture by some major stars that lost money. Yet he keeps making pictures because he keeps the financial wheels of Hollywood greased. A lot of people work when he makes pictures. Grips and gaffers, line people, and studio executives. He's made good pictures. He's made some very good pictures. He's made stinkers that made lots of money.

If the movie is made, you, as the writer, will probably not see profits with your net points. Net points represent the profit left over after all expenses. The studios have been playing hide the profit for so long they are nearly impenetrable. The old story about the producer taking his mother-in-law, his wife and four kids, and his mistress to Capri for the week—and there goes your net profit—is not far from the truth.

There is also something called the *rolling breakeven* and *triple-entry bookkeeping,* both designed to hide money in the serpentine studio account network. The rolling breakeven is that method of accounting by which the studios roll the profits of the money-making films into the ones that lose money, and somehow all the net-point profit due to writers and other creative types never leaves the studio's tight little financial wheel. Triple-entry bookkeeping is just what it sounds like: three different sets of books, depending upon who wants to see them.

The Studio Executive

The studio executive's main job is to successfully anticipate trends; otherwise he doesn't last long. In any case, the average life of a studio executive is five years. Most studio executives can't say yes to a project. They can only pass it on to a higher-up with the power to say yes. The studio executives can only say no, however, because no is safe. This is a very conservative business, and a no represents fiscal responsibility. They work on percentages. If they say no to your project, the reasoning goes, everyone else will, too. If another studio makes your picture, chances are it won't make money. In which case, he's a hero for saying no in the first place. If, however, another studio makes it and it's a big hit, the studio executive will by that time be somewhere else, and he can blame others for the mistake.

How many times have we seen a bad picture that's made money and a great picture that's gone under? Studio executives are always looking for a good script with a good hook, or a high concept. From this they can put a package together, supervise the production and the ad campaign, and pray that the review audiences like it.

To find this initial great script they employ a herd of readers who write a four- or five-page evaluation on each screenplay they read. This is called *coverage.* If you've been turned down by major studios and later decide to do a rewrite, change the title and resubmit. This way, when new readers look for coverage on the new title, they won't find it. You don't want to get shot down because of a title. And don't worry about the same person reading your script; there's a huge turnover at the studios.

Everybody in the business is looking for a good story. Story is the foundation to any screenplay. You also need a compelling character who has a strong attitude. Someone who bears a grudge or has an eccentric point of view.

If, in your case, the producer can't find a studio to put up money to produce your script, and he gives up, the option period expires and all rights revert to you. And of course, you get to keep the option money. At this point, your agent will send the script back into the marketplace.

Let's say, on the other hand, that you get lucky. The producer finds a star, a director, and the money to go forward. At this point—with your movie a real possibility—the producer has the option of hiring you for more money to do a rewrite or getting another writer to put his or her spin on it. You, of course, will get more money in either case.

At this point things look good. There's activity. You work on rewrites. The producer gives you a hand. Maybe there's a director or star on board; they put their two cents in. You finish the rewrite and a final polish, you turn it in, and you wait. You get nervous when you haven't heard anything. You call your agent, who has heard nothing. You feel left out, you get irritated. You wonder why you're not being kept up to date. You get an inkling that you're not that crucial anymore. And you're right. Your job is done, or is about to be. The process has transcended you and is now in other hands. Budget. Preproduction. Producers wrangling with studios, wrangling with stars, who are wrangling with the director.

This is where the writer needs to let it go. Higher powers are now in control. As they should be. You have made your significant contribution to this intricate collaborative process. Just as the casting agent has, as the agent has, as the stars have when the acting is done, as the director has when the directing is done, as the editor has when the film is cut, as the marketing people have when the ads are out, and so on.

Let it go. Because at this point there is nothing you can do about it. What you *can* do is to turn all that negative grousing into starting your new screenplay. Then, one rainy morning while you try to pick through this new idea, you get the word: It's a go project, a green light. There's even a start date. January 1. Happy New Year! You sweat it out, along with everybody else. If everything goes according to plan, next year you'll be in a much higher tax bracket.

The day—January 1—edges closer. You've gotten no sleep. You call your agent twenty times a day. You can't stand the silence. You leave the house and at every phone booth you call in for messages. One day, the latest in a string of hopeless days, your agent's voice comes over the answer phone. "Call me." It's too cryptic. You try to interpret the tone. Is the agent holding back? You are sure it's bad news, otherwise something would have been said. Your hands tremble as you make the call. The agent is somber, he says in a deep funereal voice, "The word is in. And the word is . . . Yes! The cameras will roll! You're set for life!"

You can't stand it, you feel so *good*!

This is where you really cash in. Remember that $250,000 purchase price? It's yours, minus what you've already received, and the ten percent fee to your trusty agent. You're strutting around town with a big check in your pocket.

I'm reminded of the Oscar Wilde line about the difference between an Oxford man and a Cambridge man. The Oxford man, said Wilde, walks down the street as if he owns it. The Cambridge walks down the street as if he doesn't *care* who owns it.

You, newly born, are the ideal amalgam of the two.

The Pitch

INT. STUDIO OFFICE — DAY
SCREENWRITER A & SCREENWRITER B sit before the STUDIO EXECUTIVE (STU).

>   A
>   Listen to this and tell me if this isn't
>   the best movie idea you've ever heard.

>   STU
>   Already I'm worried.

>   A
>   We open. Julia Roberts has been married
>   to Macaulay Culkin for six months.

>   STU
>   Macaulay Culkin is a teenager. Julia
>   Roberts is in her thirties.

>   B
>   The marriage is on the rocks.

>   STU
>   No kidding.

>   A
>   Julia had been the girlfriend of
>   Macaulay's older brother.

>   B
>   They robbed banks together, very good at
>   it. Stashed away lot of dough. One day
>   he's killed. His teenage brother . . .

>   A
>   Macaulay Culkin.

>   B
>   . . . inherits the dough.

                          A
Julia's beside herself with grief.

                          B
Not to mention broke.

                          A
She's worked hard for that money.

                          B
She deserves it.

                          A
Look what she's been through.

                          B
Julia woos the kid, marries him.

                          A
Oh, but this kid's a monster.

                          B
We open. Six months into the marriage.
She hates it, her life's a joke. But if
she leaves, she loses everything.

                          A
She can't leave.

                          B
She can't stay.

                          A
What does she do?

                          B
There's the story.

                        STU
Can you deliver the two stars?

                          B
It's a lock. They both love it. Their
agent is our agent.

                        STU
How much is it going to cost me for you to
write this masterpiece?

                                    A
                          (whistles)
                          Howie! You're on!

Enter HOWIE, agent.

                              HOWIE
                      A half million up front against another
                      half million when the cameras roll, with
                      boosters, some exotics; we can work it
                      out.

This pitch session, with some variations, actually happened. The writers got their half million. Julia Roberts and Macaulay Culkin are no longer attached to the project.

Great pitching is high art. Louis B. Mayer in the old days and Stephen Cannell today are considered top pitch men. Top pitch men plead, beg, play all the roles, get down on their hands and knees, whimper, cajole, and bleat. You may not have the brilliant thespian in you, but you do have two minutes to get the producer interested and another fifteen to keep him interested.

How do you do this? By using simplicity. Stay with the structure. Pitch a simple story about ordinary characters in crisis. Start with concept. A rich older man offers a young couple a million dollars to spend one night with the wife.

Beginning, middle, and end, with major turning points.

Hook them with your Opening Sequence, offering up a strong sense of place, mood. Dazzle them with the Inciting Incident, lower the Plot Point I boom, challenge them in Act II with your main character's demons. Wow them with the big moment of decision in Plot Point II and bring home the bacon in the final rising dramatic action in Act III. And just when they think you've done it all, spin them around one more time with a rousing Climax.

Remember that you're pitching people who are always in the market for good ideas. They're eager to buy what you have. Go with confidence. Producers buy the idea, and they also buy the writer. If they like you, you're halfway home.

Bring notes with you. Refer to them. Keep it simple. Stay with the game plan. Be prepared for them asking questions; this is a good sign. They're interested. Let them in; you've got them hooked. Keep them on the hook. Listen to what they say, answer them, and get on with your pitch.

You're in control. You've got the product. Stay within yourself. Don't get rattled. You're not responsible for their feelings, or even what they think. All you have is your carefully thought-out, wonderful story, which they want to buy and turn into a movie. This should be your only concern.

If you start to worry about what they think, you'll falter. Be congenial. Don't be defensive. Smile. This is your baby. Remember to keep it short, no rambling. If you need to get up and move around, do it. Bring visual aids if you need them. Before you arrive, practice!

Try it out on friends, the dog, people with short attention spans. This could be worth millions and a career. Remember, you're the pitcher, they're the catcher. The story is the baseball. Keep it in the strike zone.

Good pitching!

14

Writing for Television

The question my entertainment attorney asks when I call him is not, "How are you?" or "How's the work going?" or "When are you coming to visit?" but "Why don't you create a television series?" Translated, this question implies that if I were to create a television series and he negotiated it, we could both retire. It's hard to write for television. Not necessarily because of the writing itself but for others reasons: red tape, censors, network executives, the system itself.

My attorney gives me facts and figures about the money I could make creating a television series. I ask him if he's ever been to a county fair and tried to knock wooden milk bottles off the perch they've nailed to the platform from the bottom. Those are the odds against getting a TV series on. But for the sake of dreams, let's suppose a miracle happens.

When I think of the world of television, I don't see art, I see commerce. If you work in television, you can expect to make good money. If you do nothing more than create a series, you receive a royalty check for at least $10,000 each time an episode airs. If the show goes into syndication, you could make millions. If you are hired to executive-produce someone else's series, or you have another series of your own, you can earn $30,000 to $75,000 a show. Let's say the paperwork is too much in this capacity and you want a more hands-on, creative approach as the director. A hired gun earns $50,000 to $75,000 per episode. Let's say you want to run the show from a distance and produce. There are different breeds of producers on every show: producer, co-producer, associate producer and co-executive producer, who make $20,000 per episode. Down another notch, is the story editor. The story editor listens to ideas, assigns writers to the story, or may even write a few episodes, all while making $20,000 or more a week. And finally, at the bottom of the list, you guessed it, is the writer, who makes around $20,000 for a half-hour story and teleplay, plus $7,500 or more for a rerun.

The World of Television

There's not as much free-wheeling originality in television as there is in movie writing. Producers run television, which means that you as a writer have to answer to another set of gods: the God of Appropriateness (censorship), the God of Commerce (commercial breaks), the God of Speed (form over content). This is not to say that some television is not first rate. *NYPD Blue,* some PBS programming, and some BBC imports are as good as many excellent motion pictures. In writing for television, you operate under the same solid character and story principles as you do in other forms.

Tips on Television Writing

1. Remember that in television, conflict is the moving force of all drama: character in conflict.

2. Your main character has a central problem that must be resolved by the end of the show.
Make the problem as difficult as possible to resolve. This is important in all forms of television.

3. In a sitcom you have a half hour to present the problem, hurl it at each character, and by the end bring the characters to some life-enriching conclusion.

4. Clearly state the problem up front, why and how the problem exists.

5. Before you write one word, know how the problem is resolved.
Not *exactly* how, of course; allow for twists and turns in the writing process. The resolution gives you direction; you have no time to wander. Treat the half-hour sitcom the way a comedy writer writes his jokes. Start with the punch line and build up to it.

6. Each act must rise to a crisis. Make sure that the story, whether it's in a sitcom or an hour-long show, always moves forward, through the escalation of crises or plot points.

All action leads to an essentially unsolvable problem. This moment usually comes at about three-quarters of the way through the story. Solid dramatic writing is getting your character into a spot from which he cannot escape, and then in Act III you get him out of it. Or rather, he gets *himself* out of it.

For example: Two kids run away from abusive parents. They know they cannot go back home. They meet a kindly old man who takes them in, and for the first time in their lives they find warmth and friendship and caring.

During the course of events, the old man learns that the kids have run away and that the parents are probably searching for them. The old man does not want to give them up, especially to abusive people, but he feels he must. The kids tell him what kind of life is waiting there for them. But the old man, tears in his eyes, returns them at the end of Act II. What are the kids going to do? They have nowhere to go. Their parents will certainly brutalize them worse than ever. How would you make this seemingly impossible situation dramatically interesting, plausible, and satisfying for the audience?

7. If you're writing a movie-of-the-week, don't worry about commercial breaks or the eight-act structure.

Your main job is still to tell a strong story with compelling characters who change.

Television Characters

Movie characters say a lot less than TV characters because movies are visual and television is oral. Yet the same basic instincts about character development apply.

1. Make your characters human, not cardboard cutouts that vaguely represent human beings.

But remember that television characters talk all the time. Producers slit their wrists over a moment of television silence.

2. Make every word count.

You may think that television characters speak real dialogue; they don't. You've become so accustomed to television dialogue you probably think it's the way real people speak. There's a big difference between dialogue that *is* natural and dialogue that *seems* natural. You want dialogue that *seems* natural because you don't have time to include every word that comes into the characters' minds and out of their mouths. Cut to the essence of what they mean. Edit out the pauses, the false starts, the getting off track, the chitchat. You don't have time for all those words that we, in everyday life, use to convey meaning. You want the pure form, stripped and packaged—dialogue that *seems* natural.

In dialogue every word counts. Watch out for the evil creature called Irving the Explainer, whose need to tell all ruins dialogue more than anything. Just because you need to get information out, don't haul Irving in to do it for you. Dramatize it.

For example: A couple sits together in their living room. You as writer need to get information to the audience about their marriage before the story can go on. Here's Irving at work:

> HORTENSE
> Darling, those two Volvos in the garage,
> remember in the twenty years of our
> marriage—and our three kids, two away at
> college—how long we waited until we could
> afford to get those cars with you making
> so little at the Chrysler factory here in
> Detroit?

> RUDOLPHO
> And how if little Rudolpho hadn't stabbed
> the milkman when he caught the two of you
> in bed and told me and I tried to cover it
> up and had to go away for four years to
> jail until I'm finally back now making
> enough money to afford those Volvos.

This is mild compared to some of the Irvings I've seen. Watch out for talking heads who explain the plot to each other. Study the way people speak. Forget about parenthetical phrases that try to explain the dialogue. In other words, let the dialogue speak for itself, make every word count. Avoid lengthy monologues, those shaggy dog stories that go nowhere and stop all action and character development. In TV movies, for instance, I become exhausted by characters recalling great moments from their childhood. Never describe what happens in characters' minds. If you can't see the action, it's useless.

3. Keep secondary characters to a minimum.
You don't really need them; they get in the way. Forget about bringing in aunts and uncles or other family members. Use the ones you've already got, especially on half-hour shows where you can't afford to clutter up the place with extras. All you need are the characters necessary to tell the story. If you have three characters performing three different functions, combine the functions into one or two characters or give them to characters already in the scene. Another benefit of this is that you give these characters more to do, and thus more depth.

4. In TV series, study the habits of already established characters.
Know their motivations, occupations, fears, habits, vices, how they walk, talk, and dress. With established series you must know all these things, and then you can devise a plot.

5. Keep the focus on the central conflict between the protagonist and the antagonist.
Otherwise it gets sloppy, and you lose the story thread. You don't have time to waver. Make the villain's argument as strong as the hero's until the end, when the hero, if not vindicated, at least comes to some understanding. Once again, if your villain is weak, and your main character can plow through him, then your story becomes flat and you bore the reader to death. You could have warring brothers, twins, stepsisters. Family battles usually make for good conflict because in families everybody knows where everybody else's buttons are. Audiences can almost always identify with family conflicts.

6. Be original.
No clichés! If you've seen it or heard it, it doesn't mean it's safe to use it. Be original. Take time to craft a character, or a sentence, in a new, interesting way. Forget about the dumb blonde or the mousy librarian or the anal-retentive accountant. Go against type. Producers and directors are interested in new, original visions and points of view. You've got one; use it.

7. Concentrate on character motivation.
Everything happens because the character needs or wants something— a burning desire to do something, get something, or escape from something. All good drama is about a character who needs something more desperately than ever before and will do anything to get it.

Questions to Ask Yourself About Television Characters

1. Is my protagonist compelling?

If you're bored with the character or the story, you're in trouble. Boredom spreads like cancer over the script. It's easy to tell when the writer is tired or lazy or going through the motions, because it shows in his work. The writer can also tell when he's bored, but it's hard to admit it to himself. "What, bored with my own creation?" he cries, dumbfounded by the notion.

If you start losing interest, try harder, walk away for a moment, drink some coffee. Boredom is the killer. Or do what most working writers do: Brainstorm. Write yourself back into the scene. Don't worry about getting it perfect. Getting it down is all that matters. By brainstorming, you can write whatever comes into your head, as far as the scene is concerned. By doing this, you work your way through the problem or blockage, and eventually get back on track. Try it.

2. Are my main characters active or passive?

Remember that your character wants something and is willing to do anything to get it. This makes the character active, actively pursuing the objective. Sometimes the writer forgets this, allowing minor characters to take over, leaving the main character in the dust. Don't forget that this is the most critical time in your character's life. Your main character might be a little crazy (most likely is) and vulnerable. He does things he has never thought of doing before. But *actively* crazy, *actively* vulnerable.

Make your character do something, even if it is wrong-headed. Make your character take risks, make mistakes. Main characters do this; they're human, they screw up. Then the audience will start to root for them to get back on the right track.

3. Is my antagonist worthy of my protagonist?

We've covered this in motion pictures, but it is worth repeating. Without a strong villain, you have no story. It is as simple as that. If your hero or heroine has an easy time jumping the hurdles thrown up by the villain, conflict peters out, the story sags, and the reader goes to sleep. Spend time on your villain. Make this character so evil or sinister or wily that your hero has to dig way down deep inside to find ways to combat him.

4. Is my opening scene so powerful and provocative that the reader cannot help but go on?

This opening scene should be so powerful that it acts as a model for the rest of the screenplay. Work your tail off in rewriting this opening scene, then use it as a standard below which you promise never to go with the rest of your scenes.

Reasons for Rejection

1. Bad writing

Mix up the words; be creative. You are after the *essence* of things, not a piling on of details and blocky, chunky, descriptive paragraphs, or *Architectural Digest* renditions of rooms. Simple, declarative sentences with strong verbs work best.

2. Silly plotting

Plug up holes in the plot that trucks can drive through. Fix contrivances and cheap plot devices. Eliminate sudden miracles that save your character.

3. Bad form and unprofessional presentation

To a reader, poor presentation or formatting is as bad as poor characterization. For proper formatting, see the chapter in this book entitled "The Format." Also read as many scripts as possible. I receive scripts from writers who didn't bother to learn the form, or who misspell words. To me this means that the writer probably didn't bother to write a good script. Right away I develop a prejudice, a burden no writer can afford to bear.

4. Ill-timed characterization

I don't want to know too little about the character; neither do I want to know too much, all at once. A key to successful screenwriting is knowing when to leak information into the script. In William Goldman's Academy Award-winning *Butch Cassidy and the Sundance Kid,* we don't learn that Butch has never killed a man until late in the script, when he is confronted with the reality of it. Don't ruin surprise by letting the cat out of the bag too soon. Don't tell your audience anything until the audience needs to know it or will be impacted by it.

5. Clunky dialogue
In the initial stages, the important thing in writing dialogue is to get it down on paper. Don't worry about how it sounds. When you're on a roll, go with it, get the characters speaking, have them use words that move the story forward and reveal something of themselves. If you can't get the right words, use any words. If a character doesn't feel good, have him simply say, "I feel like hell," and refine it later on.

6. Improbable locations
If writing for an established television series, don't get creative with locations. I have seen perfectly good spec scripts by writers who, on a creative whim, put *Seinfeld* in an Arab bunker and *NYPD Blue* in an upscale village on Long Island Sound.

7. Derivative plots
Don't copy a familiar plot with a tennis pro and turn him into a golf pro and think you've done something original.

8. Plausibility
Is there something that you can't put your finger on that doesn't seem to work? Are you trying too hard to make something fit, but no matter how hard you try, you just can't get it to work? Your audience will think less of your work and of you as a writer for not taking care of this problem.

9. Budgets
Don't go crazy with new locations or characters. Stick with what already exists and play with it. Once again, simple plots and complex characters, not the other way around, make for the best drama. Remember that the making of film and television shows is a business whose aim, along with art, is profit. In addition to looking at character and story, the producer reading your script is very much aware of the financial bottom line.

10. Remember, writing is a study in labor and management.
The first draft is labor; the ones that follow are management. In the first draft, labor to get it down; in the subsequent drafts manage the words and images to best convey action and character.

Exercise

Write an outline or *treatment*—a narrative story of what happens in your plot to your characters for a TV sitcom. Write it in simple, straightforward prose, as if you are telling someone with a five-second attention span a story that will hold their interest.

Once you have the treatment or story, break it down into acts. Then further break the story down into individual scenes. Put each scene on a 3 × 5 card (not each entire scene, only the essential elements). Once that's done, stack the cards. Remove the top one from the stack, and begin to write.

Drive straight through to the end. Do not rewrite. If you have changes along the way, write them in the margins or in a notebook. Your job with these cards is to get the first draft done, fast.

Don't look back. Eliminate the fear of going on. You're on automatic pilot here. You've already broken the scenes down. There is no excuse for stopping, or hesitating, or looking over your shoulder. Train your eyes on the last page and go for it.

15
The Adaptation

Every great man nowadays has his disciples, and it is always
Judas who writes his biography.

Oscar Wilde, dramatist, novelist,
and author of *The Importance of
Being Earnest* and *The Picture
of Dorian Gray*

What happens when you want to turn a book, short story, or play into a
movie? The true art of adaptation, so the saying goes, is *not* being true
to the original. Let me explain. Adaptation is the transformation of a
story from one medium to another. Remember that a book is a book, a
play is a play, a short story is a short story, and a screenplay is a
screenplay. The trick here is how to turn the story from one of these
other media into a sharp, incisive screenplay.

Look at *Ironweed,* or rather, don't look at *Ironweed.* Read *Ironweed.*
The novel is wonderful. The movie is a mess. William Kennedy, who
wrote the book, also wrote the screenplay, which was a big mistake.
Hector Babenco, the director who gave us *Kiss of the Spider Woman,*
loved the novel *Ironweed* so much that he couldn't solve the problems
inherent in switching from one medium to another. He made the critical
error of staying too close to the original. Nicholson and Streep carried
what they could of the movie on their shoulders, but they collapsed
under the weight of a story that should have remained only as a novel.

Ironweed, the movie, will go down in history as an excellent example
of why certain literary properties should never be adapted into other
mediums, especially movies.

When you adapt something, try to think of the book or short story as
research material only, and the screenplay you're writing as original.
Some of it you keep; some of it you throw out. Forget about kneeling

before the altar of the book. Your job is to turn it into something else. The book will always remain as it is. You need to make a *movie* out it.

Be true to the original material only insofar as it applies to your version of what the screenplay should be. Your sole responsibility is to turn the material into a good screenplay, which will hopefully become a good movie. If you find a short story, novel, or play, take a good hard look at what you're attracted to. Ask yourself if the story is visual enough to be a movie. Is the story strong enough? Do you care about the people?

Why did Tom Wolfe's novel *The Bonfire of the Vanities* fail as a movie? A main reason was that the producers who bought it could not adapt the novel's strongest point, Wolfe's voice, his way of telling the story. Wolfe's words. If you love the way the book is written, wonderful, but make sure the story is strong enough if you're trying to turn it into a movie.

Key Points on Adaptation

1. If you're adapting a novel to the screen, forget about what the characters think.
You can't see thought. You have to turn thought into visible or visual action.

2. In movies, what you see is what you get.
If you can't see it, it doesn't belong in a screenplay. If the material is too internalized, it's probably not good movie material. A screenplay deals with externals. A novel or play deals with words. Can you turn those words into effective dramatic action? Can you open it up so that it feels like a movie?

I had the task of adapting four of my books—*The Hunter, The Crossing, The Maximus Zone*, and *The Huntress*—to the screen. Adapting your own work is not easy. That old adage about every cliché being a precious gem can come into play. In *Dangerous Company*, I adapted a man's life into a movie. The best advice I received was to take what I needed from his life, what worked dramatically, to make a good screenplay and forget about the rest. His life (in this case, career criminal Ray Johnson's) was loaded with drama. I had to choose what was best for the story I wanted to tell.

3. If you have no story line, you have no story.
Make certain you take elements you need from the source material—characters, events, lines of dialogue—and pour them into your screenplay structure. Divide your new story into three acts, as you would with an original, and start fine-tuning. Facts should be used only to support the story you're trying to tell. Don't let your knowledge of too many facts get in the way of good storytelling. Forget about informational gems you find, if they don't fit. Get rid of them. Source material is only a starting point. Once again: The true art of adaptation is *not* being true to the original.

4. Compress time.
Novels often cover long periods of time. Screenplays are rapid accelerations of events in short periods of time. Time pressures move stories along at good clips, so it is your job to compress the time of novels into shorter periods for dramatic effect. Hollywood turned the novel *Six Days of the Condor* into *Three Days of the Condor,* because there just wasn't enough time.

5. Reduce the number of characters.
Novels often have a cast of dozens. Screenplays focus on one or two main characters. Take only the characters you need, or combine many characters into one or two in order to tell the best story. Remember, in adaptation you're trying to capture the essence of the novel.

6. Watch out for too many subplots.
Some novels thrive on multiple subplots. As a screenwriter, you have two hours to tell the story. Get rid of subplots that do not feed the spine of the story you want to tell.

The Business of Adaptation

Let's say you read a book, a play, or a short story and something sparks to life in you. You know this would make a good movie, and you want to write it. First you have to find out who holds the rights. Is the book or story in the public domain? Has it gone out of copyright? Has the story been publicly told? If not, you must obtain the rights.

Call the publisher and ask for the name of the writer's agent or attorney, whoever handles the rights. Once you obtain this information, call or write to this person, expressing your interest in developing the property into a screenplay. The representative will tell you whether the property is already under option, or unavailable for other reasons, or that it is available. In which case you begin to negotiate.

If the property is recently published, the price will naturally be higher. If the property has been around for a while, been shopped, or perhaps optioned by others, the price drops. This becomes your negotiation base. If the property has been around for a while you just might, with your fabulous persuasive abilities, be able to convince the representative that you are sincere but haven't got a lot of money. "What the hell, there's nothing going on with it anyway," you argue. "Why don't you let me have it for a year or two for a pittance, or even free, and maybe we could all make a killing on it." Whatever you agree upon, the next step is to finalize a contract on paper. For this you may need an entertainment attorney.

Once this is accomplished, you begin the adaptation process. One word of caution: When you contact the writer's representative, you should have an idea about how you're going to turn the property into a screenplay. Without going into vast, numbing detail, sound as if you know what you're doing. Don't bore them. Sound positive and authoritative. With a long rambling rendition, they'll think you'll produce a long rambling screenplay. If you're brief, enthusiastic, and direct, they'll tend to believe your screenplay will possess those qualities. Don't give too much away—tease them. Also, don't tell the representative that you have worked on this for months because he or she will turn that into a negotiation point.

The Adaptation Process

Remember that adaptation is the process of shaving away what you don't need and adding what you do: reduction and addition.

1. Re-read the property (i.e., book, play) at least three times.
Read the first time for pleasure, looking for pacing and the general feeling you got the first time through, the second time for story strengths and weaknesses, and the third for character.

2. Write a step outline.
This is a chapter or scene breakdown of everything that happens in the story from one scene to the next. Just what happens—no description, no character development.

3. List all the characters in the story.
What do they look like? Their quirks? Their attitudes? Their fears. Their pasts. This is what you'd do when developing characters in an original screenplay.

4. Ask yourself what the concept, or premise, is.
Not the concept of the book or play but the *concept of the movie.*

5. Make a master list of all actions relevant to the *movie* you have in mind.
This will help you separate the movie story from the book story and also to break the story into three acts, along with creating conflict and tension.

6. After completing your master list, put each scene's salient details on an index card and start to write.

16
Collaboration

Two people writing a book is like three people having a baby.

> Evelyn Waugh, novelist and
> author of *Brideshead Revisited*
> and *Men at Arms*

Sometimes collaboration can be difficult, as evidenced by the words above. However, with the right person, the process can be enjoyable.

One day not long ago my friend Michael Blowen, a *Boston Globe* columnist, and I were on our way to the driving range.

"Did you hear what happened to Diane and me when you were away?" he said, referring to Diane White, his wife, also a *Globe* columnist. "*Boston Magazine* named Diane 'Best Journalist' in Boston," he said.

"That's fantastic," I exclaimed.

Michael paused a minute and then, with that sly look for which he's notorious, he added, "And they named me 'The Worst.' "

For years, Michael had been taking shots at *Boston Magazine* in his column, and it was payback time.

"What do you think?" he said.

"Think?" I said. "I think it's wonderful and not so wonderful."

"No, about the story. How do you think this would play as a movie?"

"Ah," I said. "A movie."

"A screenplay," he said, as if to say, *"Yoo hoo, Chris, wake up."*

Collaboration happens when two or more people decide that one person is not enough to write a screenplay. It's a decision based on a combination of talents. In this case, Michael knew the story and characters; I knew how to develop the information into a workable screenplay structure.

Michael's and my movie premise sounded something like this: what would happen to a professional husband and wife, with the same career

Everybody from Robert De Niro to Henry Winkler, Robert Redford, and a host of others have been attached to it. It's been frustrating. I've been to the brink and back so many times with this project that if it ever did get made it would be an anti-climax.

The Crossing has been called a great war story, a character-driven masterpiece, a dated monolithic white elephant. It's been too long, too expensive, too foul-mouthed. It's been said to have too many characters, too many locations, too few women, too much poker, not enough poker. It's been too claustrophobic, too rambling, too big, too small, too little, too much.

Everyone who's tried to make the movie has agreed on their love for the characters and the concept. *The Crossing*, about the biggest poker game of World War II, concerns five men, the top poker winners of World War II, playing for a half million dollars, in a winner-take-all five-card-stud game aboard a liberty ship heading home from war, sailing from Antwerp to New York in the summer of 1945. There's death, deceit, and a big sting in the end. As the book stumbled along Hollywood's rocky road, producers suggested getting rid of the poker, getting rid of World War II, taking it off the ship and putting it on land, making it Vietnam, updating it to the Gulf War. They have suggested turning two of the male leads into females, bringing nurses and steamy sex on board.

The story of *The Crossing*'s journey through Hollywood began in the late seventies when a wealthy young heir, Stephen Dart—whose father owned Dart Industries and was a member of Ronald Reagan's Kitchen Cabinet—and his partner, Eddie Palmer, a veteran industry type, optioned the book. I was living on Malibu Beach at the time and the three of us would meet once or twice a week for story sessions, during which time we transformed the book into a screenplay. After one year and many close calls with studios (Paramount, Universal, Fox) and stars (Dustin Hoffman, Redford, Elliott Gould) the option lapsed and the rights reverted back to me.

But now I was ahead of the game. I no longer had just a book, I had a screenplay. And a pretty good one. My price went up. At Columbia, David Begelman (the infamous David Begelman who cashed Cliff Robertson's check by mistake) heard about *The Crossing* and called my agent, making an offer, another one-year option, this time for five times the original option price.

So now Columbia had *The Crossing* and I was hearing more noises about Robert Redford, along with De Niro, and Martin Scorsese to direct, and even that Jack Nicholson was ready to play Animal. Meanwhile, I was writing another book and getting calls to do other projects not because of the buzz about *The Crossing* project but because *The Hunter,* my book about a modern-day bounty hunter, was rolling at Paramount, with Steve McQueen. Hot, hot, hot.

Then the phone calls from Columbia became a trickle and turned to silence. What happened? Who knows? *The Crossing* was quietly passed back across town to my agency and was, for all intents and purposes, dead in the water.

But wait. My agent had been rooting around over at MGM and found a producer who "loved Keane's work" and had been waiting to pounce. This pounce turned out to be worth a lot of money. Not only did MGM take out an option on *The Crossing*—which I was told had more to do with *The Hunter* coming out than it did with *The Crossing,* but, hey, this was the nature of the business—but they also made an offer to buy my brain on a yearly basis. They were willing to pay me big bucks in return for getting first look at all my new projects. In other words, I had to run my ideas by MGM before they went anywhere else. Simple. Wonderful. But wait. There was a catch. Behind, or beneath, this stipulation was another, silent stipulation, which said that I, and my optioned brain, also had to listen to the ideas of other brains-under-option (most of whom were producers with development deals) on the MGM lot.

Meanwhile, according to the producer who had *The Crossing* under option, Paul Pompian, a very nice guy from Chicago who made mostly movies-of-the-week, the script needed work. It was the eighties now and people wanted to see romance in their movies, he pointed out. What about having a few nurses on board ship, maybe for one or two of the players to *schtumpf* in between poker hands? When I didn't snap to that idea, he suggested making one of the players a woman. This is what Hollywood producers do. They follow a bad idea with a worse idea, thinking that the worse idea would be so bad that the writer will go for the bad idea in the end, thinking it's not so bad after all, compared to the worse idea. It's takes a while to catch on to this.

Henry Winkler wanted to play Animal, the gruff-talking Brooklyn-born player of intimidation poker. "Against type," was how the producer described it. I couldn't see it, but who was I? I, who out of some obviously misguided casting notion, wanted Marlon Brando or George Scott over Steve McQueen, who was ready to sign, to play Papa Ralph Thorson in *The Hunter.* It's no wonder the people at Paramount stopped asking me for advice.

De Niro's name popped up again. I was told on at least five occasions by people close to his people that he was on the verge of signing. This wish-list thinking is, as I was to learn, a Hollywood sport that everyone plays, and on whose emotional life everything is hinged until proven otherwise. A rumor mill worse than the army. Supported by a five-star gullibility quotient.

Lord Lew Grade, the legendary British producer, got ahold of the script. Through one of his emissaries, I learned that *The Crossing* was not an American picture in the first place and that that misconception was behind why, according to this emissary, it had not been made. This was a truly universal picture if he had ever seen one, said the man, on a grand scale, a war story of a different ilk. I kept nodding my head. Roger Moore. Sean Connery. Richard Harris. International cast. Massive budget. Shot in wartime Europe recreated, where its seeds were sown. British-American coproduction. All of these words, these promises, made me dizzy. But what did they mean? What had happened to the five American guys playing poker, coming home from war? What about the murder and mayhem, the deaths. What about the logline: Agatha Christie meets *The Cincinnati Kid*?

This hyperbole went on for weeks. I wondered where it was going. I found out. Lord Grade read the script on an airplane between London and Rome. "Too much profanity," he had said, and passed. What I was told was a done deal—a script on which the papers were already being drawn up—had not even been read by the only person who held the power of yes and no.

In the mid-eighties I moved from Los Angeles to a quiet beach house on Florida's Gulf Coast near St. Petersburg to write a novel. At the time, *The Crossing* was under option number two to MGM, which had decided not to exercise its option on my brain any longer. I was no longer hot, and no longer in town. I periodically received news that this actor or that director was ready to sign to do it as a movie. One day I got a call from my agent. *"The Crossing* is going out of option at MGM," he told me. "There's a guy who for the last two months has been panting for it. A producer, Herb Solow, who wants it. He's the president of Bunker Hunt's new production company, Sherwood Productions."

"Bunker Hunt, of the Texas oil billionaire family?" I said, *"that* Bunker Hunt?"

"The same. Calls himself Bunky."

The MGM option expired, and Herb Solow paid $75,000 for a one-year option on *The Crossing*. We talked. He loved the concept, the characters, the script. Herb, an art collector and producer of many movies, said he would get this movie to the big screen where it belonged. I continued to work on my novel. Three months later I received a call from my agent. "Have you heard from Herb?" he said. No, I replied.

"You will."

This sounded ominous. My agent, revealing nothing, said to call him when I had news.

Later that day the phone rang. It was Herb. After talking about his art collection and chatting about the weather, he asked me if I'd received anything in the mail from the University of Southern California. I told him no.

He then told me how much he loved *The Crossing,* which, he was more convinced than ever, would become a hit movie, but . . . A warning light flashed.

"Our marketing people have done some research, Chris, and they have come up with some startling news. First, as you know, today's movie-going audience is between seventeen and twenty-four. Not only do these kids not care about World War II, most of them never even heard of it. And they don't know how to play poker. You're *sure* you haven't received anything in the mail from USC?"

That slight warning bell in my head was now a five-alarmer. "What are you trying to tell me, Herb?"

"That there's good news."

"For whom?"

"You know how much I love this project."

"You keep telling me."

"I love the characters, I love their interaction, the concept—five people playing the game of their lives, winner takes all, life and death. All or nothing."

"Hang on, Herb, there's somebody at the door."

The UPS man stood there with a large moon-shaped package. I signed for it and went back to the phone.

"It's a package," I said, "from USC."

"Yes!" Herb exclaimed. "Open it."

Inside, I found a plastic multicolored, dome-shaped object with five miniature cockpits plugged into a girdle around the dome.

"What is it?" I said.

"A scale model of what your poker game will look like in our new movie. Instead of a World War II poker game, Chris, I've commissioned a USC professor of psychology—an expert in the study of games—to have this scale-model video game built."

I stared at the thing.

"Instead of a World War II poker game on a ship," Herb informed me, "we're going to hold a modern day video game championship in Las Vegas. We keep the characters. We keep your fabulous concept. We keep everything but World War II and poker, which no one wants anyway."

This was possibly the worst idea I had ever heard. After a brief discussion, he told me he wanted me to rewrite the script. Getting ill, I told him I couldn't talk to him right now, and told him to call my agent.

Well, you guessed it, like Holden Caulfield's brother Allie, in *The Catcher in the Rye*, who had moved to Hollywood to be a prostitute, I became a prostitute and rewrote the script, but not before warning Herb that my heart—or anything else except maybe my bile—was not in it. Herb assured me that once I began, I'd see the light.

I saw no light but I did my best. My best was not good enough to get the picture made, and the project went into turnaround, a Hollywood euphemism which, in this case, meant that Herb Solow and Sherwood Productions couldn't find the money to produce *The Crossing*, and didn't want it around anymore to remind them of how much money they had spent on a project that had gone nowhere. The rights reverted to me, and the project, an orphan once more, crawled off, searching for another home.

For a year and a half nothing happened. I continued on the novel I had left California to write.

One day while I was in Florida, through an acquaintance, I met the O'Leary Brothers, Nick and Dick (their names have been changed for reasons that will become apparent), who made movies. They said. They had lived in Las Vegas and in Europe where they had sold real estate. They now lived in a palatial home peering out on the vast Gulf of Mexico.

The O'Leary brothers made short subjects, quasi documentaries. Vanity films disguised as industrials. They had made one on a Boys Club, which they had sold to Boys Clubs throughout the country. When I met them they were making one on firefighters, which they were going to market to fire departments across the nation. For these endeavors, they raised money. Lots of it. From local dentists and doctors and other private investors who were rich, bored and wanted to be a part the film world.

The O'Leary brothers, in their mid-forties, were tall and wiry and spoke with Brooklyn accents. Nick was the filmmaker, Dick was the financial procurer. They threw investors' parties and when I met them were on the brink of going big time. They said. They also said that I couldn't have come along at a better time. They had read *The Crossing* and loved it. This was the vehicle, they told me, that would launch them.

I was a proven commodity and they were going to raise the money and make *The Crossing* right here in Florida, recreating WW II Antwerp docks. They would rent uniforms and clothing circa 1945. Dick knew a Navy man who could get a Liberty ship out of dry dock. They told me they wanted to run with my script. I told them they had to pay for the privilege. When they balked I told them that as a member of the Writers Guild of America, I couldn't just give it to them.

"How much?" said Dick.

I told them I'd have to call my agent.

"They want to what?" said my agent, who started calling the O'Leary brothers the Be Leary brothers.

The O'Leary brothers negotiated with the agent, a price was agreed upon, the deal was set and I was paid $10,000. They went about the project with vigor. They gussied it up, put a palm-tree-be-side-a-Liberty-ship design on the cover and sent it off to investors. They called the papers, issued a press release. They threw parties. They continued shooting the fire-safety film, which in truth was a rollicking, fast-action thirty-minute extravaganza, with local firefighters as the stars.

Then one day they disappeared. All of them. Nick and his wife, and Dick. Vanished from sight. It turned out that the lavish home they abandoned belonged to one of their investors. The cars had been leased, along with the furniture. Days passed. Debtors arrived. Investors called, and stopped by. Hundreds of thousands of dollars were missing.

Last year I got a call, from Nick, the filmmaking O'Leary brother. He said he and his family were doing okay, living out West somewhere. We talked about the old days. Before we hung up, he wished me well, and said, "You know, Chris, you were the only one we ever paid."

At this writing, for the first time in many years, *The Crossing* is not under option. The further away from World War II we get the lower the chances are for getting the thing made. But wait! Just last month, a front page *Variety* headline read: WWII SLATED FOR COMEBACK: War Stories Grip Studios.

Fix Bayonets!

The Annotated Breakdown

I've included the entire text to *The Crossing* for a couple of reasons. One is to give you an idea of what a screenplay should look like on the page. Another is to give you an annotated edition of the screenplay so you can see how I've tried to follow my own screenwriting principles.

As you read along you'll see that I've used the major turning points to form structure: The first ten pages. Inciting Incident. Plot Point I. Midpoint. Plot Point II. Climax. I've also located other turning points and thought processes I went through while writing *The Crossing*.

I've broken down characters and established story building blocks, opened up scenes to expose their mechanics through pacing, beats, action, and dialogue.

An important thing to remember is that structure is not the rigid beast some might think it is. Each screenplay is different. Not every plot point has to fall at a specific place or the work will fail. Structure sets up—for the writer and the audience—the world in which this story will live. That's the message structure delivers.

These principles exist for one reason—to help you through the process of writing your screenplay. Think of these points as oases in the vast desert of possibility that any written work presents to you. You reach each oasis and take a breather. You gather your forces, you set your direction and head out again into the heat of the working day. Eventually, by your wits, along with those of your characters, you will reach the end of the journey.

I wrote this screenplay in the early eighties and though some say it's old and moldy and will never get made—and they could be right—the thing still has legs. It may never make another dime. It may get picked up tomorrow and arrive at your local theaters by the end of next year. I don't know. Nobody does.

That's one of the big reasons—the unknown, the unpredictability, the gamble—why I write for the movies.

The Crossing

by

Christopher Keane

Based on the novel *The Crossing,*

by Christopher Keane

FADE IN:

EXT. CENTURY HOTEL, ANTWERP, AUGUST 1945 - EARLY AFTERNOON

A taxi pulls in front of the Century Hotel—Antwerp's finest.
Flags of the Allied nations hang over the hotel's entrance. The
war is over. Soldiers and pedestrians walk the street.

PFC EDWARD "ANIMAL" PODBEROSKI, chunky, short, in his mid-
thirties, exits the taxi. He wears a sloppy, wrinkled Army
uniform, as if he has just crawled out of a trench. He carries a
bird cage, covered by an Army-issue rain poncho.

The TAXI DRIVER opens the trunk. Animal pays the driver. A
BELLHOP takes the duffel bag, and goes for the bird cage.

                        ANIMAL
          That's okay, pal. I'll carry this myself.

INT. HOTEL/LOBBY - DAY

Lavish, with high ceilings and hand-carved moldings. Paintings
on the walls and Louis XIV furniture. Animal is at the front
desk.

                        ANIMAL
          I'm Podberoski. You have a reservation
          for me?

                        CLERK
          Yes, sir. We've been expecting you.

The CLERK pulls a message from the slot, hands it to him.

                        CLERK
          Mr. Santini would like you to join him at
          the Cafe Lucarne, at five o'clock.

The Bellhop takes the duffel bag and Animal carries the bird cage
as they head for the elevator.

INT. HOTEL SUITE - DAY

Elegant. Murals on the walls, a magnificent view of the city.
Animal pulls the poncho off the bird cage, revealing a CANARY.

                        ANIMAL
          Hello, sweetheart, you look terrific.
          Hang on. I'll be right back.

He pulls out a wad of bills and hands the Bellhop a tip.

                         BELLHOP
          Ah, merci, monsieur. Merci.

                         ANIMAL
          You bet.

Animal spills the contents of his duffel bag onto the couch:
crumpled uniforms, crusty dirty clothes. He pulls out a bag of
bird feed.

INT. BEDROOM - DAY

Animal carries the bird cage in, places it on the window sill.
Opens the cage door.

                         ANIMAL
          Chow time, sweetheart.

He pinches bits of feed from the bag, and the canary eats from
his hand. He pulls out the desk message, waving it at the bird.

                         ANIMAL
          Right here, kiddo. Half a million
          bananas.

Inspecting himself in the mirror, splashing on cologne.

                         ANIMAL
          I'm heading downstairs right now to meet
          a guy who's gonna make us rich. I get to
          pay off the family market and marry my
          beautiful Shirley. You get your gold
          cage, your ten stud canaries, the works.

He straightens his tie, gives a kiss-kiss to the bird.

                         ANIMAL
          Be a good girl. Papa's going to work.

EXT. SIDEWALK CAFE - ANTWERP - DAY

Surrounded by greenery in planter boxes. Fashionable women and
soldiers in uniforms of the victorious Allied forces sit at the
tables. SOUNDS of Chevalier-like tunes filter out from a piano
bar. A postwar gaiety prevails.

MICHELANGELO SANTINI, a man in his late thirties, sits alone at
a table. He wears a rooftop mustache and a finely tailored suit
of the period. He sips a glass of red wine. His chilly,
analytical eyes dart and skip, taking in everything at once. He
checks his watch.

                         ANIMAL
                         (O.S.)
            Santini!

Santini sees Animal peering over the waist-high planter,
searching right and left.

                         ANIMAL
                         (louder)
            Michelangelo Santini!

Animal sees Santini motioning to him and barrels through an
opening. Grabbing Santini's hand, he pumps it vigorously.

                         ANIMAL
            Jesus, Santini, whatta pleasure. I been
            following your career.

Santini guides him to a seat.

                         SANTINI
            What would you like to drink?

                         ANIMAL
            Scotch.

Santini signals to the WAITER.

                         ANIMAL
            I mean it, it's a real pleasure sittin'
            down eyeball to eyeball like this. You
            been one of my heroes a long time now.

                         SANTINI
            How are the cards running in Cripple
            Village?

                         ANIMAL
            Be nice. They're called field hospitals.

He flicks the combat medals on his chest.

                         ANIMAL
            I been in the real war, Santini. Life and
            death. Krauts. Guineas. Living in the
            mud, day in, day out. While you were
            playing in them parlor games.

                         SANTINI
            Not exactly parlor games.

                    ANIMAL
I don't see no calluses, no wrinkles, on
yous.

                    SANTINI
They're all on the inside.

                    ANIMAL
               (inspecting him)
You look like you're already pretty well
off, Santini. What's in this game for
you?

                    SANTINI
The satisfaction of winning.

                    ANIMAL
Half a million dollars can buy a lot of
satisfaction.

                    SANTINI
It's not the money.

                    ANIMAL
It never is . . . but what it can buy.
               (beat)
So, I heard you recently clobbered one of
the guys who's gonna be in the game with
us.

                    SANTINI
Captain Hubbard.

                    ANIMAL
That's something, beating him. He's
supposed to be the best.

                    SANTINI
An excellent poker player. But, alas, a
tormented man.

This is the *Opening Sequence:* Here we see the entire setup. It's wartime Europe. We meet Player #1 and Player #2, two of the main characters. We learn there's a very high-stakes poker game about to begin.

The lay of the land: the end of World War II.

A key here is in the characterizations. Animal is a slob who loves a canary. He's unpretentious. He's not intimidated, very much his own man. Santini, in direct contrast to Animal, is sophisticated, precise, rigid. We'll learn that he's a student of the philosophically rigid eighteenth century, during which Versailles was built. He looks down on Animal, though he respects him.

The two men play a cat and mouse game here. After all, they're about to begin the poker game of their lives.

As a screenwriter your main objective is to grab the readers' attention and keep it. Don't confuse. Don't get cute. Tell the story. Remember that the readers know nothing when they open the script. You've got to reel them in, dazzle them, and at the same time patiently usher them into this world you've created. Remember: You don't have to let the audience know something until it needs to know it. In other words, don't feel you have to load up on bio or character details up front. Sprinkle them throughout the story, as they logically fall into place.

EXT. CASABLANCA - STREET - NIGHT

CAPTAIN EVAN HUBBARD IV, in dust-covered goggles, peers over the windshield of his Army jeep as he barrels down Rue Barathon in the Casablanca ghetto. He pulls the jeep to a halt under a street light. He climbs out, removes the goggles, and dusts off his uniform.

He is tall, fair-haired, and built like a basketball forward. The name tag pinned above his left breast pocket reads HUBBARD. He looks toward the bar across the street.

EXT. T'AL RASHID CAFE - NIGHT

A musty looking Arab bar. Hubbard crosses the street.

INT. T'AL RASHID CAFE - NIGHT

Hot and noisy, the stink of cheap Arabic tobacco. A group of RAF fliers in sweat-stained uniforms at the long bar, which is tended by a fat ARAB. A large pillored room with small dingy tables with mural-covered walls picturing nomads leading camels over the dunes, the Rif mountain range.

Hubbard moves to the bar and asks the bartender a question.

                    BARTENDER
          No, sir, he has not yet arrived.

Hubbard sits at a table. The waiter serves him a glass of wine. Hubbard looks slightly on edge.

At the end of the bar an RAF MAJOR, drunk and obnoxious, wields a riding crop and harangues his fellow RAF Fliers.

Hubbard, sipping his wine, observes the Major's antics. The
Major sees Hubbard, the only American in the room, and weaves
toward his table.

                    MAJOR
          How do, Captain?

                    HUBBARD
          Major.

                    MAJOR
          In the bit, are you, Captain?

                    HUBBARD
          I'm quite well, thank you.

                    MAJOR
               (taps table with riding crop)
          Don't we stand in the presence of a senior
          officer?

Hubbard inspects the man. He is short,
neatly outfitted with a brown shoulder
strap, belt, and a holster containing a
Luger pistol.

                    HUBBARD
          The war's over, Major. Sit down and have a
          drink.

                    MAJOR
          In this bar we stand, my friend. Up!

Hubbard makes no effort to rise. The Major leans forward,
breathing into his face.

                    MAJOR
          On your feet, Captain!

Hubbard, ignoring him, takes out a wad of yellow seal dollars,
places two on the table and rises.

                    HUBBARD
          Excuse me, Major, I have to go.

                    MAJOR
          Absolutely not!

                    HUBBARD
          Why don't you just drop it.

                         MAJOR
          I shall not drop it. Nor shall I tolerate
          your impudence.

Hubbard starts for the door. The Major seizes him by the arm and
spins him around, a vicious drunken scowl on his face. Hubbard
uses his large hand to flick him away as he would a fly.

The unsteady Major staggers back against the bar where a couple
of smiling RAF Fliers prevent him from falling over.

EXT. STREET, RUE BARATHON - NIGHT

Hubbard exits and heads for his jeep. It's gone. He scans the
street, disgusted.

                         HUBBARD
          Goddamn it.

He heads down the street until he feels a TAPPING at his back. He
turns and finds the Major standing there.

                         HUBBARD
          Major, I've had enough. Go home and sleep
          it off.

                         MAJOR
          You insulted me in front of my own men!
          You are disobedient. Disrespectful! You
          are insubordinate! Captain, you are a
          coward!

Without warning, the Major slashes Hubbard across the face with
his riding crop. Hubbard reels back, anger flaring. Sensing
danger, the Major drops the crop and gropes for his Luger.

Hubbard clamps a grip on the Major, pinning his arm behind him.
The major squeezes off two ROUNDS. The explosions roar down the
Rue Barathon in a series of diminishing echoes.

The Major's head snaps back and his body goes limp. Shocked,
Hubbard lowers him to the ground. He sees powder burns on his
chin.

The SOUND of a whistle. Hubbard sees RAF Fliers pouring out of
the café. Another whistle. Frightened, Hubbard glances down the
street.

EXT. STREET - MOMENTS LATER - NIGHT

Running, Hubbard turns into an alley and stops, panting. He
looks back down the empty street. Safe? For now. Shaking off the
fear, he steals away.

Here we've just met Player #3: Hubbard, an officer, sophisticated, and
in trouble, in Casablanca. The scope of the poker game expands. The
complexity of the game is enhanced through the introduction of a very
different character from the exotic world of Casablanca.

This is also the INCITING INCIDENT. A murder is committed, for
which Hubbard will later be held responsible. This death sets up a
problem that will have to be resolved by the end of the story. In fact,
this death in the Casablanca street sets off a number of other grisly
incidents that form the basis for a subplot in the story—a threat that
hangs over the players and the game, throughout.

The Inciting Incident establishes the story's spine. This murder must
be resolved in the end. This is no longer just a poker game but a murder
mystery, a story of a different kind of suspense.

What else do we have here? Atmosphere. Lots of it. Intrigue. Danger.
Contrast. An American officer, about to leave for a big poker game, will
drag his past with him. Hubbard wears the scar on his face from the
major's whip throughout the rest of the story, a visual reminder to
him—and to us—of what has happened, and what must be resolved by
the end of the story.

                                                        CUT TO:

EXT. ANTWERP SIDEWALK CAFE – SAME EVENING

Michelangelo Santini, inebriated, sits alone. The cafe is full.
Music filters from inside.

Animal walks up behind him, zipping his fly. Silently watching
Santini, he places his hand on his shoulder, startling him.

                         ANIMAL
                 Okay, buddy, time to go.

                         SANTINI
                 Go? Where?

                         ANIMAL
                 Got a surprise for you.

                         SANTINI
                 What kind of surprise?

                         ANIMAL
          Don't ask so many questions. It's a
          surprise, now, c'mon.

Santini rises and fishes out his wallet.

                         ANIMAL
          It's taken care of.

Animal throws an arm around Santini and aims him toward the
street and hails a cab. It starts to drizzle.

INT. CAB - NIGHT

                         SANTINI
          By the way, Edward, may I call you Edward?

                         ANIMAL
          My mother calls me Edward. Animal. That's
          what my friends call me. Call me Animal.

                         SANTINI
          If you don't mind, I'd rather call you
          Edward.

                         ANIMAL
          Awright, Santini, call me Edward. You and
          my mother.

                         SANTINI
          I would like to know where we are going.

                         ANIMAL
          To the best whorehouse west of Berlin.

                         SANTINI
          No thank you.

                         ANIMAL
                    (a look)
          Why not?

                         SANTINI
          I don't like whorehouses.

                         ANIMAL
          Ah, you don't like to pay for it?

                         SANTINI
          Whorehouses are for animals, Edward.

                    ANIMAL
          Don't worry, Santini. You don't have to
          do nuthing. The best whorehouse west of
          Berlin ain't gonna make you do anything,
          which is why it's the best, you
          understand?

Santini gives Animal a curious look.

                    SANTINI
          I suppose it would behoove me to watch my
          competition—you—in a variety of
          circumstances.

                    ANIMAL
          I suppose it would.

EXT. STREET - CAB - NIGHT

Hard driving rain. They get out and scramble for cover. Animal
knocks on a door, a peephole opens on a green eye.

                    EYE
          Oui?

                    ANIMAL
          Santini sent me.

                    EYE
          Ahhh, Santini. Come in.

                    ANIMAL
          Business must be slow.

The door opens, revealing a squat, stubby woman with a cone of
red hair, a painted face and a black lace dress flowing around
her to the floor.

                    MADAME CLAUDE
          Monsieur et Monsieur. Je suis Madame
          Claude.

INT. WHOREHOUSE ANTEROOM - NIGHT

The anteroom is slightly threadbare but with its former
elegance intact. Animal and Santini enter, soaked.

                    ANIMAL
          You speak English, Madame Claude?

>   MADAME CLAUDE
>   (not wild about his looks)
>   Oui, I speak English.

>   ANIMAL
>   So do I.
>   (he winks)
>   Heh, a little joke.

>   MADAME CLAUDE
>   You would like to remove your wet
>   clothes? I have robes for you.

>   ANIMAL
>   I'm all for robes.

Madame Claude points up the staircase to the second floor.

>   MADAME CLAUDE
>   Through there. Choose the color you wish.

INT. TOP OF STAIRS - NIGHT - MOMENTS LATER

Animal and Santini, in the robes, appear and start down.

>   ANIMAL
>   Got your wallet with you?

Santini nods.

>   MADAME CLAUDE
>   Messieurs . . .
>   She gestures for them to follow her into
>   the next room.

INT. LIVING ROOM - NIGHT

A deep scarlet chamber with a fire burning, heavy satin
draperies. SOUND of downpour outside the window. Chamber music.
A staircase climbs to a second floor veranda.

>   MADAME CLAUDE
>   May I introduce my *femmes de guerre*.

Five WOMEN. Claude introduces them. Each rises and steps
forward as her name is called.

>   MADAME CLAUDE
>   Suzanne. Camée. Bette. Françoise. Lulu.

                    ANIMAL
          Hello, ladies.
                    (to Madame)
          Cognac. Bring the bottle.

Animal sits on the couch. Santini remains where he is,
inspecting the women as if they are pieces of art.

                    ANIMAL
          If I were you, Santini, I'd take the one
          on the left.

Madame Claude returns with the bottle which she puts down
beside Animal, and addresses Santini.

                  MADAME CLAUDE
          Monsieur, have you made your selection?

                    SANTINI
          Nothing, thank you.

He sits beside Animal.

                  MADAME CLAUDE
                    (to Animal)
          And you, Monsieur, you are ready?

                    ANIMAL
          I'm working on it.

                  MADAME CLAUDE
          Yes, of course, but my femmes must be off
          to their rooms very soon now, you
          understand.

Animal puffs on his cigar.

                    ANIMAL
          In which case I better get a move on.

He stands, woozily, and steps toward the women, who are not
terribly excited about the prospect of him in their bed.

                    ANIMAL
                    (holds out his arms to her)
          C'mon, Suzy baby, it's you and me.

They mount the stairs, Animal looks back over his shoulder at
Santini, a wry smile on his face.

Okay. There was a lot of ambivalence toward this scene. Some people told me to scrap it. Do you need a whorehouse scene? they said. A cliché! What's the purpose of this scene—to show that whorehouses exist in Antwerp? Does the scene contribute to the story or to the characterizations? Is the whorehouse necessary?

Good questions. The rest of this Animal/Santini scene happens later on. We'll try to answer these questions then.

From another angle, we might wonder what kind of fresh hell Animal and Santini will bring to this scene, or on themselves. The scene was also said to be sexist. Just because it was written fifteen years ago doesn't eliminate that truth.

EXT. PARIS STREET - NIGHT

A MAN rushes through the crowd. He is CORPORAL AUGIE EPSTEIN, in custom-tailored summer khakis open at the neck and brown penny loafers. In his late twenties, he has a flashy haircut that flows off his head like brown curly flowers. He has small round ears that won't hold a pencil. He's eager, intense.

He enters a building with a sign reading *Stars and Stripes*.

INT. STARS AND STRIPES NEWSROOM - NIGHT

Blocky double desks, green lampshades, a German M-42 machine gun. Over a bookcase are two signs: IT'S ADOLF NOT ADOLPH and AMMO IS AMMO NOT BULLETS.

Clippings on the walls, beauty queen posters. Crusty gluepots. A blue diaphanous cloud bank of cigarette smoke. Deskmen, copyboys. Tickertape machines. Parisian radio music.

In his glass-enclosed office, sits the corpulent COLONEL ARTHUR PEABODY, Editor-in-Chief.

Augie Epstein rushes in and up to a DESKMAN.

                         AUGIE
          That bird story we did a few months back—
          the canary that chirps just before air
          raids. Remember that?

                         DESKMAN
          I got it here somewhere.

As he rummages through his files, the phone rings. Augie goes to his own desk and answers it.

                    AUGIE
          Epstein. Yeah, General, what's up?
          Right. Listen, General, I'm leaving in a
          few hours, going home, yeah, thanks, it
          was sudden, but I'll be sure to take care
          of that for you before I go. You bet. My
          best to Mrs. Wainwright.

He hangs up and goes back to the deskman, who hands him a sheet
of newscopy. Augie reads it.

                    AUGIE
          That's the bird all right.
                    (thoughtfully)
          Edward Podberoski.

                    DESKMAN
          What's up?

                    AUGIE
          Little poker game I'm in . . .

                    COLONEL PEABODY
          Epstein!

Augie turns to see Colonel Peabody waving a sheet of paper.

                    AUGIE
          What?

                    COLONEL PEABODY
          Get in here!

Augie marches down the aisle into Peabody's office.

INT. PEABODY'S OFFICE - NIGHT

Peabody is fat and torpid, a military man in attitude but not in
appearance. Augie enters and sits, draping his leg over the
chair.

                    AUGIE
          What's up?

                    COLONEL PEABODY
                    (reads from the copy)
          In Manila, members of MacArthur's staff
          received, *with icy dignity,* the first
          envoys of surrender from Japan.

                    AUGIE
Yessir, that's how it reads. I like the
emotion you put into it.

               COLONEL PEABODY
Icy dignity?

                    AUGIE
Why not?

               COLONEL PEABODY
Too novelistic.

                    AUGIE
Novelistic?

               COLONEL PEABODY
Get rid of it.

                    AUGIE
This is a newspaper, Colonel. I'm a
newspaperman. Newspapermen ask
questions. Here's one. Why?

               COLONEL PEABODY
Were you there with MacArthur?

                    AUGIE
No.

               COLONEL PEABODY
Icy dignity is editorializing.

                    AUGIE
Emotionalizing? Think about the words.
Dignity: the quality or state of being
worthy, honored, or esteemed. Icy:
fresh, keen, boreal, piercing, cool as a
cucumber. Precisely what the photos
showed him to be.

               COLONEL PEABODY
Kill it.

                    AUGIE
The sign on the door says you're the
editor-in-chief, Colonel; you kill it.

               COLONEL PEABODY
That's an order, Epstein!

Augie gets up from his chair and leans across the desk.

>   AUGIE
> Colonel, I got three years on the *Chicago
> Tribune*. I got five years on this paper.
> You got six months on this paper and eight
> years handing out underwear in a supply
> depot. You don't know shit about a
> newspaper, never did and never will!

>   COLONEL PEABODY
>   (flushed)
> Epstein!

>   AUGIE
> The only reason you got this job is
> because you play golf with General
> Rucker. I almost got my ass shot off a
> hundred times trying to get the story.
> And you? You pick your nose and order the
> staff around like a bunch of recruits. I
> hate to break the news to you but those
> silver chickens on your shoulders don't
> mean shit around here. Sit down before
> you have a heart attack.

>   COLONEL PEABODY
>   (trembling)
> I'll have you court-martialed for this.

>   AUGIE
> Too late, Colonel, I'm going home with a
> half a million bucks in my pocket to
> invest in a small town newspaper so I
> don't have to work for an asshole like you
> again.

>   COLONEL PEABODY
> Believe me, Epstein, I will crucify you.

Augie grabs the phone and dumps it into Peabody's lap.

>   AUGIE
> Make the call.

Peabody tries dialing but his hands are shaking out of control.
Augie snatches the receiver from him.

>   AUGIE
> But consider this. For five months you've
> tried to get me transferred. Do you know

            why you've failed? Any fucking idea, you
            nitwit? I'll tell you why. Because I'm a
            good newspaperman with a lot of close
            friends who have a lot more clout than
            your General Rucker. If an MP shows up at
            my door, I'll go quietly, no problem. And
            when I get to the stockade, I'll make one
            call. And Colonel, I guarantee it, within
            a week you'll be back handing out
            underwear. Think of all the icy dignity
            you'll have to conjure up for that
            situation. Good-bye, asshole.

Augie strolls out of the office.

INT. NEWSROOM - DAY

At his desk, he dumps his belongings into a pouch. He starts out
of the newsroom, waving at the guys.

                        AUGIE
            Good-bye, fellas.

The guys let out a chorus of good-byes. In the distance is
Peabody, frozen behind his desk.

Here we meet Player #4, Augie Epstein, a reporter, who will be instrumental in solving the murder. Being different from the others in the game, he will bring a new element to the game. He's cosmopolitan, edgy, unafraid of authority, cocky, bright, and curious. He's also arrogant, self-serving, and he knows what he wants.

I like reporters as characters. They root out the truth. They dig in places they shouldn't, expose the powerful and bring them to their knees. Reporters generally have lousy love lives. They fear authority and want to topple it at the same time, usually to get back at their own fathers. They do it through their work, as writers. Is that overstatement? Am I talking about myself?

I wrote this scene hoping that the reader roots for Augie Epstein. (I named him Augie after Augie March from Saul Bellow's great novel.) In order to do that I had to make Colonel Peabody a real shithead. If you're worried about creating a main character in an unsympathetic light, make everybody around him more despicable than he is. He'll come off like a hero. Remember Don Corleone in *The Godfather?* What a brute. Then remember that miserable cast of characters with whom Mario Puzo surrounded him and you'll come to understand one of the tenets of building a well-developed character.

This scene also establishes Augie as a fighter and as somebody who can get the goods. These qualities will be utilized later on. Remember that screenplays consist of a series of setups and payoffs. Nothing in a screenplay happens by mistake. Everything matters. Your job is to make it appear seamless and spontaneous.

The following is a SEQUENCE. Call it Escape from the Whorehouse, Part II.

You'll remember that a sequence is a series of scenes tied together by a single idea or intention. In this case it's Animal and Santini running through the streets of Antwerp trying to reach the ship before getting caught and throttled—possibly killed—by an irate whorehouse contingent, led by Madame Claude and her goons.

You'll notice that the sequence is initiated by some inappropriate thing Animal has done (which is right in character), followed by the chase through the streets, and culminating in the arrival on the ship itself. When you can have your characters reach their destination in an exciting way, why just have them walk on?

                                                        CUT TO:

EXT. ANTWERP STREET - NIGHT

Driving rain.

INT. BROTHEL - NIGHT

Santini sleeps on the couch. A hand shakes him. His eyes open. Animal stands over him.

                    ANIMAL
          C'mon, we gotta get out of here.

Santini, groggy, gets up slowly. Animal pulls him the rest of the way. SOUND of a shriek.

                    SANTINI
          What's that?

                    ANIMAL
          Reveille.

                    SANTINI
          Our clothes are upstairs.

                    ANIMAL
          No time.

They head for the door.

EXT. STREET - NIGHT

Drizzling, cold and dark. They take off up a hill, freezing in their bathrobes, toward the streetlights.

                    SANTINI
          What did you do in there?

                    ANIMAL
          I don't know. It all happened so fast.

They continue running. SOUNDS of screaming behind them. The bouncer, two femmes, and Madame Claude are in pursuit.

                    SANTINI
          Down there!

                    ANIMAL
                    (looks)
          What about it?

                    SANTINI
          The name of the ship . . .

                    ANIMAL
          The S.S. *McQueen*.

                    SANTINI
          Shall we?

They climb over the fence and start down. The ground is littered with broken glass, cans, all sorts of garbage. Behind them the bouncer hurdles over the fence.

EXT. THE DOCKS - NIGHT

Ships, huge dock sheds. A smattering of lights. The harbor is misty, cast in an eerie light. They reach the dock area, running alongside the ships, searching the names on their hulls.

                    ANIMAL
                    (calling them out)
          Barbara Richie! Der Ober! HMS Binder!

                    SANTINI
          Edwaaard!

                    ANIMAL
          What!

Santini points to a ten-foot-high wall fifty yards ahead.

                           ANIMAL
            Perfect!
                    (back at the names)
            Pierre Sancerre! Patrick Henry! S.S.
            McQueen! Hold it!

The bouncer and women are gaining. A merchant marine SENTRY
with a carbine stands at the top of the gangplank.

                           SENTRY
            Halt! Who goes there?

                           SANTINI
            Santini!

                           ANIMAL
            Podberoski!

                           SENTRY
            Come back in the morning. Formation's at
            0 800.

                           ANIMAL
                    (panting)
            Morning's no good.

                           SENTRY
            I'm not authorized to let you aboard.

                           ANIMAL
            Gotta use the john. We're dying!

                           SENTRY
             Sorry.

SOUND of voices.

                           ANIMAL
            Those voices are gonna be here in fifteen
            seconds. And you'll have two dead
            soldiers on your hands.

                           SENTRY
            I'm not authorized.

Animal steps forward, the Sentry raises his carbine.

                        ANIMAL
            What if a bunch of local whores and their
            gorilla pimp are chasing me, what then?
                    (Sentry shrugs)
            A riot. Is that what you want?

The Sentry looks down boardwalk, sees the pursuers.

                        SENTRY
            All right, come on.

They race up the gangplank and duck behind the railing. They hear
approaching footsteps, voices.

                    MADAME CLAUDE
            Hey, sailor! You have seen two soldiers,
            short-fat, short-skinny?

                        ANIMAL
                    (whispers to Santini)
            She should talk.

                    MADAME CLAUDE
            Américain, you have seen them?

                        SENTRY
                    (carbine raised)
            No, Ma'am, I haven't. I did see two men
            run by that way.

Points to high wall at the end of the dock, realizing his
mistake.

                    MADAME CLAUDE
            Did they fly? Listen, sailor, we come on
            your ship?

                        ANIMAL
                    (whisper)
            Oh, Jesus, first they'll kill that poor
            bastard . . .

                        SENTRY
            'Fraid you can't do that, Ma'am.

The Sentry cocks his carbine.

                    MADAME CLAUDE
            You want justice, no? I want short-fat
            one who beat up my best girl and did not
            pay.

> SANTINI
> (whisper)

You did that?

> ANIMAL

No, no, it didn't happen that way.

> SANTINI

Oh, Edward.

> ANIMAL

It didn't.

> SENTRY

For the last time, I haven't seen the men.

> MADAME CLAUDE

Okay, sailor, see you at the guillotine.

Madame Claude turns and marches away, followed by the blond bouncer and the women. Animal and Santini listen to their footsteps departing, then stand.

> ANIMAL

Hey, thanks a lot. You saved our asses.

> SANTINI
> (offering cash to him)

Take your wife out on the town when we get back to the States.

> SENTRY

I'm not married.

Animal looks at him as if he's an idiot.

> ANIMAL

Then buy your mother a douche bag.

> SANTINI
> (interrupting)

Yes, a lovely handbag, what a good idea.

> SENTRY

C'mon, I'll find you a place to sleep.

End of sequence. Each sequence has a beginning, middle, and end. The sequence comes to a halt often after a breathtaking series of events that gains momentum and culminates, as it does here, with the end to an action, in this case the chase. That's why it's called a chase sequence.

We also establish the ship itself and add another character trait or two to each character. The two essential functions illuminate character: They move the story forward and illuminate another aspect of character.

```
EXT. MANHATTAN - NIGHT

An establishing shot of the night skyline.

INT. HOTEL SUITE - NIGHT

Five men playing poker. Vintage 1945 coats and hats on the coat
rack. A fancy leather HOLSTER with a silver-handled Smith-and-
Wesson revolver, and a cowboy hat.

The owner of this gear is PFC. CHARLIE BUCK, a baby-faced kid in
his twenties, fair-haired, with a lot of Texas savvy. He is
decked out in calfskin boots, string tie, and a fancy vest.

The largest pile of chips sits in front of Charlie. The other
players—all CIVILIANS—are losing heavily. They're in the
middle of a hand.

Bottles of booze and an elaborate buffet are on a table. Charlie
drinks a glass of milk. The game is five-card stud.

                    CHARLIE
             (looking at his hole card)
        It's like my Uncle Dandy always said,
        gentlemen, when the light shines on you,
        bake in it. I'll bet five hundred dollars.


                    MAN #1
        Do you ever check?


                    CHARLIE
        Not if I can help it, Sir.


                    MAN #1
        This is ridiculous. I'm out. What time is
        it?


                    MAN #3
        Eleven.


                    MAN #1
        I gotta get up to the Bronx.
```

                    MAN #2
Okay, cowboy, I'll see you.

                    MAN #3
              (turns his cards over)
Too rich for me.

                    CHARLIE
Real sorry to see that, suh, but when
there ain't no way home, you sleep under a
tree.

The players give Charlie an off-the-wall look.

                    MAN #4
I'll see your five hundred and bump it five
more.

                    CHARLIE
Now we're playing a little poker here.
Lemme see, that's five more to me and five
better.

                    MAN #2
              (incredulous)
On what, a pair of deuces?

                    CHARLIE
Yessir, and one in the hole.

                    MAN #2
Horseshit. I'll call.

                    MAN #4
              (sliding the money in)
My wife is going to kill me.

                    CHARLIE
Pot's right, gentlemen.
              (deals the last card)
There's a Blackeye Bear for Mr. Prentice,
and a Double Bun for my friend here on the
right and for me, well run me down, a
little threeball.

                    MAN #2
Who knows?

                    CHARLIE
Just my Uncle Dandy and the Lord. The two
balls will bet one thousand dollars.

                         MAN #4
                      (thinking)
              With anybody else, I'd raise it to the
              ceiling. I'll call.

Charlie flips over his case card, too, a winner!

                         MAN #4
              Something is wrong here!

He starts out of his seat toward Charlie, who lifts his boot and
puts it gently into his chest, pushing him back to his seat.

                         CHARLIE
              There ain't nothin' wrong, Mr. Jones,
              'ceptin' your attitude.

The door suddenly blows open, revealing MAJOR PETER TAT. Tall
and wiry, he looks like a Wall Street accountant. He heads for
the coat rack.

                         MAJOR TAT
              Cash in, Charlie, we're in a hurry.

He takes the holster and western hat from the rack and carries
them over. The other players grumble about this sudden
interruption.

                         MAJOR TAT
              Gentlemen, gentlemen, you'll have a
              chance to get your money back. My boy has
              a very important business meeting. Hurry
              up, Charlie.

                         CHARLIE
                      (cashing in)
              What's goin' on, Major?

                         MAJOR TAT
              Tell you on the way.

Charlie gathers the money and hands it to Tat who places it in a
pouch. Charlie straps on his holster.

                         CHARLIE
              Adios, fellas, nice doing bidness with
              you.

INT. HOTEL HALLWAY - NIGHT

Charlie and Major Tat hurry down the corridor.

                    CHARLIE
          What's this all about, Major?

                    MAJOR TAT
          Big surprise, Charlie. We're flying to
          Europe tonight.

The elevator door opens, they step inside. Charlie stands
looking at the Major with a befuddled expression.

INT. HOTEL LOBBY - NIGHT

The elevator door opens. Charlie, still nonplussed.

                    CHARLIE
          Half a million dollars?

They walk through the lobby toward the street.

                    MAJOR TAT
          Just the beginning, Charlie my boy. I'm
          going to turn you into the richest poker
          player in the world.

                    CHARLIE
          Jeez, I'm ready.

                    MAJOR TAT
          I've been looking for you all my life.
          Keep thinking that way.

                    CHARLIE
          I got the horse, Major, show me the way.

They move into the noise and hubbub of Manhattan.

You've just met Player #5, Charlie Buck, a Texas-born kid, and an
import. His manager will fly him in from New York for this game. The
scope widens. Charlie is cocky and brash like Augie, and likable, and
he's a kid. But he's an audience favorite because, as a kid, he has to go
up against older seasoned players, all formidable. Will youth prevail?

   This rounds out the game. My thinking on the size of the game was
twofold. I did not follow some suggestions and have six or seven players. Five is plenty. I feel the cast is already cluttered with too many
people. The fewer characters the better. Always keep the cast to the
absolute minimum by doubling up on assignments if you have to—the
result being that if one character has three or four responsibilities,

rather than assigning each responsibility to a single character, we get a more well-rounded person to work with.

In this, I feel that I have solid demographics, something for everybody, in the five diverse characters: Animal, a slob; Santini, an uptight eighteenth-century man; Hubbard, a blond WASP officer; Epstein, a Jewish reporter; and Charlie, a snot-nosed, poker-playing whiz kid. The point here is that you have to give us variety in character. Too often in scripts I find characters who not only sound alike but think and act alike, all variations on one central figure, usually based on the writer him- or herself.

                                                    CUT TO:

EXT. GARDEN - CASABLANCA - DAY

Military and Consulate BRASS are gathered in the formal garden of the American Consulate. Arab SERVANTS serve champagne to the ladies and gentlemen gathered around CONSUL GENERAL PHILIP CHADBORNE.

The Consul General finishes his farewell speech by raising his glass to Captain Evan Hubbard IV.

                        CHADBORNE
            . . . and bon voyage!

Glass raised to Hubbard. Well-wishers shake his hand. One of them, CAPTAIN BEAU SMYTH, notices the scar on Hubbard's face.

                        SMYTH
            What happened to you?

                        HUBBARD
            Momentary lapse of judgment.

                        SMYTH
            You must be more careful. How did your
            farewell-to-Casablanca game go last
            night?

                        HUBBARD
            My jeep was stolen.

                        SMYTH
            I won't ask about the rest of it.

                        HUBBARD
            Don't.

                    SMYTH
     Oh, and Colonel Morley said he spoke to
     your father, and the General wants you to
     stop in London on your way home.

                    HUBBARD
     I'll send him a postcard.

                    SMYTH
                  (shaking hands)
     Good luck with the big game.

                    HUBBARD
     I'll need more than luck. That money will
     free me in more ways than I can count.

Let's take a look at this scene in terms of beats. Beats are small turning points in each scene that propel the action along and keep it interesting.

Remember that it's the audience we always play to. Our job as writers is to keep the reader off-balance and hurtling along, spellbound, always wanting more.

We rely on the reader remembering that the last time he saw Hubbard he had killed the major in the Casablanca street. Now we find him in the Embassy setting. Therefore, we surmise, caught, he stands to lose everything. In which case, we have the built-in tension of needing to get out cleanly and quickly.

We also learn that he's connected, and that he's got a powerful father in the military, whom, because of his fears, he defies.

He's been carrying this burden for a long time and will have to deal with it before the story ends. The murder and the father problem have been planted here in order to be paid off later on.

Beat I is the fact that he's leaving. Beat II is the scar. Beat III is when we learn about his attitude toward his father, the general. Beat IV is his reason for entering the game—to be free of his father. Of course, even winning all the money will not really free him from his father, but Hubbard doesn't know this yet.

Beat IV suggests that Hubbard will have to grow during the rest of the story in order to understand that no amount of money will ever free him from his emotional angst and allow him to become a man. He'll have to do that in some other way.

Every scene is developed through a series of beats or revelations. If you construct your scenes in this manner, the process becomes much easier and far more successful. This is the craft of writing at work.

INT. LIBERTY SHIP, ANTWERP - NIGHT

Animal and Santini walk down the corridor, still wearing Madame Claude's robes. They see a MERCHANT SEAMAN.

                    ANIMAL
          Hey you! Who's in charge around here?

                    SEAMAN
          Purser Kettle. In the Ward Room.

INT. WARD ROOM - DAY

PURSER LARRY KETTLE at his desk. He is short with a mop of red hair and a sea of freckles. He speaks with a Kentucky accent. As Purser, he is third in command of the ship. A KNOCK on the door.

                    KETTLE
          Come in.

Animal enters, Santini follows.

                    ANIMAL
          You Kettle?

                    KETTLE
          What can I do for you?

                    ANIMAL
          I'm Podberoski. This is Santini.

                    KETTLE
          I heard about you fellas coming aboard
          last night.

                    ANIMAL
          Yeah, right. Listen, Kettle, we got to go
          to town. Madame Claude and her goons are
          out there and I don't know . . .

                    SANTINI
                  (interrupting)
          Mister Kettle. Edward and I need
          transportation to the Century Hotel in
          order to collect our belongings and a
          substantial sum of money.

                    KETTLE
          Yes?

> SANTINI
> We'll need a vehicle and two armed
> guards.

> KETTLE
> Gentlemen, I want to do everything I can to
> make this voyage as trouble-free as I can.

Santini opens his wallet and pulls out a few bills.

> SANTINI
> May I make a contribution to your good
> will.

> KETTLE
> (taking it)
> You'll find that all your belongings,
> including the money, have been moved from
> the hotel and are now safely on board.

They look at each other, impressed.

Kettle is the man inside. As the purser, he knows everything about the ship, where all the bodies are buried. He's a man who can get things done and, as such, could become a threat, or a boon, to the players. By this time I wanted the reader to start looking around for suspects.

Notice that I bring in this new character through dramatic means. This is the first time we meet him and he should be memorable. Here we need to take ordinary exposition and put a dramatic twist on it, through confrontation.

EXT. ANTWERP DOCK - DAY

SIR BERTRAM FOOTE, a tall, distinguished gentleman in his late fifties, and Major Peter Tat (who you'll remember as Charlie Buck's manager in Manhattan) stand on the dock. A limousine is parked behind them, bearing British Parliamentary flags.

They watch the departing ship sail out through the harbor. The sea is filled with discarded duffel bags, gas masks, all sorts of gear dumped overboard by the deliriously happy, homeward-bound troops.

> SIR BERTRAM
> We've been over this, Major Tat. I found
> the players except for your Charlie, who
> is hardly qualified to play, not having
> been in the war over here.

                    MAJOR TAT
          I cut their orders. I found the ship. You
          got your fee for this crowning
          achievement, this game of games. I should
          be on board with Charlie.

                    SIR BERTRAM
          The other players don't have their
          business managers aboard. You'll be in
          New York when they arrive, and hopefully
          your Charlie will have won.

                    MAJOR TAT
          That's not the point.

                    SIR BERTRAM
          The point is you've done a first-rate job,
          Major. I appreciate your help.

Tat says nothing.

                    SIR BERTRAM
          This is *our* crowning achievement, Major.
          The five top poker champions of the war on
          a Liberty ship, headed home to America.
          You are a part of history. Now good-bye,
          Major, and good luck.

Sir Bertram climbs into the limousine and drives off. Tat,
disgruntled, swings his head back toward the harbor.

Here we have another piece of the puzzle—Sir Bertram Foote, who has
conspired with Major Tat. Questions arise: Is Charlie Buck a ringer?
What's going on here? Are he and Tat in league? Is the game rigged?
Remember that you only have to give the reader as much information—
in this case, a tease—as the reader needs to know. Your responsibility
is to build suspense and tension.

EXT. LIBERTY SHIP - DAY

The S.S. *McQueen* is a pock-marked, battle-scarred ship about a
football-field-and-a-half long. On deck, two hundred soldiers
continue throwing gear overboard, sunbathe, play cards, stand
on the platform looking back to port.

THREE-INCH GUN PLATFORM

A group of SOLDIERS are in a contest, sailing bills into the
wind. One soldier sails a ten-dollar bill. A second betters him
with a twenty, then someone throws a fifty. A tall Georgian lets
go with a one-hundred-dollar bill.

> GEORGIAN
> All right! What's the prize?

> MAN #1
> Asshole of the month. You're it.

BRIDGE

Charlie Buck, in cowboy duds, watches seagulls swoop and dive
overhead. He pulls his revolver out of his holster and tracks a
particular gull.

> CHARLIE
> Ping!

He continues to simulate shooting the gull.

> CHARLIE
> C'mon darlin', little closer now. Ride
> that wind. Ping!

Now he takes aim for real. Using his elbow as a brace, he swings
the barrel, tracking the bird.

> CHARLIE
> There you go, darlin'.

Charlie SQUEEZES OFF A ROUND.

Merchant Seamen snap their heads at the sound. They spot
Charlie and his weapon and run in his direction.

Charlie prepares to fire again. He raises the pistol, squints
his eye.

> CHARLIE
> C'mon, little beauty, make your move.

Charlie squeezes off a SECOND ROUND. The gull shatters all over
the sky.

> CHARLIE
> Good-bye, sweet darlin'.

He hears shouting and turns to see a gang of merchant seamen storming down the deck at him. They jump him, pounding him with their fists. CAPTAIN SAM MURPHY, a big Boston Irishman, hauls the bodies off Charlie.

>   MURPHY
>   Get back to your stations! Move out!

The men stumble out away. Charlie is a bloody mess. Murphy leans him against the rail.

>   MURPHY
>   Can you talk, soldier?

>   CHARLIE
>   (through swollen lips)
>   Yessir, I think so.

>   MURPHY
>   You have any idea what you've just done?

>   CHARLIE
>   Shot a bird.

>   MURPHY
>   An albatross. Does that mean anything
>   to you?

>   CHARLIE
>   No, sir. Can't say that it does.

Charlie starts to slip back to the deck. Murphy hefts him up.

>   MURPHY
>   You just killed a sea bird, which means
>   you invited the devil on this ship.

>   CLERK
>   The devil?

>   MURPHY
>   I'd suggest you stay clear of my men,
>   because the next time I might not be
>   around. Is that clear?

>   CHARLIE
>   Yessir. About this albatross. Just
>   exactly what's supposed to happen?

>   MURPHY
>   No way of telling.

                    CHARLIE
        Well, don't you worry none, sir. I'm
        sorry about killing that bird, but when
        you got Charlie Buck on board, the
        devil's like a haymaker in a high wind.

                    MURPHY
            (no idea what that means)
        Get down to sick bay.

This is *Plot Point I*. Charlie Buck has just shot an albatross. This is now a doomed ship, a ship of death. In ancient sea lore, doomed ships never complete their voyages. They end up on the ocean floor.

At Plot Point I a giant hook comes out of the sky and grabs the action, sending it into a new direction. We are now off land and on the sea, heading for home. On a doomed ship. If Plot Point I is supposed to put the characters in greater jeopardy, overlaid with a new sense of urgency, we have it here.

We are at a point of no return. The ship has sailed, there is no turning back. Destinies are sealed. And what better place than on a ship, from which nobody can escape.

We now enter the great desert of Act II, where most scripts wander off somewhere and get lost. I always get nervous here. And no wonder. In front of me is half the screenplay to get through before reaching the next major plot point. As the writer you have to try very hard to keep the audience interested, always wanting more. Your responsibility from this point on is to build the tension through a series of tension-filled turning points and hurdles over which the characters have to leap.

By now I've set the stage. The men are on the ship. There's suspicion of collusion here. We've got five guys who will do anything to win a half million dollars, which in 1945 terms translates into about four million today. And they're on a ship destined for the ocean floor. It's your job to build tension in Act I so that the forces at work against the characters are plausible and increasingly more dangerous.

Remember that the closer you get to the end of the story the greater the tension must be. Scenes of tension increase while scenes of quietude decrease.

INT. WARD ROOM - DAY

Duffel bags are stacked against the wall. Animal's canary chirps in its cage. Liquor, ice, and glasses are on a table.

The players, minus Charlie, are here. Santini, in a tailored
civilian suit, looks peaked. Augie, in summer khakis, fingers a
deck of cards. Animal is his usual sloppy self, in need of a
shave. Hubbard, in uniform, is the tallest, towers over them.
He also wears the thick scar from his battle in the Casablanca
street.

                    AUGIE
              (indicating bird)
          This half-dead canary saved how many
          lives?

                    ANIMAL
          You don't read your own newspaper,
          Epstein? This bird's a fuckin' war hero.
          Let's have a little respect. She saved my
          ass at least a dozen times, didn't you,
          sweetheart?

Purser Larry Kettle enters, followed by Charlie Buck, with
puffy eyes and swollen lips.

                    KETTLE
          Gentlemen, I'd like you all to meet Pfc.
          Charlie Buck.

                    CHARLIE
          Howdy.

The Players don't quite know what to make of this kid in the
cowboy getup.

                    KETTLE
              (making the introductions)
          Corporal Augie Epstein . . .
          Michelangelo Santini . . . Captain Evan
          Hubbard.

                    HUBBARD
          How do you do?

                    CHARLIE
          Cap'n, sir.

                    KETTLE
          And this is Pfc. Edward Podberoski.

                    ANIMAL
              (to Hubbard)
          Fall off your horse, Captain?

Kettle pulls up a chair for Charlie.

> KETTLE
> Now that we're all here, gentlemen, I'd
> like to welcome you, and to tell you that
> if there's anything humanly possible to
> procure for you, I will get it. You'll
> notice behind you the ship's safe, where
> your money will be guarded by an armed
> sentry. You will be served meals in a
> private dining room, and you'll be lodged
> in three private fo'c'sles. Wish we had
> one for each of you, but we don't. Any
> questions?

> ANIMAL
> Yeah, Red, can you get me a dame?

> KETTLE
> Wouldn't want to be responsible for any
> distractions, Private Podberoski. If
> there's nothing else, gentlemen, I'll be
> just outside.

> AUGIE
> (to Charlie)
> Never heard of you, Buck. Where'd you
> play cards?

> CHARLIE
> Never heard of you either, Corporal.

> ANIMAL
> Bicker later, let's cut for the rooms.

Augie fans a deck of cards across the table.

> AUGIE
> Two high. Two low. Middle man sleeps
> alone.

Animal indicates Charlie and Hubbard.

> ANIMAL
> We can always put the wounded together.

Santini picks up the cards, inspects them, is satisfied they're
not marked. Animal and Santini pull a queen and ten,
respectively.

                          ANIMAL
             I coulda done worse.

Augie and Hubbard pick a three and five, respectively.

                          CHARLIE
                     (turning a seven)
             A dusty muzzle, muh God, they're runnin'
             already.

They eye him suspiciously.

Here in Act II you begin the process of resistance. In this case, not only
are we, and the characters, now suspicious of outside forces playing
with the destiny of these men—now the players themselves begin to
psychologically play against one another. We are entering the heart of
the game. Here we want the readers to take sides.

    Hopefully by this time you have given enough character details on
each to allow the reader to take his or her place behind individual
favorites, rooting them on.

EXT. MAIN DECK - FIRST DAY

A FULL SHOT on a crowd of boisterous men. Shirts have been
discarded. Soldiers hand out mimeographed sheets on the
players, tickets are sold.

A group gathers around ARTHUR WILLOW, the bookmaker, who is a
small balding man with a bland nondescript face. With Willow
are two BODYGUARDS.

Soldiers shoot dice against the bulkheads and arguments flare.
Suddenly the noise dies down as the men turn their heads
toward . . .

THE BRIDGE

High above the deck, the poker champions appear—gladiators
ready for battle. In hallowed procession, they descend the
ladder.

Animal Podberoski, slob of slobs, wrinkled uniform, no shave,
raises an arm to the men. His name patch reads ANIMAL.

Santini is trim and confident, dressed in a Saville Row suit.
Augie Epstein, in tailored khakis, is his cautious self.

Charlie Buck, in a dazzling cowboy outfit and boots, belt buckle
gleaming in the sunlight, is followed by Captain Evan Hubbard
IV, composed, fine blond hair, wearing no insignia of rank.

Purser Larry Kettle, in Merchant Marine uniform, carries a
small valise. On the deck now, the champions approach the
troops, who open a wedge for them to pass.

> SOLDIER
> (to Animal)
> Hey, Podberoski. I seen you play at
> Liege. I got a C-note on you.

> ANIMAL
> Bet the ranch, buddy. I'm a shoo-in.

MOVING THROUGH THE TROOPS

Who are feverish with anticipation. The players arrive at the
No.1 Hatch and disappear into the hold.

INT. HOLD - DAY

Specially constructed to look like a cock-fight arena, a round
wooden table and five chairs are bolted to the deck. A green felt
cloth covers the table.

Around the table are metal bleachers for the spectators.
Hanging lamps, metal ashtrays bolted to the table—everything is
bolted down to keep from moving with the pitch and roll of the
ship.

> ANIMAL
> (scanning the area)
> This looks like the inside of my fucking
> helmet.

Augie inspects the area for mirrors, hidden reflectors, angles
from which the troops can see their hands.

> CHARLIE
> Mighty fine job you done here, Mister
> Kettle.

> KETTLE
> (proudly)
> We worked day and night for two weeks.

Augie pulls out a deck of cards and fans them over the table.

                        AUGIE
            Cut for seats.

Santini inspects the cards.

                        HUBBARD
            May I?

He stacks, fans, and inspects them in his huge hands like a
mechanic.

                        HUBBARD
            Ace high and down.

Animal's ten is a winner until Charlie, going last, turns over a
queen. They take their seats. Kettle opens his valise and
spills fresh decks of cards on the table.

                        ANIMAL
                    (to Kettle)
            Okay, Red, let 'em in.

                        SANTINI
            I'd prefer not having the troops in the
            hold.

                        ANIMAL
            This is the championship of the world we
            got here, Santini. We owe it to 'em.
            Any of these jamokes get outta line, Red,
            out they go.

                        KETTLE
            Absolutely.

                        ANIMAL
            Bring 'em in.

EXT. DECK - DAY

Kettle appears and the troops let out a roar. Arthur Willow and
his two bodyguards move to the front.

                        SOLDIER
            Hey, who are they? What is this shit!

                        KETTLE
            They got season passes, fellas. The rest
            of you with tickets, line up.

INT. HOLD - DAY

Willow and his boys take their seats. Behind them, the troops
clamor into the bleachers.

At the table the players break the seals on the fresh decks,
which are passed from man to man for inspection. The discards go
into a cap, the others are placed in the middle.

Augie runs a comb through his hair and wipes off a pair of
sunglasses with his handkerchief.

                    ANIMAL
          Mr. Hollywood.

Kettle arrives with a large pouch—followed by TWO SENTRIES with
carbines who take their positions around the table. Kettle
opens the pouch revealing LARGE STACKS OF PAPER MONEY.

The players begin counting. Each man has a one-hundred-
thousand-dollar buy-in price. The cards are fanned. Hubbard is
high. He picks up the cards, ready to deal.

                    HUBBARD
          As agreed, gentlemen, this will be five-
          card-stud poker. No limit.

Hubbard deals the first card down and the second card up, calling
them out.

                    HUBBARD
          Five, four, king of diamonds. Eight.
          Five. Bet the king, Mr. Santini.

                    SANTINI
          One hundred dollars.

                    CHARLIE
          The ole double bun. What to do?

                    ANIMAL
          The what?

                    CHARLIE
               (pointing to his card)
          Double bun. The eight. Two little circles
          here. Just an expression.

Animal looks at him.

                    CHARLIE
          I'll call.

Hubbard calls, putting his one hundred dollars into the center.

>   AUGIE
>   Yeah.

>   ANIMAL
>   (he folds)
>   Good-bye.

>   HUBBARD
>   Pot's right.
>   (he deals)
>   Ten. King—jack over here. Queen.
>   Nothing. Pair of fives for me. Pair of fives
>   bets two hundred.

Augie folds.

>   SANTINI
>   Call.

>   CHARLIE
>   Well, now, my pair of ladies got to see
>   that and bump it five hundred.

Hubbard thinks, then folds.

>   SANTINI
>   (puts in five hundred dollars)
>   Call.

>   HUBBARD
>   (dealing)
>   Queen for Santini. Possible straight.
>   And a four, king high, Santini.

>   SANTINI
>   Check it.

>   CHARLIE
>   Yessir, me too.

>   HUBBARD
>   (dealing)
>   Ten. Six. King's still high.

>   SANTINI
>   Five hundred.

                    CHARLIE
        Like my Uncle Dandy said, "When you know
        it, go it." I'll bet two thousand.

A big reaction from the troops. Kettle motions for silence.
Santini ponders, then shakes his head.

                    SANTINI
        You win.

Charlie turns over his hole card—seven of clubs—a loser if
Santini had called his bet.

                    CHARLIE
        Yessir, if you know it, go it.
                (rakes in the pot)

                    AUGIE
        Cowboy, you ain't as dumb as you look.

One important element here is the setting. We have all seen a poker table before, but have we seen it in this context? This is literally a floating card game, in a specially designed hold of a ship. It's familiar on one level and original on another. When you come upon a new location, as the writer, you have to think creatively. You don't want to give us clichéd familiarity. You want to startle us by rendering the familiar in an original way.

By this time we've also established various levels of participation. The stakes run higher. We have the players, the game itself, the multitude of suspicions, and the troops watching. Many sets of eyes are on this game and the characters have bet their lives on it.

Raising stakes is all about asserting pressure on the players. You need to put your main characters in an emotional and/or physical vise. Make them *feel* the pressure.

The new pressure for everyone is Charlie's phenomenal luck with the cards. Is it luck, though?

INT. HOLD - LATER - DAY

The game has loosened up. Animal's down to his undershirt, dog tags hanging over his hairy chest. Charlie has one boot draped over his chair. Hubbard remains the same.

Augie has opened another button on his shirt, while Santini, the big loser, has sunk low in his seat, rigid and glum. Charlie has the lion's share of the money before him.

The hold is a cloud of cigarette smoke. The troops are tired,
sweaty, exhausted. Animal and Hubbard play head to head. The
others have folded.

>   ANIMAL
>   (to Hubbard)
>   You heard the Cowboy, bet the jacks.

>   HUBBARD
>   I'm deliberating right now, Podberoski,
>   do you mind?

>   ANIMAL
>   Hey, I'd be the last to interrupt your
>   thinking. I got the Kings, Hubbard, you
>   wanna bet into them or not?

>   HUBBARD
>   Check.

>   ANIMAL
>   Ah, the man checks. Now what does that
>   mean?

Animal counts out twenty five-hundred-dollar bills, pushing
them into the center.

>   ANIMAL
>   Okay, that'll be ten grand to you.

Hubbard deliberates a long time.

>   ANIMAL
>   Hubbard! I could have a nap and a sandwich
>   during this. Ten G's, right there. Yes or
>   no, it's very easy.

>   HUBBARD
>   I'll buy you an egg-timer. I'm thinking.

>   ANIMAL
>   How we can delude ourselves.

>   HUBBARD
>   I'm out.

Animal rakes in the pot; Augie leans over to him.

>   AUGIE
>   What have you got?

                    ANIMAL
Why don't you take off them fucking
sunglasses? You trying to be what's-his-
name?

                    HUBBARD
Frank Costello.

                    ANIMAL
Is that who, Eppy? I got news for
you . . .

                    SANTINI
I have to go to the bathroom.

                    AUGIE
Again?

Santini exits. A sentry automatically moves behind his cash.

                    HUBBARD
Podberoski?

                    ANIMAL
What?

                    HUBBARD
Is Santini ill?

                    ANIMAL
Hey, the way he's losing, I'd be.

                    AUGIE
Of course there's also being your
bunkmate.

                    ANIMAL
What's wrong with you, Epstein? Case of
the bad jokes? The guy is feeling punk,
you got no compassion? Tough Chicago boy
like you got no feelings for the infirm?
          (to Hubbard politely)
It was nice of you to ask after Santini,
Cap'n. I'll make a point of finding out,
the upshot of which I'll clue you in on.

                    HUBBARD
Thank you.

                    ANIMAL
You're quite welcome.

INT. FO'C'SLE - FIRST NIGHT

Plain steel lockers, a porthole, a bench and a wastebasket,
plywood bulkheads. A sign reads: ESCAPE PANEL KICK OUT. Sound
of a guitar and bad singing from somewhere.

Sweat pours out of Augie who's doing sit-ups, counting as he
goes. Hubbard, on his bunk, writes a letter.

                         AUGIE
                       (panting)
            You oughta try this, Hubbard.

                         HUBBARD
            I'm about as limber as that stanchion
            over there.

From his footlocker Augie removes a half dozen bottles of
powder. Hubbard looks at them.

                         AUGIE
            Yeast. Sunflower seeds. Makes you dream of
            home.

                         HUBBARD
            They wouldn't do me any good.

Augie, wondering what that means, bundles up in his trench coat
and, taking the bottles, exits.

EXT. ON DECK - SAME NIGHT

Charlie playing his guitar to some GOOD OLE BOYS from West
Texas.

                         CHARLIE
                       (singing)
            . . . I can't plow a field or skin a deer or
            get me a bare-hand trout, but when it
            comes to poker, boys, I can out put em
            down and out . . .
                     (rests the guitar on his knees)
            It's what my Uncle Dandy always said,
            "You got talent, my boy, but what you
            also got is a world of God-given luck."

                         GOOD OLE BOY I
            Amen to that.

                    CHARLIE
          One time I was the sole survivor in a
          cattle stampede that killed twenty
          people. Another time I was riding some
          Colorado rapids with my buddies. We went
          over. They all died. I got caught on a
          tree branch. Saved my life. One time I was
          in a hotel fire down in Laredo, wiped out
          the whole damn place except me. I fell out
          of a window into one of them big iron
          garbage bins. Like Uncle Dandy said, "It
          ain't just your good luck, boy, it's
          their bad luck."

                    GOOD OLE BOY II
          Well, you sure got these slickers in a
          heap of shit.

                    CHARLIE
          I been easin' up on 'em. We got eight
          days, fellas, and I ain't never been one
          to rush. I got the plan all worked out.
          Uncle Dandy always told me, "When the big
          fish is runnin' keep the deep water on your
          flank."
                    (sadly)
          Dandy passed away two months ago. I'm
          gonna win this one for him, fellas. I just
          gotta.

Here we've got a little character wrinkle with Charlie. He's been born with extraordinary luck, but it also seems that those who oppose him are saddled with bad luck. We also have his motivation for winning, his beloved Uncle Dandy.

I tried to build sympathy for Charlie, who will meet a terrible end. As I mentioned elsewhere, I got many letters, some of them angry, about Charlie having to die. A writer can't hope to get a better validation of character.

This is also where BACKSTORY can work to advantage. Here he's talking with some good ole boys about his past. This is probably not the best way to do this, however. I tried to come up with some way to deliver this information about Charlie's past dramatically. I couldn't find one, and had to rely on this.

INT. WARD ROOM – SAME NIGHT

Kettle at his desk, making entries in his ledger. A KNOCK at the door. He closes the ledger and slides it into a drawer.

                              KETTLE
          Yup.

Augie enters, carrying his bottles of yeast, etc., which he
deposits on Kettle's desk.

                              KETTLE
          What have we got here?

                              AUGIE
          A little something I want you to mix up
          for me three times a day.

                              KETTLE
          The cook can do it for you.

                              AUGIE
          I want you to take care of it personally
          for me, Kettle—you know, so it's right.

                              KETTLE
                            (shrugs)
          Be glad to.

Augie takes out an emery board and does his nails.

                              AUGIE
          Couple other things. I want my uniform
          pressed, sharp creases. Shoes shined
          daily. I'm sure you've got some good
          French wine in store. Serve that up with
          the dinner meal. Fresh linen each day,
          along with my room scrubbed down. And my
          pillow is like a rock.

He pulls out a wad of money, peels off some bills and edges them
under a picture frame on the wall.

                              AUGIE
          'Preciate it.

EXT. 5″ GUN PLATFORM - SAME NIGHT

Animal sits on the platform, his bird cage and a bottle of
Scotch beside him. A trail of foam follows the ship.

                              ANIMAL
                            (to bird)
          Rough day, kiddo. I'm losing my ass to the
          cowboy. I don't know shit about Pfc.
          Charlie Buck, except he's the luckiest

sonofabitch I ever seen. No, fuck it, I
gotta give the kid credit—he knows his
poker. You shoulda seen what he did to
Santini. What he's doing to Epstein.

He takes a swig from the bottle.

> ANIMAL
> Epstein, he gives Jews a bad name. Mr.
> Wonderful, with the shades and the gold
> chain and the holier than thou. The guy
> has this ego problem. Whassamatter, a
> little windy for you. Here, lemme . . .

He covers up the cage against the wind.

> ANIMAL
> How's that?
> (beat)
> How 'bout Hubbard? Mr. Emotion. He's got
> two expressions, this and this. It's like
> reading a tree. Very tough, sweetheart,
> but I'll get to him. The old fatal flaw is
> in that bastard somewhere.
> (another swig)
> But the way things are going with the
> cowboy, I gotta do some fancy fucking
> dancing. I cannot go home empty handed.
> The family, Rosalie, they're all
> depending on me. I gotta win, which, my
> little yellow banana—depend on it—I
> will do.

In the above sequence we move from the general to the particular. Once
we've established the place, the mood, and the players themselves, we
begin to catch them in private moments, in which they reveal to us
individual anxieties, predilections, fears. We move closer to the characters, in private moments away from the poker table.

INT. HOLD - SECOND DAY

The players are hot and sweaty. Charlie Buck continues to win
big. The troops are seated behind their respective favorites.
The sentries and Kettle stand by. Arthur Willow makes book.

> CHARLIE
> And we got the blackeye bear for Cap'n
> Hubbard. A Little Plow for the

Sunglasses. Yessir, and Baby Jane for the
Pod.

                    AUGIE
Will you cut that out.

                    CHARLIE
                 (looks up)
Beg pardon!

                    AUGIE
Read 'em like they are.

                    CHARLIE
              (continues dealing)
That is how I read 'em, Mister Epstein. A
Mailbox for Mister Santini, and a double
bun for me. Bet the pair, Cap'n.

INT. HOLD – LATER – DAY

On Animal, looking ragged, chewing on a half-smoked cigar.

                    ANIMAL
       . . . five grand.

Animal and Santini play head to head. The others have folded.
Lots of money in the pot. Santini, nervous, has a low pile of
cash.

Animal has a low straight working to the eight. Santini shows
two tens. The last card has just been dealt.

                    SANTINI
I don't believe your straight, Edward.
I'll call.

Animal turns over a nine—he has it.

                    ANIMAL
You should have believed me, buddy.

Santini is unraveling.

Even before writing *The Crossing*, I knew I would have a problem
keeping the readers' interest on the game itself. Most readers might
know the game, but how many would look forward to reading about, and
then seeing, five guys sitting around a poker table. How, I asked myself,
could I keep them interested?

Some people told me not to worry. If I got the characters right, the reader would follow them anywhere. Maybe. My inner voice said: Think about it, Chris, would *you*, who knows poker, be willing to sit still for a lot of poker on the page? Would *you* take the time to figure out how each hand was unfolding? I think not. Watching movies (at least on the big screen), you don't get to stop and start. Things go by quickly. They must be clear, and if that fails, you must capture the essence of what's going on.

Consequently, I felt that I had to move quickly through the games until I landed on moments of big conflict.

As the writer, you have to be able to recognize lag time and be willing to adjust—to move everything through the story dramatically. To find a way to pump up the reader in the momentum of the moment.

Surprisingly, I got a lot of fan mail from women readers of the novel, few of whom wrote about any great interest in poker, but many of whom seemed very interested in the characters. The lesson here is that readers, or moviegoers, will follow strong characters when what the characters are doing might not be that fascinating.

INT. FOC'S'LE - NIGHT

Animal sleeps, a half-empty bottle of scotch by his head. We hear the faint strains of a guitar. The ship pitches and rolls. Animal opens an eye, sees Santini on his bunk scribbling in a notebook, a nightlight beside him.

                         ANIMAL
          Santini?

                         SANTINI
          Yes, Edward?

                         ANIMAL
          You can't keep doing this.

                         SANTINI
          Hmmm?

Animal pushes off the covers and sits up.

                         ANIMAL
          This. The scratching on the paper. The
          light. I know we all gotta make notes. I
          make mental notes. You write them down,
          that's terrific, but not at one in the
          morning. I can't sleep. I can't stay
          awake. It's one of them either-or

> situations. Either you turn off the light
> or I turn it off for you. I ain't a bad
> guy, but for chrissakes.

                    SANTINI
          I apologize for the inconvenience but
          there is little either of us can do,
          except to embrace the situation and all
          of its ramifications. I must win this
          poker game because my logic must prevail.
          Except that my system, once nearly
          infallible, is breaking down.

Animal cocks his head, bewildered.

                    SANTINI
          Discipline, Edward. Cerebral symmetry.
          The balance of nature. Eighteenth
          century. The Age of Reason. Versailles!
          Man's perfect gift to his perfect
          universe. God has been at Versailles.
          Alexander Pope. Leibnitz. The Great
          Chain of Being. Monads. Cause and Effect.
          Rousseau.

                    ANIMAL
          Santini, what the hell's this got to do
          with you scratchin' in your pad at this
          time of night!

                    SANTINI
          Rousseau believed that the Lisbon
          earthquake was caused by too many people
          living in Lisbon. Their weight caused it.
          The Age of Reason collapsed into
          Romanticism. Is this what's happening
          here. My God.

                    ANIMAL
          And this Rousseau was a thinker?

                    SANTINI
          Of the most imaginative kind.

                    ANIMAL
          I can believe that.

Santini pinches the St. Christopher medal around his neck.

                    SANTINI
          My mother used to tell me—and I am

>convinced she was right—that I am the
>natural inheritor of the consciousness
>of these great men's thoughts. In the
>system of things, I am the conduit
>through which history passes. Locke.
>Diderot.

>   ANIMAL
>Hold it!

Santini looks at him.

>   ANIMAL
>You caught something! Back at Madame
>Claude's. I don't know how but, for
>chrissakes, why didn't I see it before?
>You know what a disease like this can do
>to somebody's brain? Look what it's done
>to yours.

>   SANTINI
>Excuse me, Edward, I must get back to my
>system.

>   ANIMAL
>To sleep, Santini.

He gets up and turns off the light.

>   ANIMAL
>   (in darkness)
>To sleep.

Let's take a look at elements in the above scene in terms of *Context:* Santini is losing and it's important to show the effect it has on him. He's going a little strange, as witnessed through Animal's eyes. He is breaking down. His system is fallible. Against pure luck, what system isn't? Santini, the thinker, is trying to use history to explain it. Animal hasn't got a clue what he's talking about, but in his own way he tries to give him solace.

From a technical point of view, we should always begin a scene at The Last Possible Moment. In this case, I thought about starting the scene up on deck, or in the mess hall, and then moving them down into the fo'c'sle. But why bother? Get to the crux of each scene. Ask yourself what the scene's *purpose* is. And then get to it.

It's been a long day. Animal needs sleep and Santini is obsessing over his losses. This is creating problems.

You also ask yourself if the scene adds to the heroes' chief goal? They both want to win but each has a different attitude about it. This creates conflict and tension.

Does the scene have its own beginning, middle, and end? I think so. It starts with Animal trying to get some sleep while Santini scratches away on his system. The light is on or the light is off. They can't have it both ways.

How does each character feel? Animal wants sleep, he's lost money at the table, he wants to be fresh. He's irritated at Santini. We also see Animal's sympathy toward Santini showing through. Santini, in the throes of despair, has lost a lot and is in jeopardy of losing everything, including his grip.

Leave us wondering at the end of the scene: Will Santini recover? Is he losing his mind? What will this do to Animal?

Another element here is BACKSTORY. Earlier I used Charlie's scene with the good ole boys to show how it shouldn't be done. Here we find out about Santini through his discombobulated mind. He's entering a kind of madness. He tells the story to his new buddy, Animal. And his method is painful confession. Much more effective. Try never to deliver this kind of autobiographical information through conventional exposition. Juice it up, make it work through the drama.

EXT. DECK - DAY

Overcast. Troops are lined up, waiting to go into the hold. A MERCHANT SEAMAN holds a cap with small pieces of paper.

> SEAMAN
> Step right up, gentlemen. Place your bet
> on the moment of Santini's death at the
> card table.

He holds up a few slips of paper.

> SEAMAN
> I got four o'clock. I got four-fifteen. I
> got four-thirty. I got the winner in my
> hand. For ten dollars—one thin sawbuck—
> take a fortune home to your family.

Animal, in a wrinkled uniform and thick beard, comes down the ladder.

> ANIMAL
> Good morning, you degenerates!

He pulls a cigar from his pocket. A number of matches are struck.

                    ANIMAL
          Awright, the forecast of the day, Santini
          makes a comeback.

"Bullshit!" "No Way!" Laughter.

                    ANIMAL
                (holds up his hands)
          Hey, I didn't say he was gonna win.
                (beat)
          As for my own playing, I can personally
          guarantee you that I have discovered bad
          habits in two of the players—which gives
          me a major shot at taking it all. So,
          that's it. Santini comes back. Hubbard
          and Eppy take a dive. The cowboy remains
          the same. For you day-by-day bettors, I
          recommend me.

Animal pushes through the crowd and disappears into the hold.

INT. HOLD - NIGHT

The players, minus Santini, are at the table. The money has been
divided, the decks ready. Kettle and his sentries are in
position. The troops clamor above deck, waiting to enter.

                    AUGIE
          Where the hell is Santini?

                    ANIMAL
          Last time I seen him was in the john.

                    HUBBARD
          Mister Kettle, would you send one of your
          men to find him?

                    KETTLE
          Right away.

                    SANTINI
                (O.S.)
          Edward . . .

They all turn toward the ladder where Santini hangs desperately
onto a stanchion. His face is dead white and his eyes are black
studs driven back into their sockets. Animal gets up and goes
over to him.

                        ANIMAL
            What's the matter, buddy?

                        SANTINI
                    (barely audible)
            My system. Somebody stole my system.

                        ANIMAL
            Stole your system?

                        SANTINI
            The notebook's not in the room. It's not
            anywhere. I must ask you, Edward, did you
            have anything to do with it?

Animal starts to protest.

                        SANTINI
            You said it was a waste of time. I thought
            perhaps you were trying to do me a favor.

                        ANIMAL
            I didn't take it.

                        SANTINI
            You understand why I had to ask?

                        ANIMAL
            Sure, sure . . .

Animal leads him back to the table.

                        ANIMAL
                    (to the others)
            Somebody swiped Santini's system, his
            notepad. Anybody know anything about it?

                        AUGIE
            I'd have thought about it if he was ahead.

                        ANIMAL
            Hubbard?

                        HUBBARD
            Nothing.

                        ANIMAL
            Cowboy?

                        CHARLIE
            When did it happen?

                    SANTINI
When I was in the shower . . .

                    AUGIE
Where were you, Podberoski, when he was
in the shower?

                    ANIMAL
Goosing him with the soap. I was right
there with him.

                    AUGIE
Hubbard and I were in our room.

                    CHARLIE
Looks like I'm the varmint.

                    ANIMAL
Don't sweat it, Cowboy. My canary is a
better suspect.

                    AUGIE
                (to Kettle)
And where were you?

                    KETTLE
Setting up down here.

                    AUGIE
Who is normally around our quarters at
that time?

                    KETTLE
Nobody in particular.

                    AUGIE
And everybody in general.

                    HUBBARD
The question is whether Santini wants to
continue.

                    ANIMAL
                (to Santini)
Think about that, buddy. You were doing
shitty with the notes, without them you
might shake up the cards.

                    HUBBARD
. . . or you can take what you have left
and spend it in a better place.

                              SANTINI
                              (a beat)
              I'll play.

A cheer comes up from the troops.

Okay, here we go. The stakes climb higher. Somebody has tried to
sabotage Santini by stealing his system. This is the first real indication
that things are not what they seem. Who stole Santini's system? One of
the players? Somebody else? Here I had to start planting more clues in
the fields of suspicion so that I could later reap the rewards.

INT. HOLD - MONTAGE - NIGHT

A montage of card playing scenes. Charlie, pulling
extraordinary hands, continues to win. His rooting section
grows and has to be quieted by Kettle. Hubbard seems to be
getting irritated by Charlie's luck. Santini remains the big
loser.

We treat the passage of time by using a montage. A montage is the rapid
acceleration of short scenes to create the impression of zipping through
a few days or hours. In a script that takes place over a few days' time, as
this one does, a montage works wonders. In longer time periods, you
can show time passing through the changing of the seasons, through the
length of one's hair, or the wear and tear on one's face, on the occasion
of birthdays or other celebrations.

INT. HOLD - NIGHT

Charlie deals the first card down.

                              CHARLIE
              Benny's Bullet for the Cap'n. Quatro One.
              A Sixeroo. Next-to-you, Mistuh Santini,
              and a deucer. Bet the Bullet, Cap'n.

                              HUBBARD
                              (snaps)
              One hundred.

Augie calls. Animal folds. Santini calls.

                    CHARLIE
Adios.
                (folds)
Pot's right.
                (he deals)
Dusty Muzzle, Lady Lou, and a double bum
for Mr. S. Bullet still lives, Cap'n sir,
that's you.

                    HUBBARD
                (flash of anger)
Yes, I know. Five hundred.

                    AUGIE
I'm in.

                    SANTINI
Make it fifteen hundred.

                    CHARLIE
That's a thousand, Cap'n.

                    HUBBARD
I know that, Buck!

                    CHARLIE
Jeez, sir, ah was just tryin' to be
helpful. When my Uncle Dandy . . .

                    HUBBARD
Buck!
                (beat, calms down)
I'll call.

                    AUGIE
I won't.

Charlie taps the table with his knuckles and deals. Hubbard
shows an ace, seven, and two of different suits, Santini a
different ten, eight, seven.

                    HUBBARD
Check to you, Santini.

Santini nervously counts his nearly depleted pile of cash.

                    SANTINI
Five . . . five thousand . . . one, two,
three, four hundred. Five thousand, four
hundred dollars. That's my bet.

He slides the money in.

> HUBBARD
> I'll call, and raise . . .

> SANTINI
> That's all I have, Captain.

> HUBBARD
> In that case, deal the last card, Buck.

> CHARLIE
> Comin' up.

Deals a spade jack to Hubbard and a diamond nine to Santini.

> CHARLIE
> Straight working on the right. Bullet's
> still king.

> HUBBARD
> No bet.

> CHARLIE
> Turn 'em over.

The hold is silent. Hubbard turns over his hole card, a seven.
He has two of them. Santini turns over the case eight, giving
him the high pair. A cheer goes up. He rakes in the pot, a smile
on his face.

Here I wanted Santini to win, if only to reverse the reader's expectations. Reverse expectations when you can. It generates surprise and
drama. But don't milk it. Then it feels false.

INT. OFFICER'S MESS - THIRD NIGHT

Charlie and Augie eat. The exercise-conscious Augie has his
health drink, a small portion of food, a bottle of French wine.
Charlie eats heaps of mashed potatoes, gravy-covered biscuits,
a big glass of milk.

> AUGIE
> You know the difference between us,
> Charlie?

> CHARLIE
> (with a mouthful of potatoes)
> Whassat?

                    AUGIE
          You eat. I dine.

Augie dabs his lips with his napkin. Hubbard enters.

                    AUGIE
          Hello, Hubbard. Enjoy your dinner, if you
          can keep it down.

He exits. Hubbard sits.

                    CHARLIE
          Cap'n.

                    HUBBARD
          Hello, Buck.

Fumi, the chief cook, a Filipino, enters and hands Hubbard a
mimeographed copy of today's menu. Hubbard points to numbers
one, three, and six. Fumi exits. Hubbard inspects the label of
Augie's bottle of wine.

                    HUBBARD
                 (over his shoulder)
          And a glass, please!

Charlie continues to stuff himself.

                    HUBBARD
          Tell me, Buck. How was the poker back in
          New York City?

                    CHARLIE
          Mighty fast, sir.

                    HUBBARD
          The officer who visited you on board in
          Antwerp, Major Tat? He's your commanding
          officer?

                    CHARLIE
          My business manager.

                    HUBBARD
          And what is his association with Sir
          Bertram Foote?

                    CHARLIE
          Far as I know, Mister Foote heard about my
          playing and invited me in. What other

> questions would you like to ask me,
> Cap'n?

                    HUBBARD
> You've won a quarter of a million dollars
> in three days, plus the fact that no one
> knows anything about you. I'm curious.

                    CHARLIE
> If I wasn't so easygoing, I could take
> real offense at what you're suggesting
> here, Cap'n, but I ain't gonna start
> defending myself 'cause there ain't
> nothing to defend against.
>   (beat)
> My Uncle Dandy once told me that a great
> poker player never has to look at his
> cards, just the other fella's faces. And,
> I'll tell yuh, I've been looking at your
> faces these past two days, and I ain't
> seen a winner in the bunch.
>   (smiles)
> No offense, sir.

Hubbard looks at him without expression.

Here we have Hubbard starting to ask questions. He doesn't trust anyone. He's already looking over his shoulder as a result of the murder in the Casablanca street. Here character comes to life through suspicion. In movies nobody ever agrees with anybody. Conflict moves things forward. Hubbard pushes, but Charlie doesn't back down. The kid has moxie.

INT. FO'C'SLE - EARLY FOURTH MORNING

Animal sleeps. The CANARY suddenly SQUAWKS. Animal's eyes pop open. Over the PA system the SOUND of airplane engines.

                    ANIMAL
> Hit the deck!

He flies out of bed and scrambles under the bunk. Santini sits erect in his bunk.

Animal, under his bunk, covers his head. The SOUND of the Army Air Corps theme song, "Off we go, into the wild blue yonder." Animal lifts his head and sees Augie in the doorway with a big smile.

                    ANIMAL
Very fucking funny!

                    AUGIE
So that's how she does it. What a bird!

EXT. DECK - DAY

Sheets of rain, tumbling seas.

INT. HOLD - DAY

Air thick with cigar and cigarette smoke. Charlie and Augie
play head to head. Charlie turns over a pair of kings.

                    CHARLIE
My Black-Eyed Bears.

Augie throws his cards in disgust.

                    AUGIE
It's like playing against God.

INT. HOLD - DAY - LATER

Santini turns a winning hand and rakes in the pot. His confidence
is showing.

                    ANIMAL
You and your system.

INT. HOLD - DAY - LATER

Animal deals the first round down, the second up.

                    ANIMAL
Jack bets.

                    AUGIE
One thousand.

                    ANIMAL
Already? I'm outta here.

                    SANTINI
Call.

                    CHARLIE
By me.

                         HUBBARD
          No.

                         ANIMAL
                   (picking up the cards)
          Very boring.
                      (deals to Santini)
          Seven on the six and for Mr.
          Wonderful . . .
                   (he deals Augie an eight)
          Nothing. Still the jack.

                         AUGIE
          Two grand.

Santini drums on the table as if it's an adding machine.

                         SANTINI
          Call.

                         ANIMAL
                   (dealing)
          Hot king for my roommate, and a nine, and
          a possible straight. Bet the king.

                         SANTINI
          I'll check to the power.

Augie removes his sunglasses and wipes them with his
handkerchief. He runs his fingers through his hair, checks his
nails.

                         ANIMAL
          While we wait for the beauty parlor,
          Kettle, would you get me a glass of water?

Kettle motions for a steward, who brings the water.

                         AUGIE
          Two more.

He puts two thousand dollars in the pot.

                         SANTINI
          I'm in.

                         ANIMAL
          Last card coming. Pair of sixes and eight
          balls. Poker goes up. Okay, Eppy, go
          wild.

The troops lean in for a closer look. Money changes hands.

                    AUGIE
               (counting bills)
          Ten big ones.
                    (puts ten thousand dollars in)

                    ANIMAL
          Ten big ones, he says.

Kettle motions for the bleacher noise to quiet.

                    SANTINI
               (long beat)
          Call . . .

                    ANIMAL

          Okay . . .

                    SANTINI
          . . . and raise. All that I have, twenty-
          eight thousand and change.

                    AUGIE
          Forget the change. I'll call the twenty-
          eight G's.

Santini turns over his hole card. Tension builds.

                    SANTINI
          Three little sixes.

He reaches for the pot. Augie holds up his hand.

                    AUGIE
          Uh, uh. Read 'em and weep.

He turns his third eight, a winner.

Santini is stunned. The hold is DEADLY SILENT—a moment of
repose for the game's first casualty. Santini is bust. After a
moment, he stands.

                    SANTINI
               (with great dignity)
          Thank you, gentlemen.

He walks slowly away from the table, draping a rain poncho over
his shoulders, and climbs the ladder out of the hold.

                          CHARLIE
                    (breaking the silence)
              A fresh deck, Mister Kettle, if you
              please.

Kettle hands him one.

One down, four to go. Santini, having lost his system, goes south. The
plot thickens. You want your reader to wonder who's next.

   I thought I'd mention something about dialogue here. From the beginning I knew I would have to give each character a distinctive voice,
a way of saying things all their own. In the poker scenes I needed to
jazz up the dialogue to keep it interesting.

   As far as each individual character is concerned, I decided to give
Charlie a folksy confidence, Animal a Brooklynese dees, dems, and
doze quirky way of saying things. Augie the journalist is educated and
sly and confrontational. Santini, a man in love with the past, and very
precise, very orderly, as his penchant for the eighteenth century would
suggest, is also scholarly and, when things goes awry, his facade breaks
down and he becomes emotional. Hubbard, the only officer, is a wasp
and military brat rebelling against authority. I tried to show him as
someone caught in a vise between what he should do and his need to
break free of the regimen. At times he's shy, at others abrupt.

   The language they use reflects these aspects. I chose this point in the
story to bring up dialogue because it was here, during the first-draft
writing of *The Crossing*, that for the first time the characters began
speaking in their own voices. In your own work you'll experience the
same thing.

   Suddenly, whether it's halfway through the story or near the end of
the first draft, the characters start talking to you. They take on lives of
their own, over which you begin to have less control. When this happens it's a signal to the writer that the characters are growing into
themselves. This is an excellent sign; it shows that the true collaboration—that which exists between a writer and his characters—has begun
to change and grow.

   This relationship begins to work in the following sequence as the
focus settles on Augie, when he confronts Hubbard, Fumi the cook, and
the purser, Larry Kettle.

   Augie the journalist starts to dig aggressively. He senses that things
are not what they seem. He also, as a poker player, knows with Santini's
departure, that his own chances to win just went up. He begins with one
of his opponents, Hubbard, asking questions, taunting, all the while
gathering information. With Augie suspecting that something is amiss,

he uses his journalistic talents. He worries aloud about Charlie Buck's phenomenal luck, hoping to get from Hubbard his own thoughts on this. He suggests that something has to break Charlie's rhythm.

On one level this script has now become a mystery—soon to become a murder mystery—but you don't want to give the bad guy away. It's your job to now create suspicion.

INT. FO'C'SLE - 4TH NIGHT

Hubbard is propped up in bed, writing a letter. Augie, fully dressed, sits on his bunk.

> AUGIE
> . . . sounds like you had it made in Casablanca. The Consulate. Afternoon teas . . .

> HUBBARD
> (ironically)
> Utter paradise . . . except for the boredom, the heat, the stench, the food . . . the squalor.

> AUGIE
> A rich kid like you would be attracted by that. There must have been some good money games.

> HUBBARD
> I had to travel for the big ones. In fact, Santini once buried me in a game in Marseilles.

> AUGIE
> I'm glad he's out of this one. Something's got to break the cowboy's rhythm. Any suggestions?

Hubbard looks up at him, expressionless. Augie stands and wraps a trench coat around himself.

> AUGIE
> Think about it. See you later.

He exits.

In the next scene Augie moves ahead. He goes after Fumi, the cook, using intimidation tactics. He uses something small—the absence of meat—to create something large. He will take whatever he can from

this confrontation and build upon it in the next. He's direct, knowing
there isn't time to beat around. Things he can't identify have been set in
motion. As a journalist, he smells it.

INT. GALLEY - SAME NIGHT

Fumi, the first cook, sits at the metal table. The galley is old
but clean. The cabinets are metal, some with rusted handles. A
meat locker. Chopping blocks.

Fumi's pet CAT, a black scraggly thing, eats off a plate. Fumi
wears filthy, food-stained whites, his baker's cap squashed into
his rear pocket.

                         AUGIE
                         (O.S.)
            Hey, Cookee.

Fumi looks up and sees Augie.

                         AUGIE
            I want to talk to you.

Fumi taps his chest with his index finger.

                         FUMI
            I am Fumi, no Cookee.

He stands as Augie approaches him.

                         AUGIE
            I got a question for you. The last couple
            of days I've been noticing on your
            sparkling uniform there, blood.

Fumi looks down at his uniform and sees the stains.

                         AUGIE
            That's steak blood, Cookee, which means
            somewhere on this dreamboat is steak.

                         FUMI
            No, no steak.

                         AUGIE
            How about roast beef? Roast beef blood?

Augie pulls Fumi closer so that their faces nearly touch.

                         AUGIE
          You serve me rotten potatoes. Your
          sandwiches make me sick. The coffee? What
          can I say, Cookee, sometimes it's brown
          and sometimes it isn't. It tastes like
          shit, which in fact it may be. I want to
          know about the blood. Uncle Augie's gonna
          count to three. One . . .

Fumi tries to break Augie's grip.

                         FUMI
          I no know! I no know!

Augie grips him tighter.

                         AUGIE
          Two . . .

Fumi's eyes are bulging from their sockets.

                         AUGIE
          Three . . .

Augie looks ready to do real damage.

                         FUMI
          Okay, okay . . .

Augie loosens his grip and lets him down. Fumi relaxes, turns,
starts off. Augie grabs him, hauls him off the floor, and bashes
him against the cabinets.

                         FUMI
          Over there! Over there!

Fumi, dazed, leads him toward the meat locker.

INT. MEAT LOCKER - NIGHT

Six sides of beef hang from overhead steel runners on meat
hooks. Augie inspects them.

                         AUGIE
          What's the weight?

                         FUMI
          Nine hundred, a thousand pounds.

                         AUGIE
          A thousand pounds of beef? For what?

FUMI
(smiling nervously)
For you.

AUGIE
And the reason I haven't been getting
any?

FUMI
No can tell.

AUGIE
Who does the meat belong to?

FUMI
(beat)
Purser. Mister Kettle.

AUGIE
Is that right?

FUMI
I have told you nothing. You have not
talked to Fumi.

Augie gives him a deadpan look.

The next scene builds upon the last, completing the sequence. Here the dialogue reveals the characters' emotional states along with their moods, intelligence, temperaments, and attitudes—told through the twin veils of conflict and tension. Nothing moves forward in any story except through tension and conflict.

INT. CORRIDOR OUTSIDE LAUNDRY - NIGHT

Purser Larry Kettle exits with Charlie's neatly pressed cowboy pants and shirt draped over his arm. He heads down the corridor and makes a turn. He is startled by Augie, leaning casually against a bulkhead.

AUGIE
Hello, Kettle, how are you?

KETTLE
Jes' fine, yourself?

He starts past Augie, who puts a hand on his shoulder and walks alongside.

                    AUGIE
         Did you know that within the last five
         weeks twenty-five thousand tons of black-
         market butter changed hands in Paris, and
         that bombed-out bridges held up legal
         goods while black-market trucks crossed
         rivers like magic.

                    KETTLE
         Interestin'.

                    AUGIE
         And that whole trainloads of food have
         been reported lost, including the
         locomotives?

                    KETTLE
         Really, now?

They reach the ladder but before Kettle can climb up, Augie
steps in front, blocking his way.

                    AUGIE
         Have you ever heard of Rabbit Toland,
         Mister Kettle?

                    KETTLE
         No.

                    AUGIE
         Rabbit Toland was the purser on the
         Liberty Ship *Robert Louis Stevenson*.
         Sold eight hundred jeeps to the Krauts in
         Sicily.

Kettle says nothing.

                    AUGIE
         Old Rabbit was caught and tried, but he
         was innocent as a lamb, he told me, wanted
         the world press to know that. Then he told
         me about Merchant Marine pursers who
         weren't so innocent.

                    KETTLE
         Why is it you're telling me all this?

                    AUGIE
         By way of introduction, Mister Kettle, to
         inquire as to the reason why a thousand
         pounds of beef are hanging in your
         freezer.

Kettle shows a sudden flicker of uncertainty.

>   KETTLE
>   What beef?

>   AUGIE
>   Six sides . . . on hooks.

>   KETTLE
>   What about it? I own it. I paid for it.
>   It's mine.

>   AUGIE
>   Let me put it to you this way. You have
>   some two hundred—odd troops being fed
>   slop because you probably sold all the
>   good food to a black marketeer. If just
>   one of those troops learns about that
>   beef, you'll have a mutiny on your hands.
>   You want that?

Kettle says nothing.

>   AUGIE
>   I want steak. I want it served to me and
>   the other players. Every day.

>   KETTLE
>   What about all your poor underfed troops?

>   AUGIE
>   That's your problem. Tonight, Kettle.
>   Steak. Got it?

>   KETTLE
>   Yeah, I got it.

Augie looks down and sees that Kettle has squashed Charlie's
clothes into a ball.

>   AUGIE
>   You'd better give those another press.

Kettle does an about-face and stalks back to the laundry.

>   AUGIE
>   Oh, and Kettle . . .

Kettle turns back.

                              AUGIE
           The steak . . . I like mine rare.

The following sequence adds fuel to the inciting incident—when Hubbard kills the major in the Casablanca street. Remember that as the
writer you have to reap what you sow. You plant little reminders along
the way that whatever problem occurred at the Inciting Incident has to
be resolved by the end of the story.

    In this case Hubbard has a nightmare, followed by Animal finding
evidence that he will later use against Hubbard to try to throw the
officer off his game.

    One of the most difficult things about writing is to keep the entire
story in your head as you move forward scene by scene. Extensive
outlining in the beginning will keep you from spiraling off and giving
up, hopelessly lost and confused.

    Exercise patience in the beginning. Resist getting to the "real writ-
ing" before doing the gut work of outlining. The more you outline and
foreshadow in the beginning the easier it will be for you to keep the
story in your head and go forward.

INT. FO'C'SLE - SAME NIGHT

Hubbard sleeps, perspiring heavily. He is in the middle of a
nightmare.

EXT. CASABLANCA STREET/DREAM - NIGHT

A reenactment of the night Hubbard shot the RAF Major in the
Casablanca street. He inspects the Major's body, the Major's
face metamorphoses into that of Major General Evan Hubbard III,
Hubbard's father. His name plate reads: HUBBARD. We hear the
SOUND of a whistle.

INT. FO'C'SLE - NIGHT

Hubbard jerks up in his bed, bathed in sweat. The whistle
belongs to the ship. Hubbard drops back in his pillow, staring
at the ceiling.

INT. FO'C'SLE - EARLY SAME MORNING (4:00 A.M.)

Animal wakes, climbs out of bed and into his unlaced boots.
Wrapping a trench coat around himself, he trudges out.

INT. LATRINE - NIGHT

Stalls with metal dividers, a bank of sinks. An overhead bulb
sways in the pitch and roll of the ship. Animal, dopey with
sleep, enters and eases himself onto the cold toilet seat. He
rests his elbows on his knees and drops his head. He sits for a
moment.

He spots something on the floor—two sheets of handwritten paper.
He picks them up.

                    ANIMAL
                  (reading)
          "Dear Father, read this letter
          carefully; it has been a long time in the
          making . . ."

He mumbles another line or two, then:

                    ANIMAL
          ". . . furthermore I am aware that you
          transferred Colonel Morley to the
          Casablanca Consulate to spy on my
          activities . . ."

He mumbles another line or two, then:

                    ANIMAL
          ". . . and I heard through reliable
          sources that you are openly seducing
          British secretaries while your wife—my
          mother—waits at home . . ."

He drops the letter, thinks, then reads on.

                    ANIMAL
          "I have my own life now. Stay away from
          me. Send no more spies. Do me no more
          favors . . ."

Animal goes to turn the page but there isn't one. He searches
the floor.

                    ANIMAL
          C'mon, Hubby, don't lose me now.

He's wide awake, studying the pieces of paper. A wry smile
crosses his lips.

Once again, all screenplays are built on a foundation of setups and payoffs, the glue that holds story and plot together. Here we return, through Hubbard's dream, to Casablanca, and to his problems with his father—which torment Hubbard. We might wonder if this is another ploy by the saboteur to try to drive somebody else out of the game. Has someone purposely left these pages for Animal to find, or do they just happen to be there? We'll see.

INT. FO'C'SLE — DAY

Charlie does fancy tricks with a deck of cards. He senses something, turns. Animal stands there in a towel, carrying toilet gear.

>   ANIMAL
>   Your Uncle Dandy teach you that?

>   CHARLIE
>   That's right.

>   ANIMAL
>   Classy stuff.

>   CHARLIE
>   (big smile)
>   Thank you, Mr. P.

EXT. CORRIDOR — DAY

Animal nods and goes down the corridor to Augie and Hubbard's door. Augie exercises, Hubbard is dressing.

>   ANIMAL
>   (a little wave)
>   Hi, girls.

He gives Hubbard an exaggerated wink.

INT. FO'C'SLE — DAY

Santini sits rigidly on his bunk. Animal enters, puts his shaving gear in the wall locker, and takes out an envelope.

>   ANIMAL
>   Santini.

Santini's normally slicked-back hair springs from his scalp like electrician's wires.

                              ANIMAL
          Santini?

                              SANTINI
          What?

                              ANIMAL
          Over here.

                              SANTINI
                    (his voice is hollow)
          Yes, Edward.

                              ANIMAL
          It can't be all that bad, buddy. I mean,
          Christ, you're goin' home which you ain't
          been back to in how long?

                              SANTINI
          Seven years.

                              ANIMAL
          So, cheer up, for chrissakes.

Animal pulls the rain poncho off the bird cage and peers in.

                              ANIMAL
          Good morning, sweetheart. Chow time.

He opens the cage door and places feed inside. He sits on the
bunk with the envelope.

                              ANIMAL
          What are you gonna do when you get home?

                              SANTINI
          Continue to play cards, I suppose.

                              ANIMAL
          With what?

                              SANTINI
          I'll manage.

                              ANIMAL
          You got some dough stashed back home?

                              SANTINI
          In fact, I'm rather without funds at the
          moment.

                    ANIMAL
        In that case, there's something I want to
        talk to you about.
                    (holds up the envelope)
        I didn't get a chance to tell you last
        night, but the other guys and me, we got
        together and . . .

He hands the envelope to Santini.

                    SANTINI
        What is it?

                    ANIMAL
        Open it and find out.

Santini pulls out a wad of money, looks at it, returns the bills
to the envelope and hands it back.

                    SANTINI
        I can't accept this, Edward.

Animal looks at him as if he's crazy.

                    ANIMAL
        I don't want to hear it, Santini. You've
        got it. It's yours. End of story.

He starts to dress.

                    SANTINI
        I mean it, Edward.

                    ANIMAL
        I can't hear you.

Over Santini's whimpering protests, Animal finishes dressing.

                    SANTINI
        Then may I say thank you for . . .

                    ANIMAL
        Nope.

INT. GAME — DAY

Augie, Animal, and Charlie have been dealt their fourth cards
by Hubbard, who has dropped from the hand. Augie has a jack-
nine-king showing; Animal a king-eight-six; Charlie a ten-
queen-jack.

                         HUBBARD
          King-jack.

                         AUGIE
          Five grand.

                         ANIMAL
          I should live so long. Good night.
                         (folds)

                         CHARLIE
          Yessir, I'll call that.

                         HUBBARD
                         (dealing)
          Four . . . and a possible straight.
          King's still high.

                         AUGIE
          I'll bet another five.

                         CHARLIE
          Only five, Mr. E.? Now, what would my Uncle
          Dandy do under these conditions?

                         AUGIE
          Not what you're about to do, Cowboy.

                         CHARLIE
          How much you got over there, Mr. E., in
          your pile of cash.

Augie makes a quick count.

                         AUGIE
          Forty seven thousand.

                         CHARLIE
          That's my bet.

He counts the money and puts it in. Augie leans back surveying
the situation. He takes a linen handkerchief from his pocket
and cleans his sunglasses.

                         CHARLIE
          You ain't gonna find the answer there.

                         AUGIE
          That's one thing you haven't learned,
          Charlie, my boy—to button it up at
          critical moments. I'll call.

                    (puts in the money)
          Show me that straight.

                         CHARLIE
          Don't have it.
                    (turns over hole card, an ace)
          But I got the big one.

                         AUGIE
          Close . . .
                    (turns over the second jack)
          . . . but no cookie.

Charlie shrugs, but the irritation is there.

                         CHARLIE
          'Scuse me, gentlemen.

He rises. The guard steps behind his pile of cash. Augie rakes
in the winnings. He raises his water glass in a toast.

                         AUGIE
          To the transposition of fate. It's about
          time.

                         ANIMAL
          I'd like to drink to that, Eppy, but I
          ain't seen none of that fate transposed
          over here.

                         AUGIE
          You'll get yours.

Animal lights a cigar and looks over at Hubbard.

                         ANIMAL
          You know, Hubbard, you remind me of
          what's-his-name who gave up his throne to
          marry that American broad.

Let's talk about subplots for a moment. Remember that plot drives the
action, subplot carries the theme—exploring relationships among the
characters. In *The Crossing* the game drives the story—as the Liberty
Ship brings the soldiers back home from war—while at the same time
dark forces are at work sabotaging the game.

   The subplots, of which there are many, delineate the relationships. If
plot is the story's engine, the subplots concentrate on the actual moving
parts. The function of the subplot is to expand the story in a more

human way. Each subplot should have a beginning, middle, and end and move the story forward.

One of the things I had to do with this story was extricate each subplot from the main story and take a look at it. Did I need it? Did it go somewhere and not peter out? Did each subplot support, and intersect, the main plot and not become just a creative indulgence?

In this case, Hubbard's relationship with his father is key. Not only does it go right to the heart of Hubbard's character, it is now being used by another player as ammunition in the poker game. Furthermore, Hubbard's trouble with his father sparks our memory of Hubbard's murder in the Casablanca street. In other words, one function of the subplot is to use it as a lightning rod to spark other story elements throughout the story. Think of it as a snake that appears and disappears as it slithers through the story, creating all sorts of tension and drama.

> HUBBARD
> The Duke of Windsor.

> ANIMAL
> You ever been to England?

> HUBBARD
> On occasion.

> ANIMAL
> Yeah? Whaddaya think of them British
> secretaries?

> HUBBARD
> (beat)
> British secretaries?

> AUGIE
> I'll tell you about British secretaries.
> Blotchy skin. Rotten teeth. Lazy lovers.
> (to Animal)
> I have a question for you. What happened
> with you and Santini in the Antwerp whore
> house?

> ANIMAL
> Do you mind, I'm talking to the captain
> here.

> AUGIE
> C'mon, Pod, don't be modest.

                    ANIMAL
        It was nothin' you woulda lived through.
        Ambushed by a Nazi goon. Chased down a
        mountain of broken glass. In five years of
        battle, I never came so close to cashing
        it in.

                    AUGIE
        All because you wouldn't pay the poor
        girl? You oughta be ashamed of yourself.

                    ANIMAL
        I hope you had better sources of
        information at your newspaper.

                    AUGIE
        C'mon, Pod, you can level with a son of a
        rabbi. Admit it. You couldn't get it up.

                    ANIMAL
        My heart goes out to you, Eppy, but don't
        put your life story on me.

Charlie returns from the john.

                    CHARLIE
        Okay, fellas, I lightened my load and now
        I'm gonna be tough to beat.

                    ANIMAL
        You're such a charmer, Cowboy. It's your
        deal.

INT. GAME — LATE AFTERNOON

The hold is filled with smoke. The troops are hot and tired.

Augie is the dealer. He and Charlie have folded. Animal and
Hubbard play head to head. After four cards, Animal has a ten
high, Hubbard a queen high.

                    ANIMAL
        You were stationed down in Casablanca,
        Hubbard, that right?

                    HUBBARD
        That's right. I'll bet five hundred.

                    ANIMAL
        Didja ever run into an old buddy of mine
        down there by the name of Colonel Morley?

Hubbard reacts to the name.

                    AUGIE
          You guys still playin' cards or what?
          Five hundred to you, Pod.

                    ANIMAL
          I'll match that five hundred and a
          thousand dollars more, in the name of my
          old pal, Colonel Morley. How about it,
          Captain? You gonna chase me?

                    HUBBARD
                    (beat)
          No, I don't think so.

Animal turns over his hole card, a loser.

                    ANIMAL
          Can't afford to get rattled, now, can we?

Hubbard's problems in Casablanca take on new life, now being used by Animal as a psychological weapon in the game. This piece of information not only shows Hubbard's state of mind, but also reinforces that psychological glitch—fear of father—that has bugged him for as long as he can remember.

As the writer you have to carry these character traits throughout the script, searching for places where they can be used to shake things up.

INT. CAPTAIN'S STATEROOM — NIGHT

Captain Sam Murphy sleeps. A SOUND as if the ship is under attack, pitching and rolling violently. Murphy's eyes pop open. He bolts out of the sack, pulls on his clothes and boots. Groggy, he makes his way to the door.

EXT. CORRIDOR — NIGHT

Murphy crawls out as towering wave crashes over him. He holds onto a rail, barely able to make out the bridge lights through the storm.

Merchant Seamen struggle by him in life jackets with small red lights blinking on their lapels. Murphy struggles forward and reaches the ladder leading to the bridge. He starts up. A huge wave snaps him back. He manages to hang on, continues up.

INT. WHEELHOUSE — NIGHT

Radio operator FLYNN beeps out an SOS. Larry Kettle tries to
navigate. Sam Murphy bursts through the door.

>   MURPHY
>   I knew shooting that gull was bad news.
>   (to Flynn)
>   Anything?

>   FLYNN
>   No, sir.

>   KETTLE
>   The bridge steering is gone, Cap'n. We're
>   on emergency gear.

>   MURPHY
>   Terrific.
>   (he grabs the microphone)
>   Engine room! Engine room!

>   ENGINEER (O.S.)
>   Engine room.

>   MURPHY
>   Quarter speed. You hear me?

>   ENGINEER (O.S.)
>   Quarter speed.

>   MURPHY
>   Get somebody up to drop the starboard
>   anchor.

>   ENGINEER (O.S.)
>   The anchor chain is stuck, Captain. Sent
>   three men with hacksaws to cut it free.
>   Holy Fuck!

>   MURPHY
>   What? What!

>   ENGINEER (O.S.)
>   Fire! Fire broke out. Oh, My God! The
>   hoselines are . . .

>   MURPHY
>   Hello! Hello! Jesus H. Christ, Kettle,
>   get your ass down there and find out what's
>   going on.

                         KETTLE
          On my way.

Kettle bundles up and heads into the storm.

EXT. DECK — NIGHT

Storm rages.

Crewmen pass Kettle and enter the wheelhouse.

INT. — WHEELHOUSE — NIGHT

                         CREWMEN
          Man overboard, sir!

                         MURPHY
          Can't help that now. Get the soldiers to
          the boats. Knock 'em over the head if you
          have to.

The ship takes a drunken roll, hurling Murphy, Flynn, and the
crewman to the floor. The crewman crawls out. Murphy struggles
to the wheel, looks through the window.

He sees a huge wave curl up and snap crew members out of sight.

EXT. DECK — STORM — NIGHT

Charlie Buck comes into the storm, bundled up in his cowboy
duds, wrapped in a pea jacket. His eyes are wild. He's never
seen anything like this. He struggles along the bulkhead,
hanging onto the rail.

INT. SHAFT ALLEY OF THE ENGINE ROOM — NIGHT

An OILER slides crablike through the shaft alley, which is
tight and filled with steam lines. One of the lines bursts,
burning away the oiler's face. He screams and slides back down
the alley.

EXT. DECK — NIGHT

Troops and crewmen race back and forth, in total confusion.
Monstrous waves pound over them. Troops huddle in the
lifeboats.

Charlie Buck, transfixed, on the ride of his life, stands at the
rail. Uptake valves behind him break the waves.

INT. WHEELHOUSE — NIGHT

Flynn raps out the SOS. The list is nearing seventy degrees.
Murphy stands at the window. A crewman rushes in.

> CREWMAN
> No lifeboats, sir. Davits are all rusted.
> Crank handles missing.

> MURPHY
> Fuck it, then. Get the troops below. Keep
> 'em balanced on either side of the holds.

The crewman takes off. Murphy turns back toward the window.

> MURPHY
> Say a prayer, Flynn.

> FLYNN
> Yessir, I am.

INT. HOLD — NIGHT

Water surges. The troops fight their way toward the ladders,
carried back by the current and slammed against the bulkheads.
The noise is deafening.

EXT. DECK — NIGHT

Charlie Buck grips the rail, edging back toward the hatch. The
ship rolls violently, taking him so low that his boots are in
seawater.

Suddenly a BLOW comes from behind. He's dazed, his knees
buckle. He turns to see what has hit him.

An ENTRENCHING TOOL strikes him again. Charlie falls. HANDS
grip his shoulders, pushing him down. Charlie loses his grip on
the rail. Weakening, his eyes glaze over. The hands continue to
push. Charlie's strength is gone, he sinks to the deck.

The hands push him toward the edge. Charlie tries to resist, to
no avail. His body slides beneath the rail and over the side
into the sea.

This is the midpoint. The midpoint of any script is another oasis in the
vast desert of Act II. At this point a subplot could kick in or an event—
like Charlie's murder—that serves as a dramatic and emotional turning
point in the story. The midpoint always ups the stakes for the major
characters.

As I was writing this, I asked myself: What good is a sea voyage without a storm? But is it a cliché, and an expensive special-effects one at that? Maybe it is a cliché, but I also reminded myself that I had set up the storm by having Charlie kill the seagull, thus inviting an albatross to join the crossing. According to legend, by killing a bird, one must pay. The storm hits and Charlie pays for his indiscretion with his life. Except that this is human and not divine intercession that takes Charlie down.

By creating a big additional expense, I had to keep asking myself if the storm is here for the storm's sake only. I feel that it turns things around dramatically, showing that evil does in fact lurk on board.

One other thing: If I were the bad guy trying to sabotage this game, I would think fast and use the storm to my advantage. The reader has seen the hands. Eventually the rest of the body—and the identity—will be revealed.

This is called: Taking the story from the villain's point of view, which as the writer you must always do. The villain's main function is to drive the story toward catastrophe.

EXT. SEA — DAY — SAME ANGLE

The sea is calm, the storm has passed.

Augie and Hubbard stand on the bridge watching a BURIAL DETAIL, presided over by Captain Murphy, committing the dead to the sea.

                        AUGIE
          The cowboy's luck finally ran out.

                        HUBBARD
          A real heartfelt epitaph there, Epstein.

INT. FO'C'SLE — SIXTH DAY

Animal trudges in, downtrodden, miserable.

                        ANIMAL
          Santini, you wouldn't believe . . .

He is startled by Santini who stands in front of the porthole, his eyes rolled back, trance-like.

                        ANIMAL
      Yoo hoo.

                    SANTINI
                (in a dreamy cadence)
    Edward, I have entered a new conscious-
    ness, a state of neoteric logic if you
    will, which by its obliteration of my
    past has purified me.

                    ANIMAL
    Yeah? Well, it's about fucking time. You
    been off on some tangent. Glad to see you
    getting back to normal.

                    SANTINI
    Normal . . . in the metaphysical sense. I
    am witness to the gradual disintegration
    of my memory, opening the way for my most
    profound cerebral expenditure.

                    ANIMAL
                   (uneasy)
    Yah, memory. I can hardly remember home,
    I been away so long.

                    SANTINI
    I remember my parents, probably because,
    having passed away, I feel myself growing
    nearer to them.

                    ANIMAL
    You ain't no closer to passing away than I
    am. You may be further away for all I
    know.

                    SANTINI
    The reason behind shedding my old
    identities, Edward, and there may have
    been many of them, is that my essential
    identity is echoing me back.

Animal pulls a bottle of Scotch from the wall locker.

                    ANIMAL
                (holding up the bottle)
    How 'bout a shot?

                    SANTINI
    As a member of the Intelligence Corps I
    was called upon to assume many
    identities—a French Resistance fighter,
    an Italian partisan. I was there to watch
    Mussolini dragged with his mistress

through the streets of Milan. I was there
when Hermann Göring's hidden treasure
was found. I played poker as a German
agent, a British agent, a double agent,
an American gentleman of means, all of
them thoroughly researched so that I
could feel their presence within me. So
you can see, Edward, I am no-man anymore,
stripped of his past, ready to engage
upon a journey into the future.

Animal takes a slug from the bottle, watching Santini closely.

               SANTINI
And, ironically enough, it all began the
day I was burned to death in a fire in the
Paris hotel.

               ANIMAL
C'mon, Santini, take a shot of this.
It'll make you feel better.

               SANTINI
I was also murdered by the SS, twice.

               ANIMAL
             (humors him)
Twice.

               SANTINI
A remarkable accomplishment by any
standards. And, finally, I was castrated
and put to death in a camp at Montauban.

               ANIMAL
Listen, Santini. You ain't dead.

               SANTINI
I have a confession to make, Edward. I am
not Michelangelo Santini.

Animal stares, afraid that Santini is finally gone.

               SANTINI
Jim Belasco. San Diego, California.
Harriet and Jim Belasco Senior, a sister,
Joan, and two Labrador retrievers. You
must understand—I'm telling you this
because in seven years with Intelligence
I have never had one friend, not one. You
are my first.

                    ANIMAL
        Well, that's great, buddy.

                    SANTINI
        I've had so many parts to play that I lost
        the Jim Belasco that gave me life. And
        even when Jim Belasco died, though I've
        never felt terribly close to him, part of
        me died.

                    ANIMAL
        You are Jim Belasco . . . aren't you?
        Didn't you just say . . .

                    SANTINI
                    (sadly)
        I was Jim Belasco. In fact, he was the one
        who was castrated in the camp at
        Montauban.

Animal goes to Santini and puts his arm around his shoulders.

                    ANIMAL
        Okay, buddy. We're going to take a little
        walk.

He pulls a comb out of his pocket and runs it through Santini's
hair. Then, wrapping a trench coat around him, he leads him out.

Maybe Santini would have gone insane anyway, but it's the theft of his
system that did him in. The players face a silent enemy who knows how
to get to them. Santini's madness. Charlie's murder. Tension builds. We
wonder who will be next. Who *is* the villain?
    Or, is this a ploy on Santini's part?

INT. BATHROOM — SAME DAY

Animal sits on the john reading a *Saturday Evening Post*. He
hears something, looks up. Augie, with a sour expression,
enters in a monogrammed robe, carrying a leather shaving kit.

                    ANIMAL
        Hey, Ep.

Augie grunts, places the kit by the bank of mirrors and sits in
the next stall. Animal leans forward.

                    ANIMAL
What's the matter with you?

                    AUGIE
Nothing.

                    ANIMAL
That ain't how you look.

                    AUGIE
I saw you and Santini.

                    ANIMAL
He went a little wacko. I took him to sick
bay.

                    AUGIE
And then what? You came straight here?

                    ANIMAL
Yeah, that's right. What's with all the
questions?

                    AUGIE
Who do you think stole Santini's system?

                    ANIMAL
How the hell do I know?

                    AUGIE
Somebody did.

                    ANIMAL
Yeah? Who?

                    AUGIE
The same person who made sure Charlie
Buck was taken out of the game.

                    ANIMAL
The cowboy went overboard with twenty-
three other guys, Eppy, remember?

                    AUGIE
Charlie was not one to take stupid
chances. Witness his poker. He wouldn't
put himself in a position to fall
overboard.

>   ANIMAL
> Whaddya tellin' me . . . somebody shoved
> him?

>   AUGIE
> Santini's system is stolen. Charlie goes
> overboard. Result: two players gone by
> unnatural means.

>   ANIMAL
> C'mon, Santini blew it, to you and your
> superior card playing.

>   AUGIE
> He was acting like a wild man. Without his
> system, he was shot. Somebody wants to
> sabotage this game—one of the troops, one
> of the crew, one of us.

>   ANIMAL
> You newspaper guys are conspiracy crazy.

>   AUGIE
> I've got something to tell you.

Hubbard drifts into the john.

>   HUBBARD
> Good morning.

>   ANIMAL
> You're just in time for Eppy's big
> bulletin.

>   HUBBARD
> Oh?

Augie, upset, gets up and leaves.

>   ANIMAL
>   (shouting after him)
> You leave us hanging, you fuck, hey!

INT. FO'C'SLE — DAY

Animal enters and rummages through his pile of crumpled
uniforms. He checks armpits and crotches and chooses the least
offensive. Notices the covered bird cage.

                          ANIMAL
          Jesus, you must be suffocating in there,
          sweetheart.

He snatches off the rain poncho—and is horror stricken. The
canary, frozen in death, lies on the cage floor. Her head and
legs have been torn from her body. Her feathers are spread
around like a funeral pyre.

One of her claws is wrapped grotesquely around a bar. Her beak
is open, and the hard, brown tongue inside cries out like a
petrified gargoyle.

Animal grasps the cage bars, looking in, silent.

We have already suspected what Animal now discovers—that his beloved bird is dead. Murdered. The players are being taken out one by
one. Why? And by whom?

From the beginning, when Animal was in the Antwerp hotel room,
the cynical among us knew that the bird would get it before the story
ended. We just didn't know how, or when, yet all along we saw more and
more how much the bird meant to Animal. The villain also knew this
and knew that the bird's death would most likely throw Animal off at a
critical time.

Are we starting to get the idea that the game is rigged after all, that
the villain might have all along had in mind one player as the winner?
And what better way to insure that than to get rid of the others one by
one?

Animal senses something behind him and turns. Augie stands at
the door with Hubbard.

                          ANIMAL
          You knew, didn't you.

                          AUGIE
          I covered the cage.

                          ANIMAL
          You know how many times this bird saved my
          life, how much we been through together
          . . . how many . . .

He drops his head and sobs uncontrollably. Recovering, he pulls
himself together and says in a steady voice . . .

ANIMAL
How much time before we play?

HUBBARD
Fifteen minutes.

ANIMAL
Deal me in.

INT. CORRIDOR OUTSIDE QUARTERS — DAY

A SENTRY with a carbine stands at the ladder leading to the
players' quarters. His name patch reads STARK. Augie approaches
him.

AUGIE
How long have you been here?

STARK
Since eight.

AUGIE
Anybody pass by here who shouldn't have?

STARK
Just authorized personnel.

AUGIE
Meaning who?

STARK
You, Hubbard, Podberoski, Santini.

AUGIE
Santini?

STARK
For a few minutes, I don't know.

AUGIE
Who else?

STARK
Captain Murphy, Kettle. Let's see, a
couple of mess boys, couple of troops, a
guy from the laundry.

AUGIE
These are authorized personnel! C'mon,
Stark, you're supposed to screen these
people.

                    STARK
          They all had very good reasons.

                    AUGIE
          Any of them offer you money?

                    STARK
          No.

                    AUGIE
          If they did, would you take it?

                    STARK
                    (beat)
          Sure, why not?

                    AUGIE
          If anybody offers you anything . . .
                    (pulls out one hundred dollars, hands it
                         to him)
          . . . come to me. I'll triple it.

INT. HOLD — DAY

The troops are quiet. The late Charlie Buck's rooting section
is glum. Arthur Willow, bookmaker, takes bets.

At the table, the players stack their money and inspect fresh
decks. Nobody's saying much.

                    AUGIE
                    (to Animal)
          How are you feeling?

                    ANIMAL
          Like a million, you?

                    AUGIE
          Think of it this way, Pod, the bird lived
          a good life.

                    ANIMAL
          Hubbard, deal the cards.

INT. GAME — LATER — DAY

In the middle of a hand. Augie, who has folded, deals. Hubbard
has a king-high.

                    HUBBARD
          One thousand dollars.

                        ANIMAL
Hubbard, you remember I was mentioning
Colonel Morley.

                        HUBBARD
I remember.

                        ANIMAL
Biggest rat I ever knew. Used to work for
the general staff, spy shit, squealed on
his own men.

                        HUBBARD
You knew Morley well?

                        AUGIE
You guys still playing?

                        ANIMAL
I knew him through some British
secretaries up in London who used to hang
around screwing the American Embassy
staff.

                        AUGIE
It's your bet, Pod. Five hundred. You in?

                        ANIMAL
Some of those American generals were in
them British secretaries' pants, big
time.

Hubbard watches Animal curiously.

                        ANIMAL
As a matter of fact,
              (beat, reflective)
Hubbard . . . I know that name. You got
an old man who's a general?

                        HUBBARD
That's right.

                        ANIMAL
Stationed in London, American Embassy?

                        HUBBARD
              (getting tense)
Yes.

>   ANIMAL
>   (snaps his fingers)
>   That's where I heard about those
>   secretaries . . . your old man . . . no
>   shit . . . say, how does your mother feel
>   about him screwing all them broads?

Hubbard bolts across the table and wallops Animal, who reels
back. Hubbard hits him again, drawing blood. Hubbard is now flat
across the table with both hands around Animal's neck.

Augie and Kettle pull Hubbard off.

>   AUGIE
>   (to Hubbard)
>   What the hell's the matter with you?

Animal spits blood into his handkerchief.

>   ANIMAL
>   (to Hubbard)
>   I'm gonna say this quick, asshole.

Hubbard stares at him with rage.

>   ANIMAL
>   In a game like this, one card player does
>   not belt another card player no matter
>   what! This ain't a fuckin' prize fight,
>   Hubbard.

He licks the blood from his lip.

>   ANIMAL
>   If you don't know by now, I play what they
>   call intimidation poker, which means I
>   take my shots where I can. Just like we
>   all do. You dish it out, you take it.
>   That's the way it is.

>   HUBBARD
>   It doesn't call for slurs.

>   ANIMAL
>   You poor fuckin' child. There ain't
>   nothing off limits, Hubbard. Except your
>   fists. If I wanna call you an asshole, you
>   live with it or get the fuck out. This is
>   for half a million bucks, Hubbard, which
>   means anything goes, short of pulling a
>   gun—which I think you woulda done if you

had one. You better straighten up, my
friend. I might also suggest you don't
drop personal letters on the latrine floor
for people like me to read.
          (watches Hubbard get it)
All right, where were we?

For every action there's a direct and opposite reaction. Nothing happens by mistake. Animal's bird dies. At the table he verbally assails Hubbard with the letters. In retaliation, Hubbard punches him. The card game now is in utter chaos. The villain, whoever it is, is watching, still running the show, according to plan.

In every screenplay an action deserves a reaction. The more dramatic the reaction the more dynamic the screenplay is. It's action-reaction-action-reaction etc., etc., throughout the story. This is called linkage—the glue that binds the story together. If you keep this in mind you'll be able to weed out extraneous actions while at the same time keeping FOCUS.

INT. OFFICER'S MESS — NIGHT

The players eat steak on a linen tablecloth. Augie picks at his
meal. Hubbard eats the way he plays cards, properly,
methodically. Animal hasn't touched his food.

                    AUGIE
The way I see it, everybody is a suspect
. . . including me.

                    HUBBARD
That's one effective way of letting
yourself off the hook.

                    AUGIE
Santini's system—okay, he could have
lost it. The cowboy overboard—could have
been an accident. Not the bird. The bird
was no accident.

                    ANIMAL
Who would have the fuckin' balls?

                    HUBBARD
A half a million dollars in cash is an
excellent incentive.

> AUGIE
> Only one man is going to walk off this
> boat with it—which leads me to two
> thoughts: there's some nut getting his
> jollies off on this, or one of us is
> orchestrating it.

> HUBBARD
> Or both.

INT. HOLD — DAY

The game. Augie deals. He seems to be daydreaming.

> ANIMAL
> Eppy!

Augie snaps out of it and looks over at Animal.

> ANIMAL
> You in?

> AUGIE
> Uh . . . no, no I'm out.

> ANIMAL
> Then be a good boy and deal the next card.

INT. GAME — DAY — LATER

Hubbard deals.

> HUBBARD
> Seven of hearts, a four over there,
> and . . .
> > (deals himself a nine)
> . . . a pair of nines bets five thousand.

Augie, looking ill, sweats like a pig. He removes his
sunglasses and puts them on the table. His eyes are puffy, his
concentration shot.

> HUBBARD
> (to Augie)
> That's five thousand to you. Are you all
> right?

> AUGIE
> Yeah, I'm . . . what is it?

                    HUBBARD
Five thousand.

                    AUGIE
Five, yeah, I'll call.

                    ANIMAL
Whaddya want, a maid? Put the money in.

Augie tries to focus on his hole card. In the bleachers the
troops wonder what Augie's problem is. Augie takes a deep
breath, wipes his forehead.

                    AUGIE
Jesus, it's hot in here.

                    ANIMAL
                (to Kettle)
Get the man a glass of water.

Kettle signals to the seaman, who pours a glass of water and
carries it over to Augie.

                    AUGIE
On second thought . . . I'm out.

He folds his cards.

INT. HOLD — DAY — LATER

Animal deals the first card down, the second up.

                    ANIMAL
In the words of our dear departed cowboy:
a mailbox for the Captain, and for the
dreamboat here, one double bun, and . . .
                (deals himself a three)
garbage for yours truly. All right,
Hubbard, bet the mighty one.

                    HUBBARD
Two thousand.

Augie calls the bet.

                    ANIMAL
Up to me . . . call and raise you two
back.

                    HUBBARD
Against my nines? I'll call.

                    AUGIE
          Yeah, yeah, me, too, I'm in.

                    ANIMAL
          Pot's right.
                         (he deals)
          A seven, a pair of eights on my right, and
          for me, paregoric.

                    AUGIE
          Five thousand.

                    ANIMAL
          Good night, Irene.
                         (folds)

                    HUBBARD
          I'll call.

Animal picks up the cards.

                    ANIMAL
          Okay. Hey, lookee here, pair of sevens
          and for Augie doggie . . .

Augie has drifted off, his face constricted in pain.

                    ANIMAL
          Augie! What's with you?

                    AUGIE
                    (shaking it off)
          I'm okay. Deal.

Animal deals Augie a four.

                    ANIMAL
          Eights are still high.

                    AUGIE
          Ten thousand dollars.

He pushes the money, lets out a GROAN, and doubles over. Hubbard
kneels next to him, pulls out his handkerchief, and wipes his
brow.

                    HUBBARD
          Kettle, get the doctor down here.

Kettle motions to a seaman, who heads up the ladder.

                    ANIMAL
Whassamatter, Eppy, gas?

                    AUGIE
                 (in bad shape)
Must be gas, cramps or something.
            (slowly straightens)
Let's finish this hand.

                    ANIMAL
You sure?

                    AUGIE
Yeah.

                    ANIMAL
All, right, the bet's ten grand to you,
Hubbard.

                    HUBBARD
Call.

The troops are noisy.

                    ANIMAL
Hey!

The troops quiet down. Animal picks up the deck.

                    ANIMAL
Last card coming. Holy fuck, Cap'n! Three
big sevens and holy fuck again! Eights
and fives for the Ep. That oughta cheer you
up. Bet the sevens.

Hubbard counts his money.

                    HUBBARD
Twenty-five thousand.

Augie is nearly catatonic, sweat pouring out of him. He
steadies himself by hanging onto the table.

                    ANIMAL
That's twenty-five grand to you, Eppy.

Augie tries to focus on Hubbard's three sevens.

                    AUGIE
What have you got there?

                       HUBBARD
Three sevens.

                       AUGIE
Three?
              (manages a smile)
Call that . . . and . . .

He goes to pick up his pile of cash but cannot do it.

                       AUGIE
Raise you . . . whatever I got left.

                      ANIMAL
              (to Augie)
Hey, listen, buddy, why don't we let this
go 'til you're feeling better.

                       AUGIE
           (with sudden anger)
That's my bet!
              (softer)
Count it for me, will ya?

Animal counts so that Augie can see what he is doing.

                      ANIMAL
You sure about this?

                       AUGIE
Count the fuckin' money!

Animal peels off the twenty-five thousand dollars and pushes it
into the center.

                      ANIMAL
That's the call.
           (counts the rest of it)
Fifty-eight thousand and change.

He looks at Augie, who is staring into space, having trouble
breathing. Animal slides the money into the center.

                      ANIMAL
             (to Hubbard)
Fifty-eight thousand, one . . . two
. . . three . . . four . . . hundred.

Hubbard looks at Augie, at Animal, then at his own pile of cash.
He peels off the money and tosses it in. The hold is deadly
silent, waiting for the big moment.

                         AUGIE
         Read 'em and weep.

Augie turns his hole card—a full house, eights up. He closes his
eyes in pain. The troops let out a burst of chatter, then . . . a
GREAT INTAKE OF BREATH.

                         AUGIE
         Pod?

                         ANIMAL
         What?

                         AUGIE
         Rake in the dough for me, would you? I'm
         not feeling so hot.

There is a long silence.

                         AUGIE
         Did you do it?

                         ANIMAL
         No.

                         AUGIE
         C'mon, be a sport.

                         ANIMAL
                   (beat)
         I'd like to, Eppy . . . but Hubbard has
         four sevens.

Augie spins violently around, knocking over his water glass. He
sees Hubbard's cards. He clutches his stomach, doubles over,
and falls. Animal is there to catch him.

                         ANIMAL
         That!
                   (indicating a trench coat)
         Over here. And get the doc.

Kettle spreads the trench coat on the floor. Animal, with
Hubbard's help, eases Augie onto the trench coat.

                         ANIMAL
         You picked a lousy time to get sick.

The ship's DOC and TWO AIDES carrying a stretcher climb down the
ladder. The DOC makes a perfunctory check.

                              ANIMAL
            What's he got?

                              DOC
            Could be anything.

                              ANIMAL
            That's a diagnosis?

                              DOC
                         (to his aides)
            Strap him in. We'll take him to sick bay.

                              HUBBARD
            Is he going to be all right?

                              DOC
            It could be food poisoning.

      Animal and Hubbard look at each other. Augie is carried out.

                              ANIMAL
            How you feeling?

                              HUBBARD
            All right. You?

                              ANIMAL
            I ain't sick but I'm pretty fuckin'
            suspicious. What you say we call it a
            night.
                         (beat)
            Unless you wanna take what we got and end
            this here.

                              HUBBARD
            I'd rather play it out.

                              ANIMAL
            You would, huh?

                              HUBBARD
            Yes.

                              ANIMAL
            Me, too.

Plot Point II.

    Plot Point II is the spot—usually following a big turning-point
scene—where the main character makes a decision. At this point in the

story the evidence has piled up and the main character knows that he must act or perish. Even wishy-washy Hamlet knew he had to do something. Whatever decision the character makes will spill over into Act III and become the story's RESOLUTION. So, what happens here?

Remember that the first person we met in the story was Animal, who despite all his problems, is still around. If I didn't know better I would have figured that Animal would be driven out of the game, leaving Augie and Hubbard.

As screenwriters you have to upset our expectations, throw us off balance, and demolish predictability. You have to keep the reader guessing, and therefore interested. Remember *The Usual Suspects*, in which the writers kept us in suspense until the last few frames? And *The Game*, a *Usual Suspects* wannabe, which didn't?

Here, Animal has seen Charlie die, Santini's system stolen, and Augie becoming mysteriously ill. He's alone now, facing Hubbard, whom he doesn't really trust. But he's got to do something because, the way he figures it, he's next.

Here's where the ticking clock begins pounding in your main character's ears. In this case, the $500,000 poker game is down to two men, the ship will be docking in New York in two days, and there's a killer aboard ship.

The first rule of screenwriting: Never make it too easy on your main character.

Now begins the real problem solving.

INT. SICK BAY — NIGHT

Filled with seasick and storm-injured troops. Animal, grungy and tired, in a trench coat, climbs down the ladder. His beard is nearly full, flecked with gray.

He stops at Augie's, whose face is the color of granite. The lines on his face, like black canals, make him look ten years older.

                    ANIMAL
                  (softly)
    Eppy?

Augie's eyes slowly open. He sees who it is and nods.

                    ANIMAL
You look terrible.

                        AUGIE
        How sharp of you to notice.

                        ANIMAL
        The Doc said your vocal cords ain't
        working so good, so I won't keep you.

                        VOICE
                        (O.S)
        Edward?

Animal sees Santini is down the aisle waving at him.

                        ANIMAL
        Hey, buddy. I'll be down in a minute.
                        (to Augie)
        Can you move around yet?

                        AUGIE
        Maybe tomorrow. We're due in New York
        when?

                        ANIMAL
        Two days, at which time I will be in the
        arms of my million-dollar Shirley.

                        AUGIE
        Do me a favor, Pod. Bring me a deck of
        cards, and a board, a hard surface,
        something to play on.

                        ANIMAL
        You bet. Take care of yourself. I'll be
        looking in on you.

                        AUGIE
        And be careful.

Animal, looking at him, continues down the aisle to Santini,
who is sitting up in bed, sheets of paper spread around.

                        ANIMAL
        What's the good word?

                        SANTINI
        Thinking about Azreal.

                        ANIMAL
        Who?

SANTINI
The bright Angel of death. I've been
formulating my own autobiographical
necrology, Edward. As a matter of fact,
here . . .

He hands Animal a sheet of paper.

SANTINI
You can see for yourself.

On it is a series of stick figures, one broken in two, another
hanging, one consumed by fire, another holding a penis and
genitals in his hand.

SANTINI
(childlike)
All me . . . all gone.

ANIMAL
Yeah, they're . . . real nice. Ah, well,
listen buddy, I came down to say hello.
I'm heading into the big showdown with
Hubbard later on, so I better get some
rest.

SANTINI
Good luck, Edward. Viva Azreal!

Santini goes back to his stick drawings.

ANIMAL
Sure thing . . . See ya, pal.

Santini is too lost in his drawings to hear him.

INT. FO'C'SLE — NIGHT

Animal in his bunk, drinking scotch. He stares at the empty bird
cage. With a angry kick, he knocks the cage off the locker. He
grabs the bottle of Scotch and exits.

INT. FO'C'SLE — NIGHT

Hubbard on his bunk, reading a book.

ANIMAL
(O.S.)
Hubbard.

Hubbard looks up, sees Animal in the doorway, scowling.

                    ANIMAL
          I wanna talk to you.

                    HUBBARD
                (laying his book down)
          Sure. Come in.

Animal flops on Augie's bunk, takes a healthy swig.

                    ANIMAL
          You know, Hubbard, I was just sittin'
          next door minding my own business when
          all of a sudden I got this idea—which I
          thought I would bring over here and share
          with you.
                    (beat)
          Do you know that all these strange things
          that have been happening to us ain't been
          happening to all of us?

                    HUBBARD
          What do you mean?

                    ANIMAL
          Just what I said. Every one of us has been
          fucked over at least once, everyone that
          is, but you. You ain't been fucked over,
          Hubbard. Why is that?

                    HUBBARD
                (shrugs)
          I don't know.

                    ANIMAL
          Santini's system . . . the Cowboy
          overboard . . . my bird . . . Eppy with
          the poison . . . and you, nothin'.

                    HUBBARD
          Maybe my turn hasn't come. Epstein's
          didn't come until this afternoon!

                    ANIMAL
          Got it all figured out, don't you. Think
          you're hot shit. Old man's a general.
          Lotta dough in your pocket. Evan Hubbard
          the Fourth. King Louis the Fourteenth.

Hubbard stares silently.

> ANIMAL
> I was wondering why I was the only one you
> couldn't get to. Kill my bird. The worst
> thing that coulda ever happened to me.
>   (tapping his chest)
> . . . but one thing you don't know about
> me, Hubby baby, I bounce back.
>
> HUBBARD
> Which I respect you for, Podberoski. I
> don't know if I could have done it.
>
> ANIMAL
> Save the horseshit. You're lucky I don't
> break this fuckin' bottle across your
> face.

He stands and slugs down the last of the Scotch.

> ANIMAL
> I met a lot of wimpy, rich kid, namby-
> pamby assholes in my life, Hubbard. So
> it's gonna be fuckin' heaven taking you
> down tomorrow.

Animal stumbles over to the door and turns back.

> ANIMAL
> And then, we'll get to the matter of my
> bird.

In Act III your responsibility is to raise the tension level. One of the ways to do this is to put enormous pressure on your characters. The moments of relaxation are gone, there is only tension and hard-driving anxiety. The scenes get shorter and so do the nerves. The climax is straight ahead and you are barreling—along with your characters—toward it.

In your rush to get to the end, be careful not to let predictability slip in. It's easy to do. You have been clever up to this point; why drop everything in a big rush of impatience? Believe me, greater screenwriters than you and I will ever be have done it. It's as if they swallowed a stupid pill and like a duck on speed crash-banged through Act III to the end.

The characters may be going crazy with fear and anxiety but the writer has to pull in his or her own reins and take a clear, careful look at what's going on. Here's where twists and turns, big and little surprises and prudent storytelling will make the difference between good and mediocre work.

Let's face it, about ninety percent of word-of-mouth advertising is based on how the audience responds to Act III. The audiences you have to get through first are agents, producers, and studio execs who do this for a living.

In *The Crossing* two main problems must be resolved in Act III. The game and the mystery.

INT. FO'C'SLE — SIXTH NIGHT

Animal in a dead sleep. We hear the SOUND of pipes tapping. His bloodshot eyes fall open, he listens to the tapping.

He picks up a boot and hurls it at the ceiling. The tapping stops. Animal rests his head on the pillow and closes his eyes.

The tapping starts again. He opens his eyes, picks up his other boot and throws it at the ceiling. The tapping stops. He waits. The tapping begins again. He stands and stares at the ceiling.

In disgust, Animal puts on a trench coat, climbs into his boots and clomps out.

INT. CORRIDOR — NIGHT

Animal peeks into Hubbard's fo'c'sle and the lump in Hubbard's bed. He continues down the corridor and meets one of Arthur Willow's GOONS.

                    ANIMAL
          Hey! What are you doing here?

                    GOON
          Taking a piss.

                    ANIMAL
          In my john? Who let you in?

                    GOON
          I let myself in.

The goon walks past Animal, who follows him.

EXT. DECK — NIGHT

A sentry, Stark, stands guard. The hatch opens and the goon walks by Stark. Animal climbs out and approaches Stark.

                    ANIMAL
      Whadda ya doing letting that guy in here?

                    STARK
      He works for Arthur Willow.

                    ANIMAL
      That's an answer?

                    STARK
      He had to go to the bathroom.

                    ANIMAL
      Who else have you let in?

                    STARK
      Nobody.

                    ANIMAL
                  (deadpan)
      If I find anybody else down there I'll
      personally see to it that your balls are
      chopped off. Is that clear?

                    STARK
      Yessir.

INT. CORRIDOR — NIGHT

Animal goes into Charlie Buck's empty fo'c'sle. He climbs under
the covers and closes his eyes. After a moment, the pipes begin
to tap. Animal opens his eyes and stares.

EXT. DECK — DAY

A bright, clear day. The troops mill around, waiting for the
players. Arthur Willow takes bets.

I leaned a little heavily on bookie Arthur Willow in these pages. By
establishing him early as an always-present force, he now edges closer
to the front as a suspect. At least this is what I tried to do. Reading it
again, it looks a little like overkill.

Larry Kettle and his armed sentries descend the ladder, moving
quickly along the deck, through a wedge of troops.

                    TROOP
      Who do you like, Kettle?

                              KETTLE
             I like everybody.

Kettle and the sentries disappear into the hold.

THE BRIDGE

Hubbard, in pressed khakis with gleaming Captain's bars, comes
down the ladder. His lanky strides carry him across deck. The
troops, shouting encouragement, clear a path for him.

                              TROOP
             What's the word, Captain?

                              HUBBARD
             I'll tell you, gentlemen, if I were a
             betting man . . .

The troops let out a burst of laughter.

                              HUBBARD
             . . . I'd bet on me.

THE BRIDGE

Animal starts down the ladder. His fatigues are clean and
pressed. The sun glistens off his brass belt buckle. His beard
is gone.

His spiffiness does not hide the fact that he is dead tired and
hung over. He approaches the men, whose cheers of encouragement
show that he is clearly the favorite.

                              ANIMAL
             Go wild, you degenerates! The king is
             about to take the throne!

He spots Hubbard standing by the rail and saunters up to him.

                              ANIMAL
             Smile, Hubbard, it may be your last.

Animal mugs for photographers.

                              ANIMAL
             Whaddya think about getting a dealer?

                              HUBBARD
             Who do you have in mind?

> ANIMAL
> Kettle knows the game, and he ain't smart
> enough to fuck with the cards.

> HUBBARD
> Did you sound him out?

> ANIMAL
> He's already practicing.

INT. HOLD — DAY

Kettle sits at the table shuffling cards. The Sentries are in
position behind the players' seats.

Animal and Hubbard drop down the ladder into the hold. They sit,
count, and inspect the cards.

> ANIMAL
> (to Kettle)
> Like a pro, Red. You're doing real good.

Kettle is clearly honored.

> HUBBARD
> (to Animal)
> What made you decide to shave?

> ANIMAL
> I had a nightmare—that underneath my
> beard was your face.

He throws three decks into Kettle's lap; he holds up the other
three.

> ANIMAL
> These are good. I'm ready.

Kettle signals for the troops to be let in.

EXT. DECK — DAY

Troops, loud and raucous, shove their way toward the ladder.

INT. HOLD — DAY

Arthur Willow and his goons descend the ladder. The troops
landslide down after them and scramble for seats.

Animal scrutinizes Hubbard, who is well rested and alert and
neatly arranging his stacks of money.

                         ANIMAL
          Being the rich bastard you are, this must
          seem like piddly-shit to you.

                         HUBBARD
          Like stealing sand from the bench.

                         KETTLE
          The game is five-card stud poker, with all
          the rules still applying. Agreed?

Hubbard nods.

                         ANIMAL
          Run 'em.

Kettle shuffles and offers the cut to Animal, who taps the deck
with his knuckles. Kettle deals.

INT. HOLD — DAY — LATER

Animal peels off a wad of thousand-dollar bills.

                         ANIMAL
          That's twenty of 'em.

Hubbard looks over at Animal's ace-king-nine, then at his own
nine-seven-two. The hold is silent, waiting.

                         HUBBARD
                         (beat)
          I'm out.

Animal rakes in the pot and smirks over at Hubbard.

                         ANIMAL
          Now that . . . is poker.

INT. GAME — MONTAGE

Scenes showing the back-and-forth struggle between the men. The
hold is hot and the troops have discarded their shirts.

Animal, frustrated, comes up second best too many times.

Once again, I used a montage here to accelerate the passage of time.
Readers should be asked to suspend just so much of their disbelief.
Most of a poker game is a slow process. Film must speed things up. As
writers, we're compelled to find the middle distance. Here, through a

montage, we get both the play of the game and the gradual tension building toward the climax.

INT. HOLD — DAY — LATER

Animal is glum. A cigar sticks out of his mouth. His fatigue shirt is draped over his chair, his dogtags matted against his hairy chest.

                    ANIMAL
          Check to the power.

                    HUBBARD
          Five thousand.

                    ANIMAL
          I can't catch a fucking cold. Call.

He puts the five thousand in. Hubbard turns over his hole card—pair of fours. Animal slams down his fist.

                    ANIMAL
          Break time.

                    HUBBARD
          Suits me.

INT. OFFICER'S MESS — DAY

Animal, Hubbard, and Kettle at the table. Fumi serves steak, and vegetables. He sets the plates down and starts to leave.

                    ANIMAL
          Hey, partner . . .

Fumi turns back.

                    ANIMAL
              (pointing to the dish)
          I want you to taste this . . .

Fumi is confused.

                    ANIMAL
          . . . so I don't end up like Epstein.

Fumi looks to Kettle for help.

                    KETTLE
          Do as he says.

Animal hands him his fork.

                    ANIMAL
      . . . and then I want you to do Hubbard's.

Fumi quickly tastes Animal's food, then Hubbard's.

                    ANIMAL
      Good boy.

INT. GAME — DAY — LATER

Animal wipes his forehead with a damp cloth. Hubbard is cool,
intense. Hubbard has a king high.

                    KETTLE
                  (dealing)
      Last card. A pair of kings for Captain
      Hubbard and an ace for Mr. Podberoski.
      Kings are high.

                    HUBBARD
      Check to you.

                    ANIMAL
      You worried about my shitty little
      eights? That ain't like you, Hubby. It's
      gonna cost you twenty-five grand.

He counts out the money and slides it into the center. Hubbard
takes a long time.

                    ANIMAL
      Do you mind . . . I'm falling asleep.

                    HUBBARD
      I don't think you have it.

                    ANIMAL
      Jesus, you know, it's been so long I can't
      remember myself . . .

                    HUBBARD
      I'm in.

Without turning over the hole card, Animal leans forward.

                    ANIMAL
      In Epstein's immortal words: Read 'em and
      weep.

He turns over the second ace, giving him two pair. Hubbard
stares at Animal's hand. Without expression, he folds his hand
and sits back. Cheers from the bleachers.

>   ANIMAL
>   Fuckin' brilliant . . . thank you . . .
>   thank you . . .
>   (to Hubbard)
>   You oughta listen, Hubby, I told you what
>   I had.

INT. GAME — NIGHT

Dense with smoke. The troops are near exhaustion, their
attention riveted to the seesaw game. Hubbard turns over his
hole card.

>   HUBBARD
>   Eights.

Animal throws his head back in disgust.

>   ANIMAL
>   This ain't fun no more.
>   (to Kettle)
>   What time is it, Red.

>   KETTLE
>   Three.

>   ANIMAL
>   What time we pulling in?

>   KETTLE
>   Tomorrow afternoon, seventeen hundred.

>   ANIMAL
>   (to Kettle)
>   Deal the cards.

You'll notice how short the scenes are now, how the pace has picked up.
This has become gladiatorial.

You cannot lower the pressure on the characters, not for one moment.
Otherwise, you lose the audience. Nobody can go to sleep, not the
audience, not the characters, and NOT THE WRITER.

INT. HOLD — EIGHTH MORNING

Kettle deals the final card. There is close to thirty thousand in the pot. Animal's pile of cash is dangerously low. Animal shows a pair of fours; Hubbard has a ten high.

                    KETTLE
          A second ten . . . and a king, no help.
          Ten's bet, Captain.

                    HUBBARD
          Five thousand dollars.

                    ANIMAL
          Ah, the big tease. Okay, Hubby, you got
          your fish, whaddya gonna do with him—and
          his twenty-thousand-dollar raise?
                    (long beat)
          C'mon, Hubby. You can't fade now.

                    HUBBARD
          Oh, yes I can.

He folds. A burst of chatter from the bleachers.

                    ANIMAL
               (raking in the money)
          Miracle time.

Something catches his eye. He turns and sees Augie standing by the ladder.

                    ANIMAL
          Hey, Buddy, how are ya doing?

                    AUGIE
          Not as well as you.

                    ANIMAL
          It's turning my way. You wanna sit?

                    AUGIE
          Just stopping by to see where everybody
          is.
                    (turns back up the ladder)

                    HUBBARD
          I'd like a fresh deck, Mr. Kettle.

Kettle hands the deck to Animal who shuffles it and then holds it up to his ear, peeling the cards.

                    ANIMAL
        Fifty-two on the nose . . . make me rich,
        babies . . .
                    (hands the deck to Kettle)
        . . . Run 'em, Red.

Kettle shuffles and offers the cut to Animal. He deals the first
card down, the second up, a heart seven for Hubbard and a spade
eight for Animal.

                    KETTLE
        Eight bets.

                    ANIMAL
        Pasadena.

                    HUBBARD
        Five hundred.

                    ANIMAL
        I'm in.

                    KETTLE
                    (dealing)
        Six of hearts with the seven and a seven
        of spades with the eight. Eight is still
        high.

                    ANIMAL
        Two grand on the come.

                    HUBBARD
        Call.

                    KETTLE
        Pot's right and we have a five-six-seven
        of hearts and a spade flush to the eight.
        Mr. Podberoski.

                    ANIMAL
        Well, now, looks like we got a coupla
        possibilities working here . . .
                    (to Hubbard)
        . . . which will cost you ten grand.

                    HUBBARD
        I would hope so.

                    ANIMAL
        The man has a sense of humor.

The troops' interest is heating up.

                    KETTLE
        Four of hearts and a straight flush for the
        Captain and four spades to the jack.

Noisy chatter. Kettle raises his arms, calling for silence.

                    KETTLE
                 (to Animal)
        Your bet, Mr. Podberoski.

                    ANIMAL
              (slightly on edge)
        I'll check to the bomber over there.

                    KETTLE
        That's a check to you, Captain Hubbard.

                    HUBBARD
        I see you have approximately eighty-five
        thousand dollars in front of you.

                    ANIMAL
        More or less.

                    HUBBARD
        Then that's my bet—eighty-five thousand.

He counts the money and places it into the center.

                    KETTLE
        Eighty-five thousand to you, Mr.
        Podberoski.

                    ANIMAL
        I heard him the first time.

He sits back, surveying the situation. He lights a cigar and
wipes his forehead with his sleeve.

                    ANIMAL
        Here we are at the old do-or-die. Eighty-
        five grand.
                 (beat)
        I gotta play.

He pushes the money in and holds up the extra four hundred.

                              ANIMAL
                            (to Kettle)
              This is for you, Red, if I win.

He then reaches down and turns over his hole card—the nine of
spades, giving him a SPADE FLUSH to the jack.

                              ANIMAL
                   Whaddya say, big fella?

Hubbard turns over his hole card. Animal stares into the heroic
red face of the QUEEN OF HEARTS—A WINNER! The troops break into
noisy chatter, then just as suddenly grow silent.

                              ANIMAL
                I knew I shouldn't have shaved.

Oh, no. I wanted Animal to win. What a bitch. Oh, well, now we go into
the lull of disappointment. Not so fast.

   Just when we think the thing is pretty much over and it's time for a
short emotional break, the writer must step in and say, hold it, I have
another surprise for you. And here it is.

EXT. DECK — MORNING

The troops sunbathe, nap, pace. A TROOP WITH A RADIO fiddles with
the tuner, picking up a Baltimore station playing Johnny
Desmond's "I'll be seeing you."

INT. WHEELHOUSE — DAY

Murphy enters the wheelhouse and runs into the radio operator,
Flynn, with a radio message.

                              FLYNN
                   Captain, read this!

                              MURPHY
                            (reads)
                   This is for real?

                              FLYNN
                   It came in twice, Sir.

                              MURPHY
              Okay, Flynn, stay at the radio.

EXT. BRIDGE — DAY

Murphy hurries down the ladder and across the deck where he runs
into Kettle. He hands the message to Kettle, who reads it.
Shocked, Kettle hands it back. Murphy continues on.

INT. NUMBER-THREE HOLD — DAY

Two merchant seamen are climbing out of the sack as Murphy
scrambles down the ladder.

                         MURPHY
               Grab your weapons.

They do, and follow him up the ladder.

This is called HIDING THE BALL. Once again, you do not have to tell
the audience what is going on until the audience needs to know it.
You've got the reader hooked, he wants to know what that telegram said,
what about it made Murphy and his men pick up their weapons and
move out.

INT. FO'C'SLE — DAY

Captain Evan Hubbard is packing.

                         VOICE
                         (O.S)
               Captain Hubbard.

Hubbard turns to find Captain Murphy with the two sentries.
Murphy steps into the room, holding the radio message.

                         MURPHY
               This just came in.
                         (reads)
               Place under arrest Hubbard, Evan A.,
               Captain, U.S. Army—for homicide, RAF
               Major, Casablanca, Four September, this
               year, positive print, weapon ID, hold for
               capture. Sent by Major Haines, MP
               Detachment, Brooklyn Army Base. Know
               anything about this?

                         HUBBARD
               I do.

> MURPHY
> Then you'll have to come with me,
> Captain.

Here we are at The Problem created by the Inciting Incident way back in Act I. Hubbard killing the Major in the Casablanca street has come back to haunt him.

He is picked up and jailed. And now, with Santini in mental disarray, Charlie Buck dead, Augie incapacitated, and Hubbard in jail, there's only one person available to find out what the hell is going on.

EXT. DECK — DAY

Animal races along the deck and up the ladder to the bridge.

INT. CORRIDOR — DAY

Animal rushes down the corridor and through a door that reads: CAPTAIN SAMUEL X. MURPHY. He carries a deck of cards.

INT. CAPTAIN'S STATEROOMS — DAY

Murphy is at his desk. Animal bursts in.

> ANIMAL
> What's this I hear about Hubbard?

> MURPHY
> What about it?

> ANIMAL
> Locked up in the brig. Is that right?

> MURPHY
> That's classified information.

> ANIMAL
> I wanna see him.

> MURPHY
> Afraid that's impossible.

> ANIMAL
> What did he do?

> MURPHY
> I'm sorry.

                    ANIMAL
          Knock off the horseshit, Murphy. The man
          won a half million bucks and now he's in
          the clink. I wanna know why.

INT. BRIG — DAY

Dank and murky. SOUND of a cell door opening. Animal enters,
carrying the deck of cards. Even his breathing sounds metallic.
A SENTRY leads Animal to a cell.

                    ANIMAL
                  (to sentry)
          Take a walk.
                        (into the cell)
          Hubbard?

A single dim bulb hangs above Hubbard's silhouette.

                    HUBBARD
                  (barely audible)
          Hello, Podberoski.

                    ANIMAL
          What's going on?

                    HUBBARD
          It's a long story.

                    ANIMAL
          Ain't they all. Go ahead, I'm listening.

INT. BRIG — DAY — HALF HOUR LATER

Hubbard finishes up while Animal listens.

                    HUBBARD
          . . . then Captain Murphy received the
          radio message, and here I am.

                    ANIMAL
          You're in a ton of shit.

                    HUBBARD
                  (indicating the cards and board)
          What are you doing with those?

                    ANIMAL
          Epstein. Always wanting something.
                  (beat)
          Anything I can get for you?

                              HUBBARD
        An extra set of wings?

                              ANIMAL
                          (smiles, nods)
              So long, Hubby. Good luck.

Hubbard listens to Animal's echoing bootsteps.

EXT. DECK — DAY

Troops cheer as they see shoreline, weep openly. This is home,
after many years.

INT. WHEELHOUSE — DAY

Captain Murphy stands at the wheel, guiding the ship in.

EXT. CARGO BOOMS — DAY

Kettle supervises the off-loading of cargo.

Now it's time for a short break before all hell breaks lose. This is the
eye of the storm, which always seems calm but which we know is only
temporary. As the writer you set the mood. Here things seem pleasant,
good-byes are said, troops prepare for home. The audience wonders is
this is it, hoping there's more, but what?

BRIDGE

Animal, Santini, Augie stand together by the rail. Augie,
looking chipper in his pressed khakis, watches Kettle down
below. Santini still looks haggard, manic, but some color has
returned to his face.

SHORE

Row of slips where the S.S. *McQueen* will dock any minute. A
crowd of CIVILIANS waits on the dock.

                              ANIMAL
              Despite everything, Eppy, it was a
              pleasure.

                              AUGIE
        I wish I could say the same.

> ANIMAL
> (to Santini)
> See you, buddy. You got my address. Come
> visit.

> SANTINI
> I will, Edward.

Animal puts an affectionate hand on his shoulder, then moves
along the rail, waving at his FAMILY, about ten of them on the
dock, who look exactly like him.

In the midst of them is a dumpy blonde with two kids at her side.
She waves at Animal, whose lips form the word: SHIRLEY.

The ship is docked, the gangplank lowered. The chain is dropped
and the troops swarm down.

Animal, struggling through them, suddenly spots a WOMAN—his
MOTHER, beaming up at him.

> ANIMAL
> Ma! Wait! I'll be right there, Ma! Don't!

Mrs. Podberoski drives through the soldiers, batting them
aside. With fierce determination, her arms, like great fleshy
oars, pull her forward. Now they stand facing each other. Tears
stream down their cheeks.

> MRS. PODBEROSKI
> (in disbelief)
> Edward?

> ANIMAL
> Hello, Ma.

They thunder into each other's arms.

DOCK

A military CAR pulls up. Major Peter Tat, in a creased uniform,
emerges.

The last of the troops depart. Among them Augie Epstein and
Michelangelo Santini.

Purser Larry Kettle has finished the cargo off-loading. Kettle
instructs a TROOP to put a crate into the back of a jeep. Kettle
climbs in and drives off.

INT. BRIG — DAY

Captain Murphy and two Sentries remove Captain Hubbard, in
handcuffs.

EXT. DOCK — DAY

Impatient, Major Tat checks his watch. There are no more
troops. It is getting dark. Tat starts up the gangplank.

EXT. SHIP — DAY

Murphy and his sentries lead Hubbard along the deck where they
meet Major Tat.

> MAJOR TAT
> Captain Murphy, I'm Major Peter Tat,
> Charlie Buck's Commanding Officer.

> MURPHY
> How do you do?

> MAJOR TAT
> Where is Charlie?

> MURPHY
> I'm sorry, Major, he went overboard in a
> storm . . .

Major Tat looks as if he had just had a coronary.

> MURPHY
> . . . along with twenty-three other men.

> MAJOR TAT
> Was he ahead?

> MURPHY
> Beg your pardon?

> MAJOR TAT
> Was Charlie ahead when he died? Was he
> winning?

> MURPHY
> You can ask Captain Hubbard here, he's
> the big winner.

> HUBBARD
> Charlie had a hundred and forty-five
> thousand dollars.

> MAJOR TAT
> Where is it?

> MURPHY
> The ward room, Major. I'll join you
> there.

Tat is in a daze as Murphy leads Hubbard down the gangplank.

INT. DOCK — NIGHT/LATER

Murphy, the sentries, and Hubbard wait on the dock. Murphy
checks his watch.

> MURPHY
> Those MPs should have been here by now.
> I'm going to call the base.

Murphy heads up the gangplank.

INT. WARD ROOM — NIGHT

Murphy on the radio to Brooklyn Army Base. Major Tat stands
behind him.

> MURPHY
> . . . that's right, a Major Richard
> Haines.

> VOICE
> (O.S)
> I'm sorry, sir, but we have no Richard
> Haines, no Major Haines of any kind.

> MURPHY
> *H-A-I-N-E-S.*

> VOICE
> (O.S)
> No, sir.

> MURPHY
> What the hell is going on here?

> MAJOR TAT
> Captain Murphy, I'd like to get Charlie's
> money, if you don't mind.
>> (beat)
> Captain Murphy?

                    MURPHY
             (puzzled by something)
       Yes . . . all right.

Murphy opens the safe—it's empty. He turns to Tat, looking as if
he has just eaten something rotten.

Things are getting complicated. What, we ask, is going on here? The
mystery deepens. The action accelerates. The scenes have gotten
shorter, the characters more frenetic. Tension is high. We are approaching the climax.
    Here is where the second story—the mystery—heads toward resolu-
tion. Now, some writers might resolve the mystery first and *then* play out
the game. That sounds like an *anti*-climax to me.

EXT. HIGHWAY — NIGHT

Larry Kettle races along. He slows the jeep and makes a turn on
what appears to be a great slab of concrete. In the b.g. the
SOUND of an airplane engine. The jeep pulls up to a DC-4, its
propellers going.

Kettle carries the crate from the rear of the jeep up the stairs
and into the plane's belly.

INT. PLANE — NIGHT

Pitch dark except for running lights. Kettle takes a seat and
straps himself in. The plane takes off.

INT. PLANE — NIGHT

We can barely make out Kettle in the semi-darkness. A light
switches on. Two MEN approach Kettle.

                 SIR BERTRAM FOOTE
                    (smiling)
       Hello, Kettle.

                    KETTLE
       Sir Bertram.

                 SIR BERTRAM
       May I present my driver and friend of many
       years—Harry Broom.

HARRY BROOM is the RAF MAJOR Captain Hubbard supposedly left
for dead in the Casablanca street.

                    SIR BERTRAM
          I trust you have the money?

                    KETTLE
          Yessir, a half million dollars, sewed up
          tight, you'll see.

                    SIR BERTRAM
          I take it Hubbard won?

                    KETTLE
          Yessir, just like you planned it. And
          your message came through to arrest him.

                    SIR BERTRAM
          Any difficulties?

                    KETTLE
          I had to sorta arrange for certain things
          to happen to the other players so things
          worked out right.

                    SIR BERTRAM
          Splendid work.

What do we have here? The whole Casablanca murder scene was a
setup! A phony! Now we see what's been going on all along. A sting! Sir
Bertram engineered it. Kettle was the inside man.

   Here we are at another moment of dramatic irony. We now know
more than Animal, Augie, Santini, and Hubbard, who know nothing but
suspect everything. Will they get it it before it's too late? No way, we
think, how could they?

EXT. ISLAND — PLANE'S POV — DAY

Of a tiny island below, and a runway, house, palm trees.

EXT. ISLAND — DAY

Sir Bertram, Kettle (carrying the crate) and Harry Broom enter
the house. The plane is in the b.g.

INT. HOUSE — DAY

Sir Bertram has opened a bottle of champagne.

> SIR BERTRAM
> And, now, Mr. Kettle, let's see the
> prize.

Kettle tears away one side of the crate and slides out a SIDE OF
BEEF. Inside the beef is a hollowed-out space. In the space is a
PLASTIC COVERED BAG.

Sir Bertram and Harry Broom stand closer. Kettle pulls out the
plastic bag. He rips it open and . . .

> SIR BERTRAM
> What is it?

Kettle pulls out its contents—a brown WOODEN BOARD (the same
one Animal had brought to Augie in sick bay) on which is pasted
Hubbard's final winning hand—the heart flush to the Queen.

Below the cards is written: READ 'EM AND WEEP. The three men are
stunned into silence.

What! A double sting! Animal had figured it out, after all, and has left
these murdering bastards with nothing. WHAT A CLIMAX! The reason
this works is that it comes as a shock, but not one of those out-of-the-
blue shocks that makes no sense except as a convenient way to end the
picture. It works within the context of the story, issuing out of logic.

The only thing we don't know yet is how it came about—which we
will find out in the following scene. This brings the story full circle,
back to the original intention of the tale—the biggest poker game of
the war.

A SOUND BEGINS: the din of conversation from a faraway place. We
HEAR Augie Epstein's off-screen voice.

> AUGIE
> Okay, fellas, now we play this game the
> way it's supposed to be played.

DISSOLVE TO:

INT. A LAVISH GAME ROOM — NIGHT

Augie, Animal, Santini, and Hubbard sit around the table, in
tuxedos. Stacks of one hundred thousand dollars in front of
each. An empty chair stands in memory of Charlie Buck. They
raise their glasses.

                         ANIMAL
          To the cowboy.

                        SANTINI
          May he be riding tall.

                          ALL
          Hear, hear.

They toast their departed friend.

                       HUBBARD
          And to our very clever friend, Corporal
          Epstein.

                        ANIMAL
          Okay, Sherlock, how did you pull it off?

                        AUGIE
          There I was in sick bay on the verge of
          death, and suddenly, like a beacon of
          light, this idea came to me . . .

                        ANIMAL
          Just the details, Eppy, if you don't
          mind.

                        AUGIE
          I asked myself: Whose time couldn't I
          account for? Who had access to the safe?
          Why would sides of beef be traveling
          across the Atlantic? One name kept
          popping up—that unsavory, red-haired,
          freckled-faced sonofabitch, Mister Larry
          Kettle. Pod here made the money switch
          and here we are.

                        ANIMAL
          Eppy, you're beautiful. Let's play
          cards.

The SOUND of the door opening turns their heads.

Major Tat, in tuxedo, enters the room. With him is a swaggering
YOUNG GUY in his early twenties. On Major Tat's signal, the kid
takes Charlie's seat. Tat tosses one hundred thousand dollars
in cash on the table.

                       MAJOR TAT
          Gentlemen, may I present Mr. Joey Fagan.

The players look at one another, at the kid, at Tat. Hubbard spreads a deck of cards on the table.

>   HUBBARD
>   Cut for deal.

They all do and the new kid wins with a king.

>   ANIMAL
>   Here we go again.
>   (to the kid)
>   Run 'em, slick.

Fagan deals the first card down, the second up, calling them.

>   FAGAN
>   Big Alice. Sex with an *i*. Ten of thumpers.
>   A red seven and a black nun. Bet the
>   Alice.

>   ANIMAL
>   Where do you find them, Tat?

>   HUBBARD
>   Five hundred.

>   AUGIE
>   What else is new. I'm in.

>   ANIMAL
>   Call that, and five hundred more.

>   SANTINI
>   How aggressive of you, Edward. Call.

>   FAGAN
>   Watch me shine, mamacitas.
>   (throws the money in)

>   ANIMAL
>   C'mon, Hubby, we ain't got all night.

>   HUBBARD
>   I'm in.

>   ANIMAL
>   Attaboy.

>   FAGAN
>   Pot's elastic. Sevenarola on the Alice. A

> jackson on the tenski. Pair of nuns
> for . . .

                    SANTINI
>   Santini.

                    FAGAN
>   . . . and for mish . . .
>   (deals himself a five)
>   one little red finger . . . bet those
>   nunners . . .

                    SANTINI
>   Two thousand.

                    FAGAN
>   I always follow the church.

                    AUGIE
>   (to Fagan)
>   On a pair of fingers? You should live so
>   long.

Their voices fade as . . . the CREDITS roll.

FADE OUT

When we think about this last scene we taste something bittersweet. This is not a wonderful, yellow-ribboned ending where the good guys win and the bad guys get punished. That happens, of course, but hanging over the game—just as the albatross's death had hung over the ship—we are left without Charlie Buck and without the villains having to *really* pay for their sins. But isn't that how life is? We never see perfect retribution, except perhaps in the movies.

Epilogue
Keep Writing

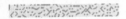

"Ninety percent of life is about showing up."

Woody Allen, writer and director
of *Annie Hall, Manhattan,* and
Hannah and Her Sisters

You, as a writer, must show up every morning to write. The more you work, the more you learn. There is no easy road, no quick shot, no fast way in. The ones who show up—who sit down and get to work—are the ones who will eventually succeed.

Some people have the mistaken impression that because they excelled at other professions, they will excel at writing. They forget how long and hard they worked perfecting their skills in their original career.

Screenplays need to be written by people who will go the extra mile. Writing is a job you love and hate to do. You have to stay with it. There are millions of excuses for not writing, and just as many ways to turn the excuses around. I park myself in my chair every day and stay there. At this point, the ideas begin to flow.

Don't be too hard on yourself. Writing is not bad or good. Get it down on paper, and you'll fix it later. Just showing up puts you way ahead of the game.

Recommended Reading

Arijon, Daniel. *Grammar of the Film Language*. Hollywood, Calif.: Silman-James Press, 1976.

Armer, Alan A. *Writing the Screenplay: TV and Film*. Belmont, Calif.: Wadsworth, 1993.

Boleslavsky, Richard. *Acting—The First Six Lessons*. New York: Theater Art Books, 1991.

Brady, John, ed. *The Craft of the Screenwriter*. New York: Simon & Schuster, 1981.

Cameron, Julia. *The Artist's Way*. New York: Putnam Publishers, 1994.

Campbell, Joseph. *The Hero with a Thousand Faces*. Princeton, N.J.: Princeton University Press, 1968.

———. *Myths to Live By*. New York: Viking Press, 1972.

Dunne, John Gregory. *Monster: Living Off the Big Screen*. New York: Random House, 1997.

Dyas, Ronald D. *Screenwriting for Television and Film*. Dubuque, Iowa: Brown & Benchmark, 1993.

Field, Syd. *Screenplay*. New York: Dell, 1982.

———. *The Screenwriter's Workbook*. New York: Dell, 1984.

———. *Selling a Screenplay*. New York: Bantam, Doubleday, Dell Publishing Group, 1989.

Gardner, John. *On Becoming a Novelist*. New York: Harper and Row, 1985.

Goldman, William. *Adventures in the Screen Trade*. New York: Warner Books, 1983.

Hauge, Michael. *Writing Screenplays that Sell*. New York: McGraw-Hill, 1988.

Kael, Pauline. *Hooked*. New York: E. P. Dutton, 1985.

Leonard, George. *Mastery*. New York: Plume, 1980.

Lord, James. *A Giacometti Portrait*. New York: Farrar, Straus, Giroux, 1980.

May, Rollo. *The Courage to Create*. New York: Bantam Books, 1990.

Pierson, John. *Spike, Mike, Slackers & Dykes*. New York: Hyperion, 1995.

Rilke, Rainer Maria. *Letter to a Young Poet*. New York: Random House, 1984.

Sautter, Carl. *How to Sell Your Screenplay*. New York: New Chapter Press, 1988.

Seger, Linda. *Making a Good Script Great*. New York: Dodd, Mead, 1987.

Vogler, Christopher. *The Writer's Journey*. Studio City, Calif.: Michael Wiese Productions, 1992.

Walter, Richard. *Screenwriting: The Art, Craft and Business of Film and Television Writing*. New York: Plume, 1988.

Zinsser, William. *On Writing Well*. New York: Harper and Row, 1976.